WOMAN-WORK

Woman-Work

WOMEN AND THE PARTY
IN REVOLUTIONARY CHINA

BY
DELIA DAVIN

Oxford   New York   Toronto   Melbourne
OXFORD UNIVERSITY PRESS
1979

Oxford University Press, Walton Street, Oxford OX2 6DP

OXFORD LONDON GLASGOW
NEW YORK TORONTO MELBOURNE WELLINGTON
KUALA LUMPUR SINGAPORE JAKARTA HONG KONG TOKYO
DELHI BOMBAY CALCUTTA MADRAS KARACHI
NAIROBI DAR ES SALAAM CAPE TOWN

First published 1976
Reprinted 1978
First published as an Oxford University Press paperback *1979*

British Library Cataloguing in Publication Data
Davin, Delia
  Woman-work.
  1. Woman—Employment—China—History—20th century
  2. Sex discrimination in employment—China—History—20th
    century
  I. Title
  331.4'0951   HD6200

ISBN 0-19-285080-6

*Reproduced, printed and bound in Great Britain by
Cox & Wyman Ltd, Reading*

ACKNOWLEDGEMENTS

I would like to thank Don Rimmington for his patient help and advice to me over the years in which this book was written. I am also grateful to Martin Bernal, Anna Davin, Mark Elvin, Raphael Samuel and Marilyn Young who read the manuscript at various stages and made valuable suggestions, and to Kato Yuzo who gave so generously of his time to guide me through the libraries of Tokyo.

Jane Tate produced an ordered typescript from my chaotic manuscript, and she, Sami Ayad, and Debbie Popper checked various drafts of the work, saving me from many foolish errors. Lastly I wish to thank friends in Leeds, London, Tokyo, Hongkong and Paris, whose warm-hearted help with my daughter Lucy enabled me to do my work with an easy mind.

Delia Davin
Peking 1975

CONTENTS

ABBREVIATIONS

CC collection: Chen Cheng (Ch'en Ch'eng) collection of Communist documents on a microfilm from the Hoover Institute Library, Stanford.

CC decisions (1943): *Decisions of the CC of CCP on the present orientation of woman-work in all the anti-Japanese base areas.* (*Zhongguo gongchandang zhongyang weiyuanhui guanyu ge kangri genjudi muqian funü gongzuo fangzhen de jueding.*)

CC decisions (1948): *Decisions of the CC of CCP on woman-work at present in the countryside of the liberated areas.* (*Zhongguo gongchandang zhongyang weiyuanhui guanyu muqian jiefang qu nongcun funü gongzuo de jueding.*)

CC of CCP: Central Committee of the Chinese Communist Party.

CCP: Chinese Communist Party.

Congress documents 1: *Documents of the 1st National Congress of Chinese Women 1949.* (*Zhongguo funü diyici quanguo daibiao dahui*)

Congress documents 2: *Documents of the 2nd National Congress of Chinese Women ZGFN No 5, 1953.* (*Zhongguo funü dierci quanguo daibiao dahui zhongyao wenxian.*)

Congress documents 3: *Documents of the 3rd National Congress of Chinese Women 1957.* (*Zhongguo funü disanci quanguo daibiao dahui zhongyao wenxian.*)

GRRB: *Workers' Daily. (Gongren Ribao.)*

LA documents 1: *Documents of the women's movement of the liberated areas of China,* March 1949. (*Zhongguo jiefangqu funü yundong wenxian.*)

LA documents 2: *Stories of the movement in which the village women of the liberated areas of China are standing up,* March 1949. (*Zhongguo jiefangqu nongcun funü fanshen yundong sumiao.*)

LA documents 3: *The campaign for women of the liberated areas of China to take part in the war,* March 1949. (*Zhongguo jiefangqu funü canzhan yundong.*)

LA documents 4: *The rural women's production movement in the liberated areas,* February 1949. (*Zhongguo jiefangqu nongcun funü shengchan yundong.*)

LA documents 5: Luo Qiong (ed.) *Documents of the women's movement*, February 1949. (*Funü yundong wenxian.*)

LA documents 6: *Selected documents of the women's movement*, March 1949. (*Funü yundong wenxuan.*)

NCNA: New China News Agency.

PRC: People's Republic of China.

QNSH: *True words of youth.* (*Quingnian Shihua.*) 1931–4. CC documents reel 18–19 008.2105/5803.

RMRB: People's Daily (*Renmin Ribao.*)

SW: Selected Works of Mao Tse-tung.

XHYB: *New China monthly.* (*Xinhua yuebao.*) (later *New China fortnightly*). (*Xinhua banyuekan.*)

ZGFN: *Women of China.* (*Zhongguo Funü.*) This magazine was a monthly entitled *Women of New China* (*Xin Zhongguo Funü*), until December 1955. From January 1956 it was published fortnighly as *Women of China* (*Zhongguo Funü*) and I refer to it always by this later title.

†: This sign indicates that the book, document, or article whose title follows is in Chinese.

NOTE ON ROMANIZATION

With a few exceptions I have used the Hanyü Pinyin system of romanization in my work. When a name is well known under another system, I give that form in brackets when the name is first mentioned, e.g. Mao Zedong (Mao Tse-tung). However, in the case of the following proper names which might be hard to recognize in Hanyü Pinyin, I have employed the better-known forms:

Canton	Peking	
Chungking	Tientsin	Chiang Kai-shek
Harbin	Yangtze	Kuomintang

I have used Hanyü Pinyin for the names of Chinese authors unless I am referring to works written in or translated into English. However, in cases where I refer to both the Chinese and English-language works of an author, I use Hanyü Pinyin for the sake of consistency.

For the translation of *funü gongzuo* as 'woman-work' see the note on p. 17.

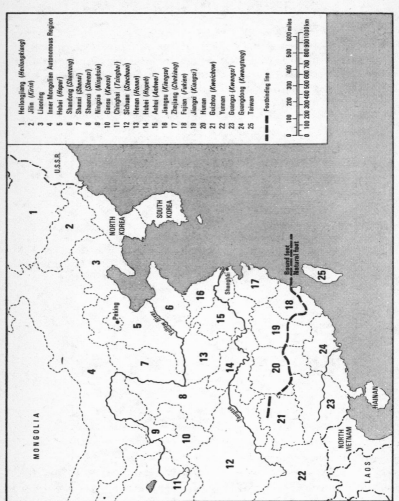

1 Heilongjiang (*Heilungkiang*)
2 Jilin (*Kirin*)
3 Liaoning
4 Inner Mongolian Autonomous Region
5 Hebei (*Hopei*)
6 Shandong (*Shantung*)
7 Shanxi (*Shensi*)
8 Shaanxi (*Shensi*)
9 Ningxia (*Ninghsia*)
10 Gansu (*Kansu*)
11 Chinghai (*Tsinghai*)
12 Sichuan (*Szechuan*)
13 Henan (*Honan*)
14 Hubei (*Hupeh*)
15 Anhui (*Anhwei*)
16 Jiangsu (*Kiangsu*)
17 Zhejiang (*Chekiang*)
18 Fujian (*Fukien*)
19 Jiangxi (*Kiangsi*)
20 Hunan
21 Guizhou (*Kweichow*)
22 Yunnan
23 Guangxi (*Kwangsi*)
24 Guangdong (*Kwangtung*)
25 Taiwan

0 100 200 300 400 500 600 miles
0 100 200 300 400 500 600 700 800 9001000 km

– – – Footbinding line

Bound feet
Natural feet

Map of China

INTRODUCTION

GREAT economic and social changes as a rule, in the long term at least, entail shifts in the economic roles of the sexes and hence in the way in which men and women live and relate to each other in the family and in society. Although there are some basic similarities between the sex roles in most human communities, the differences can also be very great. A striking example of such a difference is the extent of woman's participation in life, both economic and social, outside the home. In Asia and in Africa, some traditional societies under strong Muslim influence provide examples of communities where women scarcely leave the confines of their homes. In sharp contrast, there are other traditional communities in south-west Asia where men and women are equally responsible for farming and in Africa where all the work of cultivation is performed by women.

The effect of economic development on women naturally differs according to the nature of the society in which it takes place, and the stage of development which has already been attained. However, one can generalize that the patterns of development which are being followed in much of the modern world are not particularly favourable to women as women.[1] Where women's lives have been extremely enclosed, modernization may entail a partial breakdown of traditional barriers, and the demands of a growing economy will draw some women into economic activity outside the house. However, this activity will probably confer only low pay and status because in such a society women are quite unprepared to compete for the better-paid jobs, and it is felt natural that, as women, they should be relegated to secondary roles. But even where women were formerly economically active, economic development may begin to separate some of them from productive work. This tendency developed in England

[1] For a detailed analysis of the effects of modern economic development on women see Ester Boserup, *Women's Role in Economic Development*.

during the Industrial Revolution at the point where production ceased to be organized within the farm or city
household, and took place instead in the factory. Lacking
mobility because they had to care for children, mothers found
it more difficult to work outside the home. Consequently,
under the factory system, the individual woman's part in
commodity production became less sustained than it had been
in farm or handicraft production. In African agriculture
today, the pattern of modernization threatens to relegate
women to the most backward traditional sector, while large-
scale, mechanized agriculture follows the European-derived
preconceptions of its managers in employing predominantly
male labour. In urban development, a similar pattern is often
discernible when men are employed in preference to women,
who remain in the villages or are unemployed in urban
households. Even where women dominated the traditional
trading sector, as in the culture of west Africa, most of the jobs
in modern commerce go to men. There is some difference in
the pattern for industry. Although most new industries give
employment to men rather than to women, where a factory
industry produces goods which were traditionally made in the
home by women, as with textile manufacture, food-processing,
or garment-making, female employment may remain at a high
level even after industrialization.

Such, very briefly, are some of the possible economic
consequences of modernization for women, as it is occurring in
much of the developing world today. They may be unplanned
and indeed to some extent unnoticed. No decision is necessary
to reduce women's participation where it has hitherto
predominated, or to confine it to the least-skilled, worst-paid
spheres elsewhere; the 'normal' course of development implies
these trends.

Social and economic change in China has partly avoided
such consequences for women, because it has coincided with a
conscious, dynamic, and sustained effort to enlarge their role
and improve their status in the evolving traditional sector, and
to ensure them a more equal place in the modern sector. In
attempting to bring about equality for women, the Chinese
Communist Party had to bring the people of the traditional
communities to see their lives with critical eyes. This meant

creating a sharper awareness, and a more critical consciousness of the old social practice and the old roles. The history of rebellion in China demonstrates that a critical consciousness of the social system was certainly not a new phenomenon there, and the lesser-known history of protest and rebellion against women's place in society shows, as we will see, that here too there was an old tradition to draw upon. Moreover, since the people most disadvantaged or oppressed in the old society were the ones who could most quickly be brought to feel frustration or bitterness at their position, women were potentially a good source of recruits to the struggle for change.

Of course traditional Chinese society itself was not static, and women's position in it naturally underwent changes over the centuries.[2] Since I do not have space to discuss these here, the traditional model I build up is based largely on nineteenth- and twentieth-century conditions, although in many ways it would also hold good for earlier periods. Later, especially in my discussion of the family in chapter three, and of the relationship between women and production in chapter four, I will develop this model in detail. Here it will be sufficient to note a few of the characteristics of women's oppression, and to indicate some of the factors which underlay it.

In talking of 'the position of women in society' one is using a convenient shorthand for a complex and highly variable reality. To assess it we must consider such factors as the way in which boys and girls (or men and women) are valued by their family and society, the control which women are able to exercise over their own lives and those of others, and conversely the extent to which their lives are controlled by others. An understanding of these factors in traditional Chinese society requires that we should consider the decision-making powers of women in the various roles they played: mother, daughter, daughter-in-law, wife, widow, servant, and so on. This is of vital importance, because decisions made within the household on such matters as the organization of work, the allocation of income, the acquisition or sale of

---

[2] See Chen Dongyuan, †*A History of the Life of Chinese Women.*

property, expenditure on education, and the arrangement of marriages shaped the lives of individuals, both men and women.

Such an analysis should not be so superficial that it ignores the many variations which arise from differences of region, social class, or ethnic grouping, yet some generalizations are necessary if it is not to become swamped by a flood of detail.

In a consideration of decision-making, the value system of the society is very important. We need to know not only who is making the decisions, but also the criteria by which they are made. This is very apparent in the case of the Chinese 'matriarch', who might exercise great power in the family, especially if she were a widow, but would usually do so in what the concepts of a patriarchal ideology made appear the best interests of her family.

Closely related to the cultural pattern was an economic system characterized by a sharp division of labour between the sexes. Women's primary responsibilities were child-care, the preparation of food and clothing for the family, and general household tasks. Although such tasks were of course necessary, they were not obviously productive, and women's labour here was expended on processing the raw materials supplied to them by men. Women in many parts of China worked outside the home very little or not at all. Even in those regions where they did so, their work tended to be of a secondary nature, and, equally important, very much perceived as such. If, for example, women worked in the fields, weeding, hoeing, and gleaning were representative of their tasks. Those who worked in cottage industries producing for the market sometimes did so alone, sometimes as part of a 'family team'. Materials might be supplied by their husbands, or by a 'putter-out'. Obviously the particular conditions under which they worked had different implications for their status, but their work, whether inside or outside the home, rarely brought them independence though it did affect the degree of their dependence.

As fundamental to their status as their role in production was women's relationship to the means of production. In rich families women might own such personal wealth as jewellery which, even when taken to their husbands' households upon marriage as a dowry, remained their own property. However, they were debarred from the inheritance or ownership of what in a predominently agricultural society was the chief means of production: the land.

It has been suggested that in hunting societies women have greater power when they are important producers of raw materials (from gathering or fishing) than when they are mainly processors of meat or other supplies produced by men.[3] In a similar way, the amount and type of work performed by women aside from child-care and housework seems to have been an important variable in determining their status in China. Thus, Cantonese women who normally worked in the fields have for centuries been famed for their strength of character, and were generally considered to be *lihai* (tough and fierce). A Japanese anthropologist, writing of a Yangtze delta village in the 1930s, noted that female status was comparatively high amongst the poorer families since their women worked as agricultural labourers, made willow baskets, and did embroidery work.[4] Significantly though, even his proof of the 'high status' of the housewife, viz. that she was able to *influence* the family head, indicates the framework of subordination within which women lived, while showing that the degree of that subordination might vary.

Much of the life of a Chinese woman was lived in a state of dependence. As a child, like her more valued and privileged brothers, she was expected to submit to parental authority. Although loved, she had, unlike her brothers, to submit to the fearful pain of foot-binding. When her parents arranged her marriage she entered her husband's household as a vulnerable stranger and was expected to accept not only his authority, but also that of all her seniors in the household. Women in wealthy families had the great advantage of security from the material hardships which ordinary women suffered, but in certain ways they were less fortunate. Their seclusion, really only possible amongst the gentry who could afford servants, made these women more dependent than their peasant sisters. What Lin Yutang referred to as the puritanico-sadistic background of Confucianism, with its practices of concubinage, foot-binding,

[3] Kathleen Gough, *The Origin of the Family*, p. 12.
[4] Tadashi Fukutake, *Asian Rural Society: China, India, Japan*, p. 87.

encouragement of woman's suicide in defence of chastity, and perpetual widowhood rather than remarriage, was also at its strongest in this class.[5]

Given the nature of the work she could perform, and the fact that she could neither own nor inherit land, a woman who was alone had no place in conventional Chinese society. Women whose fate had somehow denied them family support might become servants or prostitutes in order to live, but in doing so they had to accept a loss of status and of hope for the future. It was from this hope that ordinary women drew the strength to survive the difficulties of their early lives. The most oppressed daughter-in-law in the humblest family could, if she had sons, be compensated in her old age by their love and respect, by the care of her daughter-in-law and the pleasures of her grandchildren. When young, however, women whose lives followed the traditional pattern often had much to endure. Writing on patrilineal societies, an anthropologist has characterized the treatment of daughters in their fathers' families, where they are seen as potential deserters, as stepmotherly, while he points out that they join their husbands' families as intruders and are often treated as such.[6] These misfortunes were perhaps peculiarly intensified in China by the strength of patriarchal ideology and its religious expression, the ancestor cult, to which women could contribute only as the bearers of sons.

Nevertheless, criticism of the position of women was not a new phenomenon in China. A strong current of dissent within Chinese tradition itself found voice both in literary and in popular culture. Various scholars, if not really taking up a feminist position, had attacked specific aspects of the treatment of women in their essays.[7] Novels and stories often gave very sympathetic treatment to women. One nineteenth-century novel, *Flowers in the Mirror*, by Li Ju-chen, went very much further by offering explicit criticism.[8] The author, using the satirist's device of the voyager known to us from *Gulliver's*

---

[5] Lin Yutang, 'Feminist Thought in Ancient China', p. 128.
[6] U. R. Ehrenfels, 'The anthropological background of matrilineal societies', p. 41.
[7] Lin Yutang, 'Feminist Thought in Ancient China'.
[8] Li Ju-chen, *Flowers in the Mirror*, translated by Lin Tai-yi.

Travels, imagines his hero in the 'Women's Kingdom', a land where women rule and men attempt to gain their favour. Showing a perception of the power relations between the sexes startlingly close to some present-day analyses, he has the men powder their faces, apply rouge to their cheeks, and bind their feet to attract women. Old men painted their beards black in order to preserve their youthful attractiveness.

In a passage which still has considerable power to shock, Li shows his hero, having undergone the torture of foot-binding at the hands of a bearded palace 'maid', being escorted powdered and rouged into the presence of the Queen. He has then to endure being ogled and pawed by the Queen until he is ready to die with shame.

Popular rejection of the subjugation of women is often to be found in the ideas and practice both of peasant revolts and of the secret societies which played an important part in them. The best-known example is that of the nineteenth-century Taiping movement[9] within which women were accorded equality.[10] Women had a right to an equal allocation of land under the Taiping land system, and girls could attend school, take examinations, and become officials. The sale of brides, foot-binding, prostitution, and polygamy were forbidden. Widows were permitted to remarry. Women could join women's armies which sometimes engaged in battle although they were more often used in non-combat roles.

The Taiping movement had originated amongst the Guangxi Hakka, a minority group whose women worked in the fields and did not undergo foot-binding. Its treatment of women was thus based on normal Hakka practice. This favourable treatment should not, however, be exaggerated. The extent to which the land system was implemented is doubtful. It has been shown that though the Hakka women

[9] The Taiping Rebellion (1850-64) gave rise to civil war on so vast a scale that it resulted in a population loss estimated at 20-30 million. At the height of their success the Taipings held most of Central China, and their armies fought in 16 of the 18 provinces south of the Great Wall. The Taipings intended to overthrow not only the existing dynasty, but the whole traditional social system. Their doctrine was a sort of primitive communism derived partly from Chinese tradition and partly from a bastard Christianity.

[10] The fullest discussion of Taiping attitudes to women is in Vincent Shih, *The Taiping Ideology*, from which most of the information which follows is taken.

from Guangxi did enjoy rights granted to women under the
Taiping system, the fate of women in territory newly occupied
by the Taipings was often very different. They were given as
rewards to successful generals, and the Taiping leaders built
up enormous harems in the decadent years of the rebellion.
The possession of women also became a badge of rank: the
more senior the officer or official, the larger the number of wives
permitted to him. The Taiping leader Hong Xiuquan wrote:

Women in the inner palaces should not try to leave;
If they should try to leave it would be like hens trying to crow.
The duty of palace women is to attend to the needs of their
husbands;
And it is arranged by Heaven that they are not to learn of affairs
outside.[11]

(It is perhaps significant that he had had a Confucian
education, though he had failed the official examinations.)
Even the fact that women did serve as officials in the
government and army must be qualified by the observation
that they were often the concubines of the leaders they served
and their promotions were sometimes political manipulations
on the part of their masters. However, in spite of all the
inconsistencies of Taiping attitudes to women, their ideology
and to a lesser extent their practice remain valuable evidence
of a tradition of dissent.

Secret societies were also part of this dissenting tradition.
Unfortunately, since secret societies as a vehicle for popular
discontent represented a challenge to the established order,
they were often ignored or simplistically reviled by orthodox
Confucian scholar-historians. Their own rules of secrecy have
also contributed to a dearth of information. However, we do
know that women were eligible for membership and office in
at least some of these organizations so important in the
'hidden history' of peasant China.[12] Given the place of women
in Chinese society as a whole, it seems improbable that any but
the most exceptional achieved positions of great power within the secret societies, but their participation in itself was
remarkable. It was doubtless the fact that there were already

---

[11] Quoted in Vincent Shih, p. 73.
[12] Jean Chesneaux, *Secret Societies in China*, p. 59.

female secret society members which made possible the participation of women's units in the Boxer Uprising at the turn of the century and in the 1911 revolution, both movements which enjoyed strong support from secret societies.[13]

Unorthodox ideas, however, found voice only rarely; in the mainstream of traditional thought the assumptions of female inferiority, implicit in the whole social and political system, went unchallenged. Only when national humiliation at the hands of imperialist powers forced Chinese intellectuals to reassess their whole cultural tradition did change really begin. Then some of the fiercest attacks of the new radicals were focused on the family system and the misery which it inflicted on women. Such attacks were developed from a knowledge of societies in which things were ordered differently and were often expressed in direct comparisons. As long as the criticism took this form, its influence was very limited.

Foreign cultural impact might be felt heavily in the great coastal cities, but reached the hinterland in too diluted a form to undermine traditional ways. In our time small traditional cultures can be demoralized by foreign contacts. Films, television, advertising, tourism, urban migration, and holiday visits by absent emigrants bring idealized images of Western urban civilization to the villages, and dissatisfaction sets in. The slow process of social change that this gives rise to can undermine traditional values since it is determined too much by external factors, replacing them with the new values irrelevant to the needs of that community.[14]

In China, however, the momentum for social change in the vast rural hinterland was not created by a longing for the

[13] Victor Purcell, *The Boxer Uprising*, p. 235. The main organization for women was composed of girls between the ages of 12 and 18. For widows there was an organization known variously as the Green or Blue Lanterns. This seems to imply that ordinary married women were not recruited and that Boxer attitudes towards women were less radical than is often claimed. Presumably the recruitment of married women would have been opposed by their in-laws, and family burdens might have created practical difficulties. Perhaps it can also be seen as a ritual exclusion. The Boxers believed that women were unclean and that their impurity could render Boxer magic ineffectual. If their belief system resembled others in which the idea of the polluting influence of the female played an important part, they would have regarded sexually active women as especially dangerous (See, for example, Mary Douglas, *Purity and Danger*, pp. 51-2).
[14] For an account of this process see Hugh Brody, *Inishkillane*.

rewards and luxuries of another life-style built up through mass communications. It arose rather from an intensification of the contradictions within Chinese rural society and the growing anger and frustration of the peasantry. Although the leadership of the revolution which helped the peasantry to give expression to their tensions and directed their struggle for change was in part of urban origin, the tensions themselves grew directly out of the contradictions of the rural social structure and thus owed their force to internal factors.

As the revolution mobilized the resentment of peasants, both men and women, against the old village power structure, it also mobilized women against their particular oppression. As we have seen, it was not necessary to *create* the consciousness of the bitterness of women's lives. Women down the centuries had bemoaned their sad fate in words which echoed the lines of the third-century poet, Fu Hsuan:

> How sad it is to be a woman
> Nothing on earth is held so cheap.
>
> No one is glad when a girl is born
> By her the family sets no store.[15]

In those extreme cases when an individual's life became unbearable, the characteristic female protest was the supremely negative one of suicide. In revolution, women's fatalistic acceptance of suffering had to be swept away. They had to learn to struggle together against 'destiny'.

Bound feet were symbolic of the subservience of women. A girl's feet were bound when she was about six. Her toes were turned under her feet and held in position by tightly wound bandages. As the years passed, the feet could not grow, and the bone structure became deformed. Adult women walked on three-inch stumps. Though prohibited from 1911, this custom died out slowly, at least in some northern villages, where small feet and the swaying walk that they imposed were still considered beautiful, and were necessary if a girl was to make a good match. To be crippled physically like this in a pre-industrial economy in which a peasant's income depended at least partly on strength was to be crippled economically as

---

[15] Taken from a translation in Arthur Waley, *Chinese Poems*, p. 84.

well. It is interesting that foot-binding was rare only in those areas where it was customary for women to work outside the home, notably in Guangdong, Guangxi, and parts of Taiwan. But for women in most of China except among minority peoples, the pain and the disability of foot-binding were a normal part of childhood at least until the twentieth century. I will use one old woman's account of her pain to convey what would have been the experience of countless women in Chinese history, including many whose struggles this book will describe:

My feet hurt so much that for 2 years I had to crawl on my hands and knees. Sometimes at night they hurt so much that I could not sleep. I stuck my feet under my mother and she lay on them so they hurt less and I could sleep. But by the time I was eleven my feet did not hurt and by the time I was thirteen they were finished.[16]

Foot-binding was such an obvious evil that feminists made it one of their first targets. The formidable Qiu Jin (Ch'iu Chin) (1874-1907) even gave a lecture on the subject which implied it was the sole cause of women's subjection, though elsewhere she expressed less simplistic ideas.[17] For several famous twentieth-century women of upper-class origin, a childhood refusal to allow their families to bind their feet was the first step in a long struggle to escape a traditional style of life.[18] But it soon became less important for the early women's movements since the custom died out rapidly in urban areas where they were based.

As I have implied, early feminism was often inspired by Western models. Descriptions of the lives of women in other countries, of famous women of European history, and of the feminist movement in Europe and America were carried by the rapidly growing women's press and gave rise to much questioning and debate. The women's press was itself an interesting phenomenon, and a significant one in the rise of feminism.[19] The first paper by and for women came out in

[16] Ida Pruitt, *A Daughter of Han*, p. 22.
[17] Lionel Giles, *Ch'iu Chin: A Chinese Heroine*, pp. 4-5.
[18] See accounts of childhood in the following autobiographies: Hsieh Ping-ying. *Autobiography of a Chinese Girl*. Buwei Yang Chao, *Autobiography of a Chinese Woman*. Wei Cheng Yu-hsiu, *My Revolutionary Years*.
[19] The information about the women's journals in this paragraph is from a paper on the subject, unfortunately as yet unpublished, by Charlotte L. Behan of Columbia University.

Shanghai in 1902; by 1911, sixteen women's periodicals are known to have appeared in China or in the Chinese community in Japan. Though there was a considerable variation in the emphasis and interests of these papers, they belonged to the same radical school, and shared a common concern for what became generally accepted goals for the women's movement in China, women's rights, women's education, and family reform.

Traditionally, only a minority of families sent children to school. Many of them would have had to make sacrifices and perhaps obtain aid from relatives in order to do so. Such spending was regarded as an investment for the future, for an educated boy might get on in the world and in doing so increase his family's prosperity. There was little incentive to make such sacrifices for girls who would leave their own families on marriage. The women of élite families might (depending on the period and region) be expected to acquire literacy in addition to such ladylike accomplishments as household management, embroidery, and pickle-making. But the texts provided for them, of which the *Biographies of Model Women*[20] is the best known example, were didactic attempts to inculcate Confucian propriety and the ideal of submissive femininity. However, this convention was occasionally flouted in the families of scholars who chose to educate a favourite daughter, often the only or the youngest child, as if she had been a boy. Qiu Jin, whose history is briefly related below, had been brought up in this aberrant tradition, allowed to wear boy's clothes, well versed in the classics, and left unmarried until the late age of 24.[21]

Women's education expanded very rapidly in the first two decades of the twentieth century, and a small number of women went abroad to study. A contemporary estimate for 1907 put the number of Chinese girls enrolled in Japanese schools at 100 with many more studying informally. The first Chinese woman to go, Qiu Jin, who was destined to become a heroine to future generations of rebellious girls, sold her jewellery to raise money, and leaving her husband and two children for ever, went alone to study in Tokyo in 1903. On

[20] Liu Xiang, †*Biographies of Model Women*.
[21] For the life story of Qiu Jin see Mary B. Rankin, *Early Chinese Revolutionaries*.

her return to China she devoted herself to the causes of women's education and revolutionary politics until 1908 when she was executed as one of the leaders of an anti-dynastic rising. Though Qiu Jin was the best-known, a few other women also involved themselves in radical and revolutionary émigré politics. Perhaps in the native tradition of peasant rebellion rather than under Western influence, women's armies were active in the 1911 revolution. Then, employing tactics derived directly from the West, suffragettes stormed the Provisional Parliament at Nanking in 1912, and in the next ten years, as a result of vigorous campaigns, women were enfranchised under several provincial constitutions. Unfortunately, these were rather empty victories at a time when real power was in the hands of the warlords.[22] In the decade of intellectual ferment which followed the May 4th movement,[23] no aspect of traditional society was more firmly rejected by young radicals than the subjugation of women and the old marriage system. Ibsen was immensely popular with the intellectuals of this period, and Nora became as well known as Qiu Jin as a model for young women who wished to escape from their 'Doll's House'. However, the 'Doll's House' for most of these young women was not married life, but the family into which they had been born. Successful Chinese Noras avoided arranged marriages, obtained their education, and sometimes even began an independent life in some profession, in most cases as a teacher. Most later made marriages which were unconventional for China in that they arranged them for themselves, but which were hardly revolutionary in Ibsen's terms. In 1923, Lu Xun (Lu Hsun) delivered a lecture at the Peking Women's Normal University entitled 'What happens after Nora leaves home?' His answer was that without economic rights she would either go to the

[22] This phase of the women's movement is covered in Roxanne Witke, 'Woman as Politician in China of the 1920's', in Marilyn B. Young (ed.), *Women in China: Studies in Social Change and Feminism*.

[23] A storm of protest greeted the news that Japan was to receive the former German concessions in China under the terms of the Versailles Treaty. Educated Chinese had previously expected that they would be restored to China, one of the victorious allies. A student demonstration on 4 May 1919 gave its name to the era of demonstrations, social unrest, strikes, intellectual debate, and literary activity which followed.

bad or return home.[24] In European terms, many of these Chinese Noras had never left home. Their individualistic rebellion was not against their roles as wife and mother, but rather against the family which tried to determine for whom they should play that role.

The literature of this period often reflects the concerns with love, family, and individual freedom which exercised both its creators and its readers. In works such as Ding Ling's *Diary of Miss Sophie*, we can sense the excitement and hope of the period, but also the dangers which the elevation of 'love' to the level of a holy grail could bring.[25] Hope could easily turn to the disappointment typical of the experience of the 1920s and 1930s.

The anti-imperialist May 4th movement had brought many women students into politics. Among these were Deng Yingchao (Teng Ying-ch'ao) and Cai Chang (Ts'ai Ch'ang) who have been great figures in the women's movement for over fifty years. Women campaigned for reforms in the laws of property and inheritance, and affirmed their rights to be educated, to work, to vote and hold office, and to choose their own husbands. The Kuomintang had a women's section which was led by He Xiangning (Ho Hsiang-ning, also known by her married name as Mme Liao Chung-k'ai, 1876-1973), who played a part in the Women's Federation in Peking after 1949.[26] Many women soldiers marched with the Northern Expedition (1924-5) which extended Kuomintang power to the Yangtze valley in a military drive north from Canton. More important to the future of the women's movement were propagandists from the women's section who organized a million and a half women in leagues to fight for women's rights in the rural communities through which the expedition

---

[24] Lu Xun, "What happens after Nora leaves home?", in Gladys Yang (transl. and ed.), *Silent China*.

[25] Ding Ling, *Diary of Miss Sophie*, in †*In the Darkness*, p. 124. The problems of this articulate self-conscious vanguard of women are most interestingly examined in a paper by Yi-tsi Feuerwerker, 'Women as Writers in the 1920s and 1930s', in Roxanne Witke and Margery Wolf (eds.), *Women in Chinese Society*.

[26] For details of the work of this Department, see Anna Louise Strong, *China's Millions*, pp. 96-125, and Suzette Leith, 'Chinese Women in the Early Communist Movement', in Marilyn B. Young (ed.), *Women in China*.

passed. The work of the leagues included propaganda against foot-binding and the support of women who were trying to resist arranged marriages. They were also supposed to publicize women's inheritance rights and help women who wanted divorces. They functioned in difficult times, and were faced with great problems. They survived only a very short time since, like the peasant leagues, they were products of the united front between the Kuomintang and the Chinese Communist Party and were suppressed in the reaction of 1927. Nevertheless, they were historically important as an early attempt of modern revolutionaries to organize women. Since the western arm of the Northern Expedition was dominated by the left wing of the Kuomintang and laid much more stress on mass organizations, they were especially strong in central south China, which a few years later was to be the home of the Chinese Soviets. No doubt some of the members of the Soviet women's organizations had once been members of these earlier leagues.

With the repression of this radical women's movement and the death of many of its leaders and members, the women's cause in China suffered a severe setback. It is true that many of the objectives of the women's rights movement were formally achieved in 1931 when the Kuomintang government promulgated the Civil Code.[27] Women were granted equality in civil, political, and property rights. The prohibition against foot-binding was repeated. Freedom of choice and equality in marriage were upheld. Divorce by mutual consent was permitted, but here a concession was made to custom: the father normally took custody of the children. However, the vast majority of peasant women would never have heard of this legislation, and amongst the very wealthy concubinage continued to flourish. The effects of the new laws were largely limited to the urban middle class. For the urban middle-class girl, the chances of a career were also increasing. The development of women's education accelerated, and an educated wife became an asset to a young man's career.

As Kuomingtang ideology shifted to the right, however, it

[27] For the text of the Civil Code see M. H. van der Valk, *An Outline of Modern Chinese Family Law*. It was drafted by five lawyers of whom one, Wei Cheng Yu-hsiu, was a woman. (See Wei Cheng Yu-hsiu, *My Revolutionary Years*, pp. 167-71.)

took on many anti-feminist aspects. The New Life Movement launched in 1934 at the height of Chiang Kai-shek's operation against the Communists was a neo-Confucian revival which emphasized ascetic self-discipline and obedience to the leader.[28] An important part of this moral code was support for the patriarchal family and male supremacy. The movement was not strong enough to halt the progress being made by professional women in the towns, but it influenced the nature of the work done by women's organizations amongst the masses. The organization and methods of the 1920s were abandoned. Under Mme Chiang's leadership, women's organizations did welfare work, taught domestic economy, hygiene, and child-care, and with the coming of the war, engaged in relief work and fund-raising. Wider feminist goals were ignored.

The women's movement in twentieth-century China can broadly be divided into the narrowly feminist tendency which concentrated on the struggle for women's rights in the belief that true equality was possible without a revolution in the whole social system, and the socialist tendency which held that women's liberation would only be achieved under socialism and therefore engaged in revolutionary activity. Mao Zedong (Mao Tse-tung) wrote:

A man in China is usually subjected to the domination of three systems of authority (political authority, clan authority and religious authority). As for women, as well as being dominated by these three systems, they are also dominated by men (the authority of the husband).[29]

Using Mao's imagery, we could say socialist women saw four authorities to be overthrown.

Xiang Jingyu, one of the Communist Party's leading theorists, and its main authority on women until her execution in Hankou (Hankow) in 1928, distinguished three types among China's emancipated women intellectuals.[30] One she characterized as useless to the revolution because they were

[28] For a fuller analysis of the Kuomintang backlash against feminism see Norma Diamond. 'Women under Kuomintang Rule: Variations on the Feminine Mystique'.
[29] Mao Zedong, 'Report on an Investigation of the Peasant Movement in Hunan', English-language version in *Selected Works* (Peking 1965), vol. 1, p. 44.
[30] Xiang Jingyu, †'Three types among China's women intellectuals'.

interested only in the right to marry monogamously a man of their own choice. Once they had achieved this they would immerse themselves in the cares of their small families. Other women, romantics who sought liberation in free love, became too absorbed in their personal lives to be able to change society. Among intellectuals, only the professional woman who wished to remain independent and who had a sense of social duty might work for the revolution. Such women, she argued, would be capable of uniting with the masses of working and peasant women and organizing them to fight for their own liberation as part of a movement for the total liberation of all oppressed people.[31] Although she died before the process she envisaged was firmly established, an alliance of revolutionary women intellectuals and labouring women under the Communist Party leadership did in fact take place.

Its beginnings, like the beginnings of the communist movement itself, were in the towns where Party work always included woman-work.[32] Party workers organized amongst women and set up unions, schools and newspapers for women. When the focus of the communist movement shifted to the countryside, the nature of woman-work underwent profound changes. Its new tasks and problems will be examined in the next chapter. Here it remains only to note that although the women's movement underwent unprecedented development in the Soviet period, and began for the first time to affect the nature of the society in which the great masses of Chinese people lived, the contribution of earlier feminists should not be overlooked. They did belong to a tiny élite, were largely occupied with the problems of their own class, and often appeared introverted in their own concerns. Nevertheless, they did begin the great quest for women's emancipation in China, and in some fields, notably that of education, they achieved significant successes. Even today, many of the important leaders of the women's

---

[31] Xiang Jingyu, †'Three matters to which the women's rights movement in Shanghai should give attention from now on'.

[32] I use the term 'woman-work' for the Chinese *funü gongzuo*. This made-up word seems preferable to the usual but misleading translation 'women's work'. The term covers all sorts of activities among women, including mobilizing them for revolutionary struggle, production, literacy and hygiene campaigns, social reform, and so on.

movement are women who were students in the May 4th movement, and women intellectuals have played an important part in mobilizing peasant and worker women throughout the revolution. Without the struggle of the earlier feminists there would have been no women intellectuals and the alliance envisaged by Xiang Jingyu between them and labouring women would never have taken place. This alliance, its aims, its problems, and its achievements, will be the subject of the chapters which follow.

In chapter one I describe Party policy towards women in the period of the Jiangxi Soviet, the anti-Japanese War, and the Civil War. Although social reform was often not fully implemented and sometimes even completely dropped in this period of difficulty and almost continual warfare, its evolution in these two decades is of great interest. These early communist areas served in a sense as a laboratory for social change, and experiments in them were later to determine the course of Chinese history. The currents which shaped policy towards women were complex and at times contradictory. The youthful, largely intellectual leadership of the Communist Party believed in the equality of the sexes. They regarded the emancipation of women as an important goal for the revolution. Female emancipation and the reform of marriage and family institutions were profoundly threatening to the male peasantry whose support they had also to win for survival. But even if the postponement of emancipation had been ideologically acceptable, it would have been impractical. Some goals might be modified, but the needs of the army meant that women had to be mobilized for unaccustomed roles in agriculture, handicrafts, and war support work. Such a mobilization in itself both necessitated and gave rise to rapid social change.

In chapter two, I trace the history of the Women's Federation which has directed the women's movement since 1949. This involves consideration of the contradictions which have arisen between some of the movement's goals and the economic priorities of the state. I try to show in general terms how these contradictions have been met, and the policy fluctuations to which they have given rise. More specific details of these fluctuations as they affected the villages and the towns will be found in chapters four and five.

In chapter three, I analyse more closely the difficulties of introducing a new style of marriage and family life to the conservative countryside. I conclude that although much has changed, there are still basic institutional factors which inhibit the implementation of the 1950 Marriage Law as it was first interpreted.

In chapter four, I return to the relationship between women, production, and the land in the countryside, showing the effects of land reform and collectivization on women's economic position. Although I find that women are still a long way from economic equality with men in the countryside, I argue that a fundamental change has taken place in that women now earn and receive money as individuals, and could, in the last resort, support themselves in order to preserve their independence.

In chapter five, I examine the life of women in the towns. I show that the classical Marxist solution to the woman problem did not prove quickly attainable, owing both to economic problems and to the lack of skills of much of the female population. However, other types of social participation have been evolved which imply considerable political power at the community level, and which have certainly had a profound effect on both the self-image and public status of Chinese women.

The growth and reform of the educational system and the enormous progress which has been made in public health and medicine have of course been of great importance to Chinese women. I have not, however, chosen to deal with these subjects under separate chapter headings, but in the contrasting settings of town and village so that they are among the themes of chapters four and five.

My study concentrates primarily on the 1950s. Less material is available for the 1960s, though in many spheres the pattern for change had been laid by 1960. Moreover, much is still obscure about the period of the Cultural Revolution, nor is it yet clear how much permanent change it has brought about. However, some of the most interesting material on the earlier policy fluctuations emerged only during the Cultural Revolution, and often a comparison with a later period may illuminate our understanding of the 1950s, so the limitation is not rigid.

CHAPTER 1

WOMEN IN THE JIANGXI SOVIET AND THE LIBERATED AREAS

IN 1929 the Red Army, in retreat from the Jinggangshan base on the Hunan-Jiangxi border, established a new base on the mountainous borders of Jiangxi, Fujian, and Guangdong which was to be the central Chinese Soviet for the next five years. Other, smaller Soviet bases were developed, in similar areas, where the remoteness and difficulty of the terrain combined to make defence easier. By the summer of 1930, there were already fifteen such bases, scattered over about ten provinces. The Soviets were at war for the whole period of their existence, their borders fluctuated continually, and there were serious tensions and disagreements among their leaders. Furthermore, as they were dispersed over a huge area, and communications between them across hostile territory were often difficult, any description of their administration can only be a generalized one and will not cover the situation in each base at all times. Nevertheless, the period of the Soviets during which the communists governed a population of millions was important for the testing and development of practical policies. Among them were social and economic measures designed to alter the whole status of women. A brief description of these measures is essential to this study. My account is based mainly on documents surviving from the Jiangxi Central Soviet, on which the Chinese Soviet Republic (founded in November 1931) was centred.

The equality of men and women, which was of course taken as a principle in the Soviet areas, achieved a degree of reality partly by the creation of organizations to fight for it and partly by legislation intended to favour women. The picture is confused, and in this as in other matters it is not possible to judge the degree of success achieved in Jiangxi. Agnes Smedley, using eyewitness accounts by participants, says that the Army and the Party were often too busy to assist the local

Soviets much, even with agrarian policy.[1] This was probably the case generally with social and economic policy. Moreover, it was, as we know, a period of disunity and struggle at the highest level of Party leadership, so that even had trained or experienced cadres existed to carry it out, policy on women might have been expected to lack a consistent line.

And an examination of those documents on woman-work from the Jiangxi period does in fact seem to show that there was less agreement, perhaps even less certainty, about priorities than existed in the northern liberated areas at least after 1942. We have quite a number of programmes, plans, and lists of aims for woman-work from different regions and different organizations, and they are by no means stereotyped in the points they make. Their common characteristic, and that in which they differ most from documents of the later period, is the overwhelming importance which they give to organizing women for the war effort. Often, for example, when cadres are urged to get women to work in the fields the reason they are given is not the necessity for women to lay an economic basis for their equality, but that only if women can take their place in the fields will men be willing to join the Red Army.[2] The Central Bureau of the CCP in the Soviet Areas passed a resolution in 1933[3] which stated that seeing off new recruits and caring for army dependants was 'the core of woman-work' (funü gongzuo de zhongxin gongzuo), an expression which was later to be reserved for productive labour.

The Party obviously considered that the morale of the Red Army was vital, and believed that the women's movement could make an important contribution to it. The most urgent task was the support of army dependants. Simply to pension them would have imposed too great a burden on Soviet funds; it was both more economical and administratively simpler to provide substitute labour to farm the land of absent soldiers on behalf of their dependants. This task was the responsibility of

[1] Agnes Smedley, *China's Red Army Marches*, pp. 130–40.
[2] †*Programme for the organization and work of labouring women's representative congresses.*
[3] †Resolutions on the summoning of the provincial representative congress of women workers and peasants.

the local Soviet, and literature aimed at Soviet personnel, the Youth League, the Poor Peasant League, and soldiers on garrison duty contains appeals to all of them to help army dependants.[4] Nowhere, however, are such appeals more frequent than in the documents of the women's movement.[5] The extent to which women actually performed such work presumably depended largely on their traditional contribution to the work-force in a given region; which in turn is itself linked to the labour requirement of crops grown in the area and the extent of foot-binding which had been practised in the north but not the south of the Soviet area. Though efforts were made to teach women the farming skills which they lacked, and Mao Zedong reported their wish to learn to plough and harrow,[6] inexperienced women already burdened with housework and child-care would certainly not have been able to replace men in the fields without at least a period of adjustment.[7]

Women were also organized into teams to launder and sew for the army and to carry food for it.[8] Through their representatives, they were urged to sell their valuables to buy arms for the troops. Women's groups wove straw sandals and stitched cloth shoes for the soldiers.[9] In 1933 there was a campaign to finish 100,000 pairs of shoes before the anniversary of the October Revolution. Endearingly, the Jiangxi Provincial Party Committee commented on this campaign that it was of course also the responsibility of men comrades.[10] Perhaps this may be taken as a sign of sensitivity about the fact that so much of the contribution that women were being asked to make to the war effort was a mere extension of their domestic role. If so it is exceptional; other

[4] See for example most numbers of *QNSH* (1931-4).

[5] Such appeals may be found in every women's movement document from the Jiangxi period cited in this text.

[6] Mao Zedong, 'Be concerned with the well-being of the masses, pay attention to methods of work', 27 January 1934, *SW* (1965), vol. 1, p. 149.

[7] For a fuller treatment of this problem see chapter four, 'Women in the Countryside'.

[8] †*Circular No. 74 of the Central Government: The women's movement and preparatory work for Labour Day*, 5 April 1930.

[9] †*Decisions of the joint conference of the Guangchang central county committee and the heads of the district women's departments*.

[10] †*Resolutions on the summoning of the provincial representative congress of women workers and peasants* (Jiangxi Provincial Committee of the CCP).

documents indicate that their allotted role was hardly questioned. Undoubtedly the main direction of the women's movement in Jiangxi was determined by expediency. But if the critical military situation and the needs of the army directed the work of the women's organizations, they also made it necessary to treat the politicization of women as an immediate and important task as part of general popular mobilization.

Party, Soviet, and Poor Peasant Association committees at every level were meant to make woman-work the particular responsibility of one department.[11] There were two types of women's organization, the Committee to Improve Women's Lives,[12] and the Representative Congress of Women Workers and Peasants,[13] and they should in theory have had branches in each district (xiang). In fact, a considerable number of the documents on woman-work complain that in certain districts there were only paper organizations or that none existed at all.[14] Other areas, notably Xinguo county, are praised as models for thorough work.[15] Another criticism about the performance of woman-work was that it was somewhat despised, and that men cadres tended to believe that it should be left to women. Such attitudes were attributed to feudal ideology, which underestimated the importance of women.

---

[11] For information on the Party and the Soviets see †*Circular No. 14 of the Central Bureau of the CCP of the Soviet Areas. Prepare the commemoration of International Working Women's Day and correct the errors in woman-work.* For information on the Poor Peasant League see *Regulations for the Poor Peasant Associations issued by General Political Department of the Central Revolutionary Military Council of the Soviet Areas,* 16 February 1931, translated in Hsiao Tso-liang, *The Land Revolution in China 1930–1934,* p. 179.

[12] †*Decisions of the first joint meeting of the heads of the district committees to improve women's lives of Gonglüe county.* The Committees to Improve Women's Lives were presumably modelled on a contemporary institution in the Soviet Union: the Committee for the Improvement of the Working and Living Conditions of Women. All government executive committees at Union, Republic, provincial, regional, and district levels were supposed to have such a sub-committee. Interestingly, they seem to be mentioned most often in connection with the eastern republics where the reform of marriage and emancipation of women raised problems in some respects similar to those in China. (See Rudolf Schlesinger, *The Family in the USSR,* pp. 189, 198, 201, 203, and Fannina Halle, *Women in the Soviet East.*)

[13] †*Programme and methods for promoting the struggle of the labouring women of East Jiangxi.* Ningdu central county committee of the CCP. Women's representative congresses also had counterparts in the Soviet Union, see Rudolf Schlesinger p. 202.

They are mentioned frequently and so were presumably a factor in the absence of women's organizations in some areas. The Committees to Improve Women's Lives appear to have been bodies appointed from above with a brief to propagate the policies of the Soviet and to find out what women felt about them, and what the actual difficulties of their lives were, and to transmit this information upwards.[16] They were also to check up on work of the local leadership and Soviets, especially in connection with the implementation of the marriage law; to work at mobilizing mass opinion; and to report to higher authorities any malpractice, for example where they found a woman being unreasonably refused divorce. Support work for the army was of course an important part of the committees' duties and they were also supposed to organize literacy classes for women.

Women's congresses were meant to be held in every village or in every district at intervals of three to six months.[17] Each member was to be elected by between fifteen and twenty women. These congresses were in turn to elect their own representatives to attend county congresses. Judging from the attention devoted in the surviving documents to each form of organization, these congresses, though by no means universal, and perhaps not always organized strictly according to the book, were the most important form of organization for women. Unfortunately much of what was written about them consists only of elaborate descriptions of their structure, or lists of their aims, and we have little specific information on what they did.

Mao Zedong in his 1933 investigation of the Changgang district in Xinguo county, Jiangxi,[18] reported that of the sixteen delegates at the Women's Representative Congress,

---

[14] Yang Lianying, †'Representative congresses of women workers and peasants and their work', *QNSH*, 28 May 1933.

[15] Ibid.

[16] See the Gonglüe decisions cited in note 12.

[17] See the provincial committee document cited in note 3.

[18] Mao Zedong, †*Investigation into Changgang district*, 15 December 1933. The information about women in Changgang is taken from section 8, p. 132, and section 13, pp. 163-5, of the Japanese edition (Tokyo 1970-2).

eight did their work in their villages as women's representatives very well, seeking out jobs and doing them properly. Six did not seek work, accepted the tasks that they were allocated but did not do them well and were in need of help, and the worst two did not even do the work allocated. He says that the first women's meetings called by the district Soviet to choose women's representatives were attended on average by six out of every ten village women; a high initial participation rate compared to later experience in the north. The first subjects discussed by the newly elected district Women's Congresses were:

  enlarging the Red Army;
  aid to the Red Army;
  looking after the dependants of Red Army soldiers;
  women learning to plough;
  women selling their jewellery and buying government
  bonds.

These show both in selection and arrangement a subordination of specific women's demands to the general cause of the Soviets. Mao, in fact, remarked reproachfully that during the election campaign women's health, child-care problems, and women's education had not been discussed.

The laws of the Jiangxi Soviet of most direct concern to women were the Land Laws, the Marriage Law, and the Labour Law. Under the Land Law, hired hands, coolies, and peasants, irrespective of sex, were to have an equal right to land allotments, and part of the aim of this measure was to give poor women a greater possibility of economic independence.[19] This was linked to the orthodox Party line that women could gain liberation only through participation in productive work, which in the countryside of the Soviets had been specifically linked with ownership of land. An authoritative document on woman-work stated: 'Only land

---

[19] The Provisional Land Law of the Soviets (May 1930) did not explicitly give women the right to an allocation of land. However, it only remined in force for 3 months. Both earlier and later laws, of which a list follows, promised land to men and women alike. Land law adopted at Jinggangshan Dec. 1928. Land law adopted at Xinguo county Apr. 1929. Land law promulgated by the Chinese Military Revolutionary Council 1930. Land law of the Chinese Soviet Republic Nov. 1931. English texts of these laws can be found in Hsiao Tso-liang, *The Land Revolution in China*.

reform and only the Government of the Soviet can ̶
feudal bondage and liberate women.'[20]

The Land Law incorporated another very important pr̶
consistently present in Party policy, which is that ̶̶̶ss
transcends sex. Though the patriarchal family was held to
oppress all women, the women of the exploiting classes could
not thereby be considered a part of the exploited masses: the
rich peasant's wife was not held to be landless just because she
had never held title deeds. Women also complicated the whole
task of class analysis since they joined their husbands' families
at marriage and thus might change their class. The Central
Government devoted a section of its *Decisions concerning
some problems arising from the agrarian struggle* to this
problem.[21] It ruled that in the case of marriages which had
taken place before the uprising, women, even if they had been
born into another class, should be given the class status of their
in-laws if they had lived the life appropriate to this class for a
significant time. In the case of marriages which had taken
place after the uprising, poor women, even if they had
married into a landlord family, retained their original status.
Women from landlord families who married into poor
families could lose their original status only if they engaged in
labour for five years. ('Labour' was here held to include
domestic labour.)

There were apparently cases where women from rich
families married poor men in order to obtain a favourable
classification and save their family property. Not only did the
labour condition in this decision make such a ruse ineffective,
but dowries brought by such women were only to be immune
from fine if they did not exceed 50 silver dollars.[22] The rule
that to change her status the daughter of a poor family had
actually to live the life of a landlord family was intended to

---

[20] †*A work plan for the Ningdu county women's movement.*
[21] What follows is a brief summary of a fairly complex set of decisions. The full text is translated in Hsiao Tso-liang, pp. 277-9.
[22] A clause which itself tends to call into question the extent to which Soviet law was even implemented, since the Marriage Law in force at the time forbade dowries absolutely. †'Marriage Regulations of the Chinese Soviet Republic', article 8. Translations of both the Marriage Regulations and the Marriage Law (see note 25) are available in M. J. Meijer, *Marriage Law and Policy in the Chinese People's Republic.*

cover those cases where a girl had been 'adopted' into a landlord family as a child daughter-in-law or a maid, and in effect worked for them in exchange for her possibly quite scanty food.

Another problem in land distribution which especially concerned women was that a redistribution based on the number of heads per household might result in more land than they could farm efficiently being received by families with many members who were incapable of working. (Though of course elderly men and boy children might belong to this category, they were outnumbered by women handicapped by bound feet, pregnancy, or young children.) On the other hand, if land were distributed on the basis of labour power, such families might be left without the land necessary for survival. The Land Law does not provide a very clear-cut solution to this problem but recommends that distribution should be settled on the basis of both factors, in the light of local conditions and in such a way as to favour the interests of poor and middle peasants.[23]

There were two pieces of family legislation in the Jiangxi Soviet, the Marriage Regulations of December 1931,[24] and the Marriage Law of 1934.[25] Both follow family law in the Soviet Union[26] in dealing with marriage, divorce, and the subsequent disposal of property and children. Both laws define marriage as a free association between a man and a woman to be entered into without interference from other parties and to be ended by mutual agreement or upon the insistence of either husband or wife. Registration of marriage and divorce was required under both laws, an important principle because it removed marriage arrangements from the exclusively family domain accorded them by Chinese tradition, and, since both parties to a marriage had to take part in registration, it gave cadres a chance to verify at least that crude compulsion had not been employed.

The laws are broadly similar in both tone and content. The

[23] Land Law of the Chinese Soviet Republic, Nov. 1931, in Hsiao Tso-liang, p. 186.
[24] See note 21.
[25] †*The Marriage Law of the Chinese Soviet Republic*
[26] For the texts of the Soviet family laws of 1918, 1926, and 1944 see Rudolf Schlesinger, *The Family in the USSR*.

1934 Law is slightly more detailed, and contains a few changes which are presumably the result of the experiences of the two years during which the 1931 Regulations were in force. For example, while registration was still required by the 1934 Law, Article 9 expressly recognized *de facto* marriage, presumably in order to extend the protection afforded to women by legal marriage to those who had not complied with Soviet law. Article 11 placed the first restriction on the freedom of an individual to seek a divorce even against the will of the other partner, by making the consent of a Red Army soldier (or that of the local government, if he had not been in contact for two years) indispensable in any divorce action brought by his wife. Article 14 of the law decreed that if after divorce action a woman moved to another area, she had a right to receive land there under the local land reform. Both laws tended to favour women over men in custody of children, but to give men the heavier financial responsibility after divorce. This was explained by the Central Executive Committee of the Chinese Soviet Republic in the preamble to the regulations:

Although women have obtained freedom from the yoke of the feudal lords, they are still labouring under tremendous physical handicaps (for example, the binding of the feet), nor have they obtained complete economic independence. Therefore on questions concerning divorce, it becomes necessary to deviate in the direction of protecting women, and placing the greater part of the obligations and responsibilities entailed by divorce upon men.[27]

Unfortunately we know almost nothing of the implementation of marriage law in the Soviet Republic. Eighteen months after the promulgation of the 1931 Marriage Regulations Mao found that: 'freedom to divorce existed in the Changgang district'; however, many documents on women complained about cadres who automatically refused women divorce. It seems probable, since the whole period was marked by a desperate fight for survival and by serious tension and struggles within the party leadership, that economic and social policies were unevenly and very imperfectly carried out, and the strength of conservative attitudes towards women, which, as later experience proved, it took immense efforts and long

[27] Bela Kun (ed.), *Laws of the Chinese Soviet Republic*, p. 83.

periods of time to overcome, must seriously have hampered the implementation of the marriage law in the Jiangxi Soviet. To conciliate conservative opinion, there were frequent assurances that freedom of marriage did not mean sexual licence. The Revolution was even shown to bring stricter morality. Mao in his Changgang investigation claimed that before the revolution 50 per cent of women had had secret love affairs, that after the revolution the number had gone down to 10 per cent and could be expected to decrease further in future owing to the combined effects of land reform, freedom of marriage and divorce, and the demands of revolutionary work.[28]

A commentary on the implementation of the Marriage Regulations also betrays a certain uneasiness about the potential divisiveness of the campaign, insisting that 'it is a struggle against all feudal power, in no way is it stirring up women against men for a "struggle between the sexes" '.[29] Mao Zedong's famous reference to the subjection of women to the feudal authority of the husband[30] finds no echo in this document which speaks only of their oppression by the feudal family. Only in the extreme case of a wife-murderer was a campaign launched against a man as an individual, though it is true that then moderation was not counselled. Women's meetings were urged to demand that he be shot.[31]

The Labour Law,[32] though it contains provisions extremely favourable to women, must be held to have been of little practical significance, since it was designed to apply only to industrial and handicraft workers who were a small minority in the Soviet areas. Furthermore, it seems impossible that

[28] · Mao Zedong, †*Investigation into Changgang district*, p. 164.

[29] †*Order No. 10 of the Gan county soviet government.*

[30] Mao Zedong, †'Report on an investigation on the peasant movement in Hunan,' March 1926, *SW* (1965), p. 44. quoted in my Introduction, p. 16.

[31] †*Notification No. 7 of the Ningdu central county committee of the CCP. Mobilize labouring women for the struggle against feudal oppression*

[32] † *The Labour Law of the Chinese Soviet Republic.* Regulations affecting women in this law resemble those of the Soviet Labour Code of 1922 except that maternity leave was longer for Soviet women. (Norton Dodge, *Women in the Soviet Economy*, pp. 61-3). Both in the Soviet Union and in China, dissenting voices have at times been raised against restrictions on the work which women may do, by those who claim that such limitations are detrimental to women. (Dodge, p. 60. William Hinton, *The Hundred Day War*, p. 139).)

material conditions in the Soviet areas, situated as they were in areas of China which were economically backward, could have been such as to make possible the realization of the working conditions which the law stipulated. However, it is perhaps worth summarizing the regulations governing the employment of women workers, if only to show the Party's ideals for them.

Women were to receive equal pay for equal work, but their employment was actually prohibited in the mines, in various chemical and metallurgical industries and at very high altitudes. There were also restrictions on the weights they might be required to carry and they were not to do night-work. Women got eight weeks' paid maternity leave and when pregnant or nursing were to enjoy job protection. Enterprises were to provide crèches and nursing rooms, and nursing mothers were to have thirty minutes every three hours in which to feed their babies.

Though a few exceptional women like Kang Keqing (wife of Zhu De) and Li Zhen[33] (in the 1950s China's only woman major-general) actually served with the combat troops, women were apparently less active militarily in the Jiangxi Soviet than in the Sichuan (Szechuan) or Qiongya (Hainan) Soviets.[34] However, many thousands belonged to the Women Guards, a local defence force. A larger organization than this was the Women's Aid Corps which was responsible for rescuing and nursing the wounded and for carrying supplies to the fighters. Women also took an extensive part in intelligence work and sabotage.[35]

Though the idea of the equality of the sexes was to be propagated with far more energy in future years, much effort was made to put it over to ordinary people in the Jiangxi Soviet. Attitudes must in any case have been directly influenced by women's growing economic, political, and social

[33] For biographical material on these and other remarkable women see †*Important Documents of the Chinese Women's Movement* and Nym Wales (Helen Snow), *The Chinese Communists*.

[34] Nym Wales quotes Kang Keqing on the existence of a women's regiment in Sichuan (*The Chinese Communists*, p. 218). One of the many accounts of the famous Women's Red Detachments in Hainan is in Xu Dixin and others, †*The emergence of new China*.

[35] Hu Delan †*Recollections of some revolutionary women in the old red bases of north-east Jiangxi*, in *Stories of the revolutionary struggle of Jiangxi women*.

role in actual life; but other resources were also brought to
bear. Plays with emancipated activist heroines were put on
and women were encouraged to take such heroines as models
for their own development.[36] Even sport was used to get
women outside the home. In 1933 the youth paper carried an
account of a football match between a school team and a
women's team.[37] As people learned to read, the first sentences
which they struggled to decipher in the elementary reading
texts bore important political messages, like this one:

> Men and women are all people
> Without equality, there's trouble.
> (Nan he nü zongshi ren
> Yi buping dajia nao.)[38]

In his investigation of Caixi district, Shanghang county,
Jiangxi province, Mao Zedong reported that in 1931 about 30
per cent of representatives at district congresses were women,
and that the proportion rose to about 60 per cent in 1932 and
remained at that level in 1933.[39] The rapid rise is presumably
partly to be accounted for by the absence in the army of
increasing numbers of men, but even the first figure is
surprisingly high, again perhaps implying that women's right
to participate in public affairs at the lower levels was
comparatively easily accepted in Jiangxi. Very few of these
women would have been able to continue their activities. Only
fifty women left the Jiangxi Soviet on the Long March to the
north, and of those left behind many were killed.[40] Others
must simply have resumed their former lives.

Northern Shaanxi, the new headquarters of the Communist
Party after the Long March, was to provide the base from
which communist armies fought the anti-Japanese war and

---

[36] A play of this type which seems to have been widely performed was †*On the spring
ploughing front*, edited by the Soviet education bureau of Jiangxi province.

[37] †'The Red School Youth team beats the women's team', *QNSH* 21 May 1933.

[38] †*Three-character reader for workers and peasants.*

[39] Mao Zedong, †*Investigation into Caixi district, Collected Works*, pp. 178-9. A
recent commentator, calculating percentages from the absolute figures given by Mao
Zedong, has found slight errors in his arithmetic, (Trygve Lötveit, *Chinese
Communism 1931-1934*, p. 218). My percentages are approximations intended to
illustrate the trend in both the upper and lower Caixi districts.

[40] Nym Wales, *Inside Red China*, p. 174.

the Civil War against the Kuomintang, and where the communist movement laid the political and social foundations for its later victory. Here techniques for the mobilization of popular support, including that of women, first employed in the southern Soviets, were developed and improved. Shaanxi had been the scene of considerable communist activity since 1927.[41] By the autumn of 1935, when the first battered remnants of the Red Armies which had evacuated the Jiangxi Soviet almost a year earlier arrived in the north of the province, it was the home of a fully-fledged Soviet which had carried out land reform and successfully resisted three Nationalist annihilation campaigns.

Nevertheless the communists' retreat to the north was interpreted by many contemporaries as the escape of stray sparks from a fire, which could only delay its ultimate extinction. They did not foresee a new and greater conflagration in the barren mountains of Shaanxi. And indeed it was an improbable birthplace for the largest-scale revolution of the modern world. Far more remote and backward even than the southern Soviet areas, the province of Shaanxi had experienced very little of the growing commercialization of the south, or the radicalizing influence of pre-communist revolutionary movements. The element of popular bandit tradition was stronger in early communist activities in Shaanxi even than it had been in the south.

The forces that had moulded Shaanxi's twentieth-century history had been warlord rivalries, civil wars, banditry, a chronically indebted peasantry, grinding taxation, and large-scale opium cultivation. These interconnected factors combined to aggravate the effects of famine in an area where it was anyway endemic. The China Famine Relief Commission estimated that in the famine years of 1928 and 1929, 2,500,000 persons perished, almost a third of the entire population of Shaanxi, and there were other years in which many thousands died.[42]

---

[41] This description of the economic and political situation in Shaanxi is based on Mark Selden's excellent account of the communist movement in that province (Mark Selden, *The Yenan Way*).

[42] China International Famine Relief Commission, Annual Report for 1929 cited in Selden, p. 6.

In such an environment, neither modernization nor education had thrived, and peasant society in Shaanxi was still less affected by change than in the rest of China. In the words of Xu Deli, the Commissar for Education, the province was culturally one of the darkest places on earth with an illiteracy rate of 95 per cent, and a belief that washing was harmful. He told Edgar Snow: 'But all this and many other prejudices are due to ignorance, and it is my job to change their mentality. Such a population, compared with Jiangxi, is very backward indeed . . . Here [in Shaanxi] the work is very much slower.'[43]

The position of women in the region was very low indeed. Small girls still had their feet bound although the custom was by then in decline over most of China, and was extinct in the towns.[44] Thousands of women had been sold during the great famines of the late 1920s and early 1930s by their fathers and husbands, who resorted to the sale of the human capital of their families in a desperate attempt to ensure survival.[45]

The particularly low status of women in the province probably had its origins in several interrelated factors. In part of course it was a reflection of the backwardness of Shaanxi society. The Confucian ideal that women should lead enclosed lives seems to have been more insisted on in northern Shaanxi, perhaps because it was a frontier area with a long history of border raids. As in other societies threatened by outsiders, women were 'protected' by being more closely restricted to the home. Buck showed that nowhere in China did women do less farm work than in the region of winter-wheat and millet cultivation within which most of Shaanxi lay, or in the winter-wheat and kaoling area into which the communists were soon to expand.[46] This last was a characteristic which Shaanxi shared with the Jiangxi bases. Alone amongst the southern agricultural areas, the rice-tea area of which Jiangxi was a part had a very low rate of female participation in farm work. I will return again, both in this chapter, and in chapter four to

[43] Edgar Snow, *Red Star over China*, pp. 240-1.

[44] Nym Wales, *Women in Modern China*, p. 223.

[45] Selden, p. 6. For the biographies of women who were sold see Jan Myrdal, *Report from a Chinese Village*, pp. 203-5 and William Hinton, *Fanshen*, pp. 174-7.

[46] For data on women's participation in farm-work see J. L. Buck, *The Chinese Farm Economy*, p. 235, and *Land Utilization in China*, p. 293.

the general problem of the level of women's participation in agriculture. Here it is important simply to note that the rural areas where the mainstream development of Chinese communist policies took place prior to 1948-9 were poor, remote, mountainous regions where comparatively extensive plough cultivation predominated, and the labour force was likely to be largely male.[47]

Thus when Party workers engaged in woman-work examined the oppression of women in China, the orthodox Marxist analysis that it developed from women's exclusion from productive labour seemed to fit the situation before them. Of course the need to increase production was vital to the success of the revolution, but it was not just expediency that led theorists to give women's involvement in the workforce an ever more prominent place in policy towards women; it was that in both the Jiangxi and the anti-Japanese period they found themselves in areas where women produced little and were clearly oppressed. They had no reason to seek other factors in women's oppression.

During the early years in the north-west, official policy on women apparently showed little change from the days of the Jiangxi Soviet. The Marriage Law of 1934 was reprinted in Baoan in 1936 and remained in force.[48] But women were more difficult to mobilize in the conservative north. Since footbinding was still the rule, the peasant women found the big feet of the few women who arrived from the south very odd. The feet of little girls were still being bound even in Yanan, the new communist capital, in 1937.[49] Presumably it was policy to eliminate the custom by persuasion rather than coercion, and it was taking time. In spite of this, the women's movement was gradually gaining ground. Gao Mengzhen, who directed woman-work in northern Shaanxi, claimed in 1937 that there were 7,000 active Communist Party women in the Shaanxi–Gansu–Ningxia base (henceforth Shaan–Gan–Ning), and about 130,000 had taken some part in the activities of the women's organizations.[50] She listed spinning, weaving, and

---

[47] Ester Boserup, *Women's Role in Economic Development*, p. 35.
[48] Edgar Snow, *Red Star over China*, p. 230.
[49] Nym Wales, *Women in Modern China*, p. 223.
[50] Nym Wales, *Inside Red China*, pp. 194-5

sewing to produce army uniforms and shoes, food collection for the troops, and the development of agricultural skills as the activities of women in these organizations.

A political campaign to involve women in the 1941 elections both as electors and candidates ran for many months.[51] Women were in fact elected to 8 per cent of the seats, an achievement perhaps in Shaanxi, but unremarkable by Jiangxi standards. In the following year, in a fierce debate on the women's movement, a new line on woman-work emerged which was more clearly defined and firmly orientated towards economic problems than ever before.

Westernized women intellectuals from urban areas like Shanghai, who came to Yanan in the early years of the united front, brought with them ideas of women's emancipation influenced by feminist tendencies developed since the May 4th era. They seem to have favoured an all-out attack on the feudal marriage system. The great clash between them and the Party came in 1942, when Ding Ling published an essay in the *Liberation Daily,* attacking policy towards women, saying that they were being overworked, expected to play a dual role, and subjected to criticism if they failed in either.[52] The Party counter-attacked, and as Ding Ling told the journalist Gunther Stein, she and some others were severely criticized in that year. They were told that 'full sex equality had already been established' and that their feminism was outdated and harmful.[53]

The resolution on women issued by the Central Committee in February 1943[54] follows up this attack. 'Women cadres must stop looking on economic work as unimportant.' Its sole reference to the 'feudal oppression of women' lies in the assertion that they can escape it through production. Male dominance, purchase marriage, and other such problems are not mentioned. Foot-binding is merely brought up as a practice which is 'harmful to both health and production' and in which reform is therefore desirable.

In a speech welcoming this resolution, Cai Chang accused

[51] *Party work*, Shaanxi 1936, quoted in Selden, p. 165.
[52] Ding Ling, †"Thoughts on March 8th".
[53] Gunther Stein, *The Challenge of Red China*, p. 206.
[54] CC decisions (1943), see appendix 1.

many women Party members and cadres of lacking a sense reality and a mass outlook.[55] She said that her criticism applied especially to some women cadres from the intelligentsia who, in leadership positions in the organizations responsible for woman-work, could only recite a set of slogans such as 'economic independence', 'free-choice marriage', 'oppose the four oppressions', instead of acting in accordance with the specific situation. She claimed that such cadres automatically discriminated in favour of the wife and against the husband, in favour of the daughter-in-law and against the father-in-law, so that woman-work was forfeiting public sympathy and its support became isolated. When meetings were held, women's domestic problems were forgotten and their daily routine was ignored; meetings took place too often, and what was said was hard for peasant women to understand so that they became fed up. In another speech of this period, she said, 'Our slogans are no longer "free choice marriage" and "equality of the sexes" but rather "save the children", "a flourishing family", and "nurture health and prosperity." '[56]

A brief retrospective analysis of the women's movement during the anti-Japanese War, which contained similar criticisms, pointed out that the relationship between women and the family could only be dealt with on the basis of the real situation in the liberated areas.[57] This was that the family was the basic economic unit, that this family was not the small (conjugal) family of capitalist society but the 'big family' of the village whose intention was the most efficient use of labour power. This big family was the basis of the rural economy which was supporting the resistance war. The basis for action should therefore be the reform and consolidation of this type of family. Furthermore, given the subsistence nature of the rural economy, women could not liberate themselves by leaving the family and taking a job. Thus the path for the women's movement of the liberated areas of China would differ from that taken by such movements in other countries.

---

[55] Cai Chang, †*Greeting the new orientation of woman-work*, LA documents 1, p. 5-7.
[56] Speech quoted in †*Chinese Women Stand Up*, p. 2.
[57] Ibid, pp. 1-3.

Like Cai Chang's speech, this analysis sustained the main thesis of the 1943 Central Committee resolution that the vital task for the women's movement was to involve women in productive labour.

So, for instance, according to Isabel and David Crook, when the 1943 resolution of the Central Committee was received in the mountain village of Ten Mile Inn, Hebei province:

It was realised that women's general emancipation depended on their role in production, woman-work no longer involved launching campaigns on so many fronts simultaneously, and other objectives were given attention only when they could be tied in with production. Thus by the end of the war the position of women in this village was greatly improved economically, but other advances had still to be made.[58]

Many reports of production heroines were published in this period, but there were very few models of the type later to become so common, in which peasant women fought back against ill-treatment by husbands or mothers-in-law. Each of the border regions replaced the Soviet marriage law with its own regulations of which the first were promulgated in 1939.[59] But at this stage there seems to have been little done to enforce them.

What was the reason for this soft-pedalling? The assertion made to Ding Ling that 'full sex equality' had already been achieved in the border areas is hardly consistent with later statements about the very long period of education and propaganda needed before it could be achieved. But Ding Ling was also told that for the sake of victory both men and women should get on with the political problem of improving co-operation between all groups.[60] Fear of the potentially divisive influence of a women's movement has always been a factor in communist policy towards women. It was present, as we have seen, in Jiangxi, and perhaps to a greater extent in the Shaanxi base area. There is perhaps an instructive parallel to compromise on women's issues to be observed in the history of

[58] Isabel and David Crook, *Revolution in a Chinese Village*, p. 69 and pp. 100-8.
[59] Marriage regulations of the Shaan-Gan-Ning border area, promulgated 4 Apr. 1939. Translated in M. J. Meijer, *Marriage Law and Policy in the Chinese People's Republic*, Appendix 3.
[60] Gunther Stein, *The Challenge of Red China*, p. 206.

land policy. The militant class struggle of land reform, abandoned with the establishment of the United Front in 1936, was replaced by a more conciliatory campaign to reduce rates and interest. That the fear of the women's movement became more acute and resulted in the open polemic of 1942 was due in part perhaps to the stimulus of Ding Ling's highly critical essay, but the force of the response must surely be attributed to the general military and political situation.

This was a crucial stage of the war. Under severe pressure from Japanese offensives the communist bases suffered heavy territorial losses and by the end of 1942 their population had declined from 44 to 25 million.[61] Furthermore, the Kuomintang blockade accelerated a formerly mild inflation until it became intolerable. The needs of the army caused commodity shortages and spiralling taxes. The situation was critical for a regime which depended for survival on popular support.

The rectification campaign which sought to deal with the situation by the development of a simpler and more economical administration, greater army participation in production, more emphasis on mass mobilization and on ideals of devotion and sacrifice amongst cadres has been amply dealt with elsewhere.[62] Its effect on the women's movement was to produce a swing away from militancy. Resistance to accepting this swing, since it was in the long-term interests of the revolution (and therefore of women themselves), was regarded as feminism in a pejorative sense. In the 1943 resolution the main theme of the criticism about the way woman-work had been done was:

> We have not regarded economic work as the most suitable for women, nor grasped that the mobilization of women for production is the most vital factor in safeguarding their special interests.

The resolution contains this strong emphasis on production throughout, stating for example that woman-work should be judged by how well women do in production, and that only through economic prosperity and independence can women

[61] Selden, p. 179.
[62] See Selden, pp. 177ff., and Boyd Compton, *Mao's China: Party Reform Documents, 1942-44.*

start to gain liberation. The tactics of the women's movement changed and developed considerably during the Civil War, and it is only in the late 1940s that we have a sort of miniature preview of the social struggles which were to erupt all over China after 1949. But economic strength arising from involvement in production was throughout seen as the key to women's equality and social independence, so it is important to examine this aspect of woman-work more closely and to consider the attempt to establish women as a productive labour force.

The daily routine of the northern peasant woman was hard. Before she could cook she had first to husk and grind the grain. Water had to be fetched, possibly from a distance, and she usually made both clothes and shoes for her family. But she rarely undertook remunerative work and her domestic tasks lacked status compared with the more obviously productive jobs done by men. Only exceptionally, if her family were both short of manpower and too poor to hire help, would a northern woman work in the fields, and then it was felt a cause for shame. Apart from the desirability of increased production for its own sake, the communists argued that if women could make a significant contribution to family income their status would rise in consequence. But although there are reports of women learning to plough and to hoe, clearing new land, and raising record crops in the early years of the production campaign, they are comparatively few, and it seems that in Shaan-Gan-Ning it was still unusual for them to work on the land on any scale until the time of land reform, though in other smaller base areas, where the military participation rate was higher and the need for mass mobilization still greater, their role in agriculture was probably more significant. This is confirmed by a 1948 report which says that during the anti-Japanese War, it was only in families or areas where manpower was short that women went much to the fields. The main effort of the campaign went into getting women to spin and weave, because the liberated areas, being cut off from the centres of textile production by the Japanese occupation and the Kuomintang blockade, were very short of cloth,[63] and resulting price rises were aggravated by

[63] Luo Qiong. †*Production by village women in the past year.* LA documents 4. p. 30.

the heavy demand for cloth for army uniforms.

When the problem of textile production was first faced in 1939, the solution attempted was that of joint state-private factories. But large-scale enterprises turned out to be difficult to organize in the primitive countryside, nor was it easy to find the amount of capital and the numbers of full-time workers which they required. Production did increase in the next few years, but not enough to satisfy demand.[64] In 1942 Mao Zedong set the target of making the industry supply the needs of the people, the army, and the cadres by reliance not only on factories but on cottage and co-operative handicrafts.[65]

Reviving the handicraft industry required considerable effort. The village of Zhehu in Xingtai county, Hebei, was thriving by 1948 with 196 spinning-wheels and 61 looms among its 220-odd households, yet in 1942 its few spinning-wheels had been out of use for years. Only three women had known how to weave, at least one of whom had married into the village from another county. When she started weaving early in 1942 she had to make a long journey to buy a loom. At the start she had five companions but was quickly joined by so many others that in 1943 they were already able to tide the village through a year of drought with their earnings, which obtained them added respect. By then a co-operative had taken over the purchase of cotton and the sale of cloth and organized a training class. Women were better clothed and could afford to buy draught animals so that they no longer had to push the heavy grindstones themselves. A beneficial side-effect of this was a fall in the number of miscarriages and births of deformed children.[66] Such obvious advantages were vital to the success of the campaign as they induced women, already heavily burdened with domestic work which could not be much reduced, to take on extra jobs. Older women had to help younger ones in order to get everything done. This was hard on the older women who had formerly been able to sit back a bit and supervise the household. Now they were often left with both the cooking and the children while their sons'

---

[64] Luo Qiong, †*The cottage textile industry in the Shaan-Gan-Ning border region*, p. 5.
[65] Ibid, p. 6.
[66] Liu Heng, †*Zhehu, the village where every household weaves*, LA documents 4.

wives went off to spin or weave. In Zhehu some of them were very annoyed. When their daughters-in-law returned from work, they dished up only cold food, and grumbled, 'Everything is upside down since the Communist Party came. Mothers-in-law have become daughters-in-law.' They were somewhat mollified, however, when the younger women brought back their earnings in the form of grain from the co-operative.

It was common for women to group together to spin, reel, and wind the yarn, and to set up warps. Even when the task did not actually require more than one pair of hands, they tended to work together, sharing heating and lighting expenses. So much contact with others must have had a profound effect on people who had formerly led more enclosed and solitary lives. As they worked in groups and arranged to care for each other's children they learned to organize themselves and their time. So much was the textile industry the concern of women, that at village level it was frequently managed by the Women's Association. The close relationship between the campaign to revive the textile industry and woman-work was constantly stressed in the documents and also in the literature of these years. In 1945 the *Liberation Daily* published some reportage by Ding Ling on the women spinners of Mada village near Yanan.[67] This was perhaps symbolic of the closed ranks of the women's movement in which for a time conflict, or at least open conflict, had ceased. Priority for production was accepted.

By 1947, the liberated areas of Shanxi–Chahar–Hebei and Shandong were self-sufficient in cloth and those of Shanxi-Suiyuan and Shaan–Gan–Ning partially so. In the Taihang mountains about 74 per cent of the women could spin or weave, and income from supplementary occupations, of which textile production was the most important, had risen to approximately 30 per cent of total household income.[68] (This was probably exceptionally high since Taihang is a very poor agricultural area.) It was estimated that production of cloth increased eightfold in the liberated areas between 1942 and 1944.

[67] Ding Ling, †*A Yanan collection*, pp. 40-60.
[68] Luo Qiong, †*The cottage textile industry*, p. 10.

Other supplementary occupations in which women began to play an important part included the production of vegetable oil, cured leather, and paper. Even more important were the sewing workshops which served the army. Besides cloth uniforms for the summer and quilted cotton ones for the winter, the soldiers had to be provided with Chinese cloth shoes which take one or two days to stitch but can be worn through in only two weeks of marching or a few months of ordinary wear. Bonus schemes were operated with competitions and ever-rising targets in attempts to boost production.[69]

During the anti-Japanese War, woman-work was directed by the Women's Committee of the Central Committee (Zhongyang Fuwei). In 1945 the Preparatory Committee of the Women's Association of all the liberated areas was set up in Yanan with thirteen members.[70] At village level, until the Japanese surrender, the mass organization was usually known as the Women's National Salvation Association, and afterwards, more simply, as the Women's Association or the Peasant Women's Association. It is claimed that by 1945 these associations in Shaan-Gan-Ning and seven other liberated areas had 7,100,000 members. Great stress was laid on the importance of working with women. The Party was constantly hampered by a shortage of women cadres, and by 1947 Deng Yingchao was not only urging that women activists in the villages should be given special help to enable them to become cadres, and that all the women cadres who could be spared should go to organize amongst peasant women, but even that men cadres should not despise such work or think themselves unsuitable for it.[71]

In 1948 a report was published to show the usefulness of special organizations for women. It said that in the winter of 1947 several defunct organizations for women had been abolished in Lingqiu county, Shanxi, and at the beginning of mobilizing for land reform no distinction had been made between men and women, who all joined the New Peasants'

[69] †*Chinese women stand up*, pp. 52–4.

[70] † *The movement in which the women of the liberated areas of China are standing up*, p. 28.

[71] Deng Yingchao, †*Land reform and the new tasks of woman-work*, p. 35.

Association and the Poor Peasants' League.[72] Few women spoke at meetings and they complained that it was not natural for them to hold meetings with men. They themselves admitted: 'If we're speaking with men present, those who ought to say a lot say very little.' The county leaders chose two villages in which to experiment with separate organizations for women. These were a great success; women attended meetings enthusiastically and lost their reserve in talking, so the experiment was extended to cover the whole county. Women's congresses were set up in every district, and through these 90 per cent of the women were organized to play an active part in land reform. It was concluded that the preliminary work of mobilization was best done through two organizations, one for both men and women, the other exclusively for women. The latter could hold small meetings where women would gain confidence in speaking. Such meetings should not last too long so that they did not inconvenience women with small children, and should be timed so that they did not interfere with household routines.[73]

Although they had their own regional and central headquarters, the village Women's Associations were subordinate to the local Peasants' Associations.[74] This made them vulnerable to local cadres who might consider themselves good revolutionaries and yet have very backward attitudes to women. In Ten Mile Village in Hebei, middle peasant cadres forbade their wives to attend meetings of the Women's Association which they called 'prostitutes' meetings'.[75] In Longbow village in Shanxi province, when Wang Yu-lai, vice-chairman of the Peasants' Association, forced an under-age girl to marry his son because he had already 'bought and paid' for her, the Women's Association was afraid to interfere.[76]

In spite of such difficulties, the importance of the Women's Association in village life continued to grow. In areas near the front it organized its members to sabotage or repair bridges

[72] †New forms of women's organization emerge in land reform.

[73] †Experience in mobilizing women during the land reform movement in Beiyue district.

[74] Decisions of the Land Reform Conference (1947) quoted in †Chinese Women stand up, p. 6.

[75] I. and D. Crook, Revolution in a Chinese Village, p. 107.

[76] William Hinton, Fanshen, p. 397.

and roads, to prepare food for the soldiers and carry it to them, to rescue and nurse the wounded, and to carry messages and gather intelligence under the cover of going to market or visiting relatives.[77] The importance of such support activities in mobile guerrilla warfare can hardly be exaggerated. Information about enemy movements was vital to the survival of the resistance; so were friendly villages which would extend help whenever necessary; but it had to be organized help so that even a small village could feed perhaps a hundred soldiers, though they might have to leave after only an hour. To collect so much food presented formidable problems in the mountain villages where most of the inhabitants grew little food for the market and were themselves living close to subsistence level. Women were found to be better at this work than men because they knew how much grain their neighbours had in store and who might be persuaded to sell some, and because they had more gift for talking people round. Communications were difficult and much of the fighting was in remote areas, so that several food carriers might be needed to supply one fighting man. 'Hospital' administration, also often in the hands of women, could be very complicated. In guerrilla areas which were free territory by night but all too often penetrated by the enemy by day, a 'hospital' had no centralized existence. Stretcher bearers carried wounded men to peasant homes, gave brief instructions on dressing wounds and on sterilization by boiling, and then disappeared, leaving the family to care for the patient on its own. Medical workers might come if they could, but most of the care devolved on the women of the family. If the Japanese came to search they would claim the patient was a sick son of the house, usually naming some highly infectious illness so that the search might not be too close. These activities increased women's commitment to the new society by giving them a sense of participation, and brought them experience and self-confidence which they then drew upon in land reform.

Agrarian policy underwent a radical change with the end of the anti-Japanese War and the outbreak of the Liberation

[77] The following information about women's activities is drawn partly from articles contained in the anthology LA documents 3 and partly from information obtained from an informant in Peking who had been a nurse in the liberated areas.

War. It was no longer necessary to avoid alienating the landlords. The peasant had to be given a stake in New Democracy, to be shown what it could mean to him, and so, after the implementation of 'double reduction' or in some places even omitting this stage, came land reform. The change in policy on women could not be so sharp. Too sudden and strong a campaign for women's rights would have alienated many peasants, including even many of the women themselves. In the words of the Central Committee's new resolution on woman-work issued in 1948:[78]

> It must be recognized that this is work to change the peasants' ideas and is a long and demanding job which cannot be hurried.

Nevertheless profoundly important changes occurred in the course of land reform as the resolution acknowledged:

> Women have become much more aware and enthusiastic, and consequently there has been a fundamental change in their political and economic status, and in their position in the family and in society.

Under land reform not only did men and women get equal rights to the land, but separate land deeds were sometimes issued. To quote again from the resolution:

> When a family is taken as the unit for issuing land deeds, a note must be made upon them to the effect that men and women have equal rights to the land. Every member of the family has democratic rights in the disposal of the property. When necessary, land deeds for women can be issued separately.

Women were quick to realize the significance of this; for example in Chao Chen village in Shanxi, many said: 'When I get my share I'll separate from my husband, then he won't be able to oppress me any more.'[79] Mass meetings to discuss and agree the division of land, the disposal of confiscated landlord property, and the treatment that the individual landlords should receive were an important part of land reform. Women

[78] CC decisions (1948), see Appendix 2.
[79] William Hinton, *Fanshen*, p. 397.

took an active part in all of them. In some villages where all the able-bodied men were away in the army, women were even the main force in land reform.[80] As the textile movement had encouraged women to come out of their homes and group together, so land reform got them to take more part in general village affairs. But it is significant that a disproportionate number of women activists in land reform seem to have been widows, forced by their situation to represent the interests of their families. Married women must have left this important affair to their husbands in accordance with custom.

At the same time the transition from the scattered guerrilla fighting to large-scale positional warfare brought many more men under arms, causing a shortage of agricultural labour which could only be relieved by women. At the end of the anti-Japanese War it was still unusual for them to do field work, yet Deng Yingchao claimed that by 1949, 50–70 per cent of the women in the older liberated areas were working on the land, and as many as 80 per cent in the best-organized places.[81] Frequently it was not possible to find substitutes for the absent soldiers within their own families, and though it had been the responsibility of the village cadres or the Peasants' Association to help them and see that their land was tilled, it was now more often members of the Women's Association who undertook the work. Mutual-aid teams and agricultural co-operatives were more commonly set up in areas relying heavily on women in order to overcome the shortage of really strong workers.

Both the morale and the consciousness of women had been raised by the production movement and by land reform, and women increasingly came to reject their old subordinate role in the family and in society. The 1948 resolution encouraged them to do so actively and warned against just letting things take their course:

It should not be thought that once women take part in production all the remnants of feudalism which still constrain them will just naturally disappear and there will

[80] Er Dong, † *Women and children do important work*

[81] Deng Yingchao, "Chinese Women help to build a new China", *People's China*, No. 6 (1950).

be no need to do any more work.

The resolution asserts that:

The basic policies laid down by the Central Committee Resolution of 1943 are still completely appropriate,

and that:

after rent and interest reduction or land reform has been carried out, productive labour remains the pivot of the women's movement.

However, production is no longer advocated as a panacea. The need for laws against foot-binding, infanticide, purchase marriage, and the adoption of daughters-in-law, followed by education on the equality of the sexes is specifically acknowledged. On the means to be employed in emancipating women it states:

The small number of backward elements who want to preserve old feudal customs and who constantly oppress women must be suitably struggled against where necessary. But it must be understood that this sort of struggle is an ideological struggle amongst the peasants, and should be radically different from the class struggle against the feudal landlords.

Propaganda and persuasion are advocated, and violence is by implication rejected. But as in the land reform landlords were sometimes beaten by furious peasants who took things into their own hands, so women in their struggle for emancipation did sometimes resort to violence. Jack Belden recounts how the members of one women's association beat a man to try to stop him ill-treating his wife, and when he escaped, several women told her they would bite him to death if they caught him again.[82] Reports of such incidents are quite common, but they appear to have been allowed to pass without action by the higher authorities. When women used violence as individuals it was a different matter. There were only four women in the prison in Yanan in 1946 and they were all in for the murder of their husbands.[83] Violence sometimes made it easier for the women's association to rely on persuasion alone in subsequent cases. For instance in the Shanxi village of Longbow, after one

[82] Jack Belden, *China Shakes the World*, pp. 304-7.
[83] Robert Payne, *Journey to Red China*, p. 104.

man had been beaten because he punished his wife for going to meetings, the others all became more careful.[84] Violence posed too great a threat to family and class solidarity to be condoned, and the Longbow Women's Association was acting more correctly when it persuaded a poor peasant to stop beating his wife by reminding him that it was hard enough for a poor man to find a wife at all, so he had better not drive her to demanding a divorce.[85] Women helped each other in similar ways in the new liberated area of north Jiangsu when young women fought their husbands and mothers-in-law for the right to attend meetings. Women's Association leaders would go to the home of any woman having trouble and invite the sister to go with her. If any objections were raised, she would threaten the family with the power of organized women.[86]

Such quarrels sometimes split women's associations. Hinton says that though women were united in their support of their right to own land, they did not agree on free-choice marriage, which the older women saw as a threat to their authority over their daughters-in-law.[87] Jack Belden met one young woman who, in her zeal for catching 'bad mothers-in-law', used to eavesdrop on family quarrels and, at the sound of blows, drag the offender off to appear before a reform meeting.[88] A description of the work of the Women's Association in north Jiangsu records that the Association always dragged mothers-in-law who had beaten their daughters-in-law before meetings to scold them. The younger women liked the Association, but the older ones complained that times had changed and that they felt useless.[89] In Zhao Shuli's story *The Heirloom*,[90] the mother is gradually won over to her efficient modern-minded daughter-in-law's way of doing things, but it is easy to imagine that the frustrations of older women who had reached a position of some dominance within the family only after many

[84] William Hinton, *Fanshen*, p. 158.
[85] Ibid, p. 159.
[86] Lu Feng, †*The people arise*, part 5.
[87] William Hinton, *Fanshen*, p. 396.
[88] Jack Belden, *China Shakes the World*, p. 294.
[89] Lu Feng, †*The people arise*, part 5.
[90] Chao Shu-li, *Rhymes of Li Yu-ts'ai and other stories*, pp. 69–89.

years of subordination must have been harder to resolve.

Perhaps partly because of this sort of problem, even during the Civil war there were no great marriage reform enforcement campaigns of the type that took place during the 1950s. Each border region had its own marriage laws, which upheld the principles of free-choice marriage, the right to divorce (though the grounds had to be given), and custody and maintenance arrangements which tended to favour women.[91] However, in the words of an official commentator on the Marriage Law of 1950: 'Marriage Law was not pursued with great force in the Border Areas.' If a woman appealed to government cadres for assistance in resisting forced marriage, or obtaining a divorce, they were supposed to enforce the law, though they may often have failed to do so. They did not campaign against traditional types of marriage when those involved took no initiative. Women's campaigns against family oppression most often involved the organization of a peer group to exert pressure so that their mistreatment by their husbands or in-laws might end.

In this transitional period when tradition was crumbling but had by no means collapsed, odd situations arose. A couple in their early twenties who lived in Dongnan county, Jiangsu, had been betrothed since childhood.[92] Both were Party members and she was head of her village Women's Association, so they would presumably have been considered as among the most modern young people in their area. Yet though they had seen each other by chance sometimes, and had once even attended the same peasants' conference, they had never spoken to each other. A recruitment campaign finally induced her to communicate with him because she wanted to urge him to join the army. She got the village political worker to help her write a letter, in which she promised to wait for him and to marry him when he came back. In the meantime she pledged herself to care for his family as though it were her own. Her letter

[91] For the titles, texts, and discussions of the laws see M.J. Meijer, *Marriage Law and Policy in the Chinese People's Republic*, chapter III and appendices 3-7. The many differences between the laws obviously appeal to the legalist. Since, however, the basic challenge which they offered to the old marriage system was the same, and it is doubtful to what extent their fine points were implemented. I have not chosen to discuss them here in detail.

[92] †*Qian Xiuqing and Jiang Jinzhai.*

ended with a shy suggestion that they should 'meet for a chat when you have time'. No doubt if the boy returned the marriage was recorded statistically as a free-choice marriage, one of some percentage used to prove the successful implementation of the new law. But this story probably tells us more than statistics about the way things changed.

In the liberated areas of north China between January and June 1948, 64 per cent of all civil cases were petitions for divorce, of which the great majority were brought by women. Yet the new ideas were still far from being generally accepted. The other side of the picture was brought out in figures collected by the Women's Federation which showed that of 464 cases where a woman's death had been investigated, 40 per cent had involved women who had wanted divorces, but had been unable to get them.[93] There were both murders and suicides amongst these. In 1950, Zhang Zhirang, a vice-president of the Supreme Court, admitted: 'Because the feudal marriage system is so deeply rooted, it is still no easy thing, even in the old liberated areas, to carry through the new policy regarding marriage.[94]

But at least the basis for change had been laid. Cases of young women who set themselves against tradition by insisting on choosing their own partners and who won their battle occurred more and more frequently, and they set an example in new-style family relationships. The principle of social equality for women was strengthened by the need for extra labour in the war effort as a result of which millions of women gained at least partial economic independence. Through handicrafts, co-operatives, and work on the land women played a greater role in the family and village economy. The impact of such widened horizons on the individual and her conception of herself could be revolutionary.

Many might cling to the old idea of women's subservience and dependence, but nowhere was it unchallenged. Women were to be found in the army as doctors and nurses, and even more important, in the political and propaganda departments. They worked in the new territories taken by the army as front-

[93] †*Marriage problems in New China*, p. 4.

[94] Zhang Zhirang, †'A much-needed marriage law', *XHYB* (May 1950).

line representatives of the new order. They worked in government administration, land reform, and cadre training programmes. By 1949 30 per cent of the elected village reresentatives were women. In government they numbered 20 per cent of the cadres at district level and 10 per cent at county level.[95]

The women's movement in the liberated areas was certainly not completely successful during the hectic years of the Civil War, but a great deal was accomplished. Women organized to fight for their rights on a larger scale than ever before. In April 1949 the All-China Democratic Women's Federation was formed to give unified direction to the thousands of women's associations in the old liberated areas, and to the new ones organized to struggle for women's rights in village after village as the People's Liberation Army swept south. Millions of women learned to stand on their own feet economically, freeing themselves at least partially from their dependence on men, and as they broke through the bonds which had tied them to their homes for centuries, their social and economic status began to change. Traditional attitudes to women were crumbling. In the words of the 1948 Resolution they had 'started on the road to complete liberation'.

---

[95] Deng Yingchao, †*Report on the present direction and tasks of the Chinese women's movement.*

CHAPTER 2

WOMEN'S ORGANIZATIONS

IN the great campaigns of 1948-50, the People's Liberation Army extended its control over the whole area of mainland China. In the wake of its military campaign came huge political campaigns to mobilize and organize the support of as much of the population as possible. Even before the end of the Civil War, when the Party might have been expected to be devoting its resources to the consolidation of purely military control over its rapidly expanding territory, it in fact gave great priority to organizing such events as women's and youth congresses. This was consistent with the belief that the key to victory lay in mass organization and that China's problems could only be solved through a revolution which transformed society. To achieve real change it was necessary to mobilize and involve people on as large a scale as possible, for they must understand the need for change and the ways in which it was to be carried out. Participation in organizations would give them that sense of identity and belonging which makes people give of their best. Hence the proliferation of congresses, conferences and committees which was a marked feature of the mass organizations of the 1950s. It was perhaps especially effective in the case of women, whose election or appointment to office gave them possibly for the first time in their lives a sense of direct importance to the community as individuals.

Organizations in China served as channels through which Party and government policy could be passed down to the cadres and the masses. They arranged group discussions for their members at which new policies could be explained and talked over. The function of 'downward transmission' is easy to see, but the constant meetings did more than that. The reports given so indefatigably in thousands of district, county, and provincial congresses ensured that at least some idea of what was going on at the basic level was passed upwards. Meetings also had another aim. Franz Schurmann has written that the Chinese Communist Party expects a high level of consciousness from its members and that 'consciousness is achieved by making its members speak, write and publish'.[1] Its goals for the masses are less high, but nevertheless it attempts to raise their consciousness by making them listen, comment, and act. Blind obedience to the Party's directives is not enough, it wants people to understand and agree with them. Schurmann also comments that Chinese political life has made people, intellectuals and non-intellectuals, articulate, and has taught them to analyse.[2] This has also been achieved even for the illiterate by the continuous practice of self-expression at meetings.

Documents concerning women in the 1948–50 period always stated that since very different situations obtained in the old and the new liberated areas, policies should be adapted to suit local conditions. However, such differences were certainly not going to be tolerated for ever; on the contrary, the Party wanted woman's role in society to change all over China as it had begun to in the liberated areas. Hence, ten months before the proclamation of the People's Republic, the Preparatory Committee for the All-China Women's Federation called a National Congress for the following spring to set up a body to unite women's groups and direct woman-work throughout the country.[3]

In the old liberated areas women's organizations needed rationalization. It was policy to set up separate organizations for women, and after 1948, the experience of Lingqiu county[4] was constantly quoted to illustrate that they were really necessary to mobilize women for land reform, the production movement, and hygiene and literacy campaigns, while also representing women's special interests. But as we have seen, the forms of organization remained diverse. Some areas had, like Lingqiu County, decided on women's congresses as the best way of mobilizing women, others had women's associations, and yet others were represented by the women's

---

[1] Franz Schurmann, *Ideology and Organisation in Communist China*, p. 20.
[2] Ibid, p. 48.
[3] Circular of the Preparatory Committee of the All-China Democratic Women's Federation, in †*Chinese Women Stand Up*, p. 69.
[4] See chapter 1, pp. 43–4.

section of the Peasants' Association. In other areas again all three organizations existed.

The strength of women's organizations in a given locality depended on many factors amongst which were the importance of women's role in production, the local military situation, the degree of their exclusion from village life, and the attitude of the village cadres. Perversely, the first two factors would have tended to give villages at opposite ends of the spectrum a strong women's organization. Where women had had in the past no contact with men outside their own families, the only way to organize them was through groups open only to women. This was recognized in the Beiyue report of July 1948 which concluded that though women's congresses should be held to further women's special interests after land reform, in the older liberated areas where women already customarily took part in social activities, men and women could work together in the Poor Peasants' League or the New Peasants' Association for the overthrow of the landlords.[5] On the other hand, in newly liberated areas, or in old ones which were still rather backward, where women usually took no part in village affairs, the report stated that mobilization for land reform was better done through an organization with a mixed membership supplemented by one open exclusively to women. In the opposite case, where women's role in production was or had been economically important, much attention was given to their organizations out of economic pragmatism. For example, we have seen that the textile movement in the liberated areas strengthened and extended the women's organizations.

There were also areas where women's organizations had been weak or non-existent. Local cadres might try to make a good impression with 'paper organizations'. The 1948 Central Committee resolutions, echoing documents of the Jiangxi period, condemned areas where women's organizations existed in name only, and urged the abolition of all such formalistic bodies.[6] Complaints of this kind, especially as they came from official sources, cast doubt on the reliability of the figures

[5] †*Experience in mobilizing women during the land reform movement in Beiyue district.*
[6] CC decision (1948). See appendix 2. For the Jiangxi period see chapter, 1, page 24.

given for the members of women's associations.

Much effort was put into the expansion and development of the women's organizations all over the country after liberation. In time these were given a national leadership, voice, and cohesion by the Women's Federation, with its formalized hierarchy of committees and its regulations, documents, and directives. The Women's Federation was supposed to be represented at village, district, county, and provincial level, by women's delegate congresses each of which, on the principle of democratic centralism, elected the congress immediately superior to itself. The executive committees of these congresses could still be known as the Women's Association or Congress in accordance with a ruling in the 1948 resolution:

Women's congresses are the best form of organization to bring women together on a larger scale and more democratically. These organizations should exist everywhere and at every level. The basic form of organization of this sort of congress is the village women's congress. Its delegates should be democratically chosen by ordinary women and should include women members of the people's congress, delegates from the women's organizations (such as women representatives of weaving groups, co-operatives, and literacy groups) and delegates elected directly by women (the number of women electors being settled by residential conditions). The role of this sort of congress is to represent the opinion of ordinary women, to discuss policy and priorities for work among local women, to publicize the policies, orders, and resolutions of the Democratic Government and higher authorities, and to mobilize women to carry them out. There should also be a committee chosen by the congress to carry out resolutions, deal with day-to-day work, and decide when to convene a congress. What a committee should be called depends on the wishes of the masses. Where women are already familiar with the women's association, it can be called the committee of the women's association.[7]

In fact, though there are accounts of the full system of women's congresses being established at village, district, and county level, women's associations are so much more frequently mentioned, especially by the mid-1950s, that it seems reasonable to infer they were of more enduring

[7] See appendix 2.

importance. A women's association, or local branch of the National Women's Federation, could be quite a loose organization led by the most active local women, who had sometimes but not always been inspired by a political worker from outside. A representative congress was a more complicated body necessitating, in the short term at least, much organizational work. That its early importance was soon eclipsed may imply that it was found useful as a device for the initial mobilization of women, but too demanding or unwieldy as a permanent system. This produced a tendency for the executive committee of the congress to become a permanent body known generally as the women's association.[8]

In the countryside of the liberated areas the problems of organizing women would have seemed familiar to the cadres who were brought in to deal with them. There were of course regional differences which affected the work, an especially important one being that in some areas of the south women already played a major productive role. But the difference was one of degree, for women's social and economic status was subordinate to that of men everywhere in rural China. By contrast, in the towns, communist political workers faced new problems. They had played an important role in the pre-1927 labour movement, in which both exclusive unions for women and women's departments of general trade unions had enjoyed mass support amongst women workers. But in the two decades which had passed since the suppression of these unions, communist experience in the towns had been limited to clandestine work in which contact with the mass of un-politicized women was very difficult.[9]

In both country and town, the shortage of women cadres was a serious problem. Many could only work as local cadres

---

[8] Congresses did continue to be held, however, though with increasing irregularity. As late as 1973, municipal women's congresses were held in Tientsin, Peking and Shanghai, apparently as part of a revival of the Women's Federation which the Cultural Revolution had left in disarray. *Peking Review*, 13 July 1973 and 28 Sept. 1973.

[9] A delegation from Kuomingtang-controlled China did attend the 1st National Women's Congress in 1949, and the presence among them of women from Shanghai is evidence of the Party's contacts there. However, although they spoke at length on a strike of women textile workers, neither in that nor in the rest of their report did they imply that the Party was playing an important role in such struggles. Congress documents 1, p. 51.

doing political or administrative work in their own area, for most women had family responsibilities which prevented them from accepting the unsettled life of a cadre completely dedicated to political work. The few women who had done this were liable to be transferred from woman-work to other jobs if these had a higher priority. The very low literacy rate amongst women also limited the work that they could do and the extent to which they could be promoted. For example, an article in 1950 claimed that of 1,200 women cadres in Chahar, 51 per cent were illiterate or semi-literate, and that in 1949 40 per cent of the women candidates failed a test of theory and policies for district and county cadres as against only 27 per cent of the men.[10]

Thus at the time of liberation, though production was declared to be the main priority and woman-work cadres were asked to concentrate their efforts on women workers and workers' dependants, they were urged to try also to win over women students and intellectuals quickly if there was any chance that they could be recruited to ease the worsening shortage of women cadres. The majority of the seasoned cadres assigned for work in the towns at this time had received most of their experience in land reform. Even those who had worked in the small towns of the liberated areas would have found the problems of the big industrial centres different from anything they had known. Understandably many regretted the change, and several delegates at the 1949 Congress criticized themselves for an initial reluctance to take up work in the towns.[11]

Industrial workers were probably the easiest women to organize since they were already concentrated in groups, their lives were in contradiction with traditional ideas on the place of women, and they were less afraid to speak out or to discuss with others. Moreover, improvements in the economic situation, and later the advantages conferred on them by the labour laws, gave them a deepening commitment to the new regime. However, women workers were a small minority especially in the heavy industrial centres of the north-east

---

[10]† 'Be skilled and work well', *XHYB* (April 1950).
[11]† 'Preliminary experience of mobilizing women in the newly liberated countryside', Congress documents 1, p.39.

which were the first big towns to be liberated. Far more
numerous and difficult to contact were working-class women
who did not themselves have jobs. With the peace-time
restoration and expansion of the economy, many were
persuaded to take jobs and were then organized in their place
of work. Those who stayed at home were brought into touch
with the developments of the new society by their local
women's association, dependants' association, and street
committee, or residents' association.

A fundamental difficulty for the women's movement in the
towns, and one which was to cause problems throughout the
1950s, was that according to theory women were to liberate
themselves through participation in productive labour, yet
urban women were often unable to get jobs. Dependants'
organizations were an early reflection of this sharp contradiction between theory and practice. The reasons for
unemployment amongst women will be examined in chapter
five; its existence must be borne in mind in relation to
dependants' organizations since it was a basic factor in their
creation. I will also discuss street committees and residents'
associations in chapter five, since though often run by women,
they were not exclusively women's organizations and were not
formally affiliated to the Women's Federation.

I chose to deal with dependants' associations as organizations here, because, in spite of their name, they were in
fact women's organizations.[12] Since their usual base of
operation was the burgeoning factory and enterprise accommodation blocks (*sushe*) they would often have replaced
residents' associations which functioned in residential areas
housing the employees of many different enterprises. They
worked in close association both with neighbouring residents'
associations and with the Women's Federation. The three
types of organization often performed quite similar work,
and the distinctions between them sometimes became
blurred. However, one sharp difference in the organizational
principle of the dependants' association marks it out from the

---

[12] The description of dependants' associations which follows is mostly drawn from:
†*Experience of work amongst the dependants of workers and employees* and
†*Important documents of the national representative congress of the dependants of
workers and employees.*

er two. As the name implies, membership of the association
is determined not by the work or residence of the member,
but by the job of her husband. The women of the association
were thus being viewed, and learning to define themselves,
through the identity of their husbands.

The functions of the dependants' organizations clearly
reflected this. Their basic purpose was to help the dependants
of workers to understand and assist their men folk and to
provide a harmonious home atmosphere so that they might
give their whole attention to their jobs. A whole genre of
newspaper stories extolling women who protected their
husbands from household or family worries so that their
performance at work might not be adversely affected also
boosted this image of the wife as a person who 'serviced' the
worker.

A description by an Australian woman journalist of a visit to
a model worker's home brings out excellently the significance
for women of this role at the level of an individual family.[13]
Questioned about her day, his wife, Mrs Lou, began to speak
with diffidence between interruptions from her rather brash
and overbearing husband. She planned all her work to satisfy
her husband's preferences. She even shopped twice a day
because he liked his food fresh. As the journalist exclaimed
rather caustically, to be a model worker one needs to have a
model wife. (The woman worker is thus doubly disadvantaged
when this is the prevalent view of the wife's role since she
cannot play it for her husband nor does she as a worker have
anyone to play it for her.) Though much of the work carried
out by dependants' associations was valuable or beneficial to
their own members, they did in fact ask that certain women
should make their contribution to society not as independent
producers, but as the wives and mothers of productive
workers, the limelight heroes of the new society.

This characteristic of dependants' associations meant that
the level of their activities fluctuated considerably. In the first
years after liberation when they were the means of organizing
many housewives for the first time they were often mentioned
in the press. They were then given progressively less and less

[13] Dymphna Cusack, *Chinese Women Speak*, pp. 46-8.

attention until 1955, when a difficult unemployment situation produced various attempts to reduce the number of women in the labour market by improving the status and self-image of housewives. In that year, there were reports of local dependants' conferences all over China, and the first National Congress was held in April 1956. Dependants' congresses of certain groups amongst whom a specific campaign was being waged could also be called to reinforce that campaign, as occurred for example in the period when private industry and trade were being brought under state management.[14]

Subsequently the importance of dependants' organizations seemed to wane and they were rarely mentioned in the 1960s. Later developments like the setting up of farming teams amongst the wives of oil-workers, though superficially similar, differed fundamentally: although in the first instance their members would be recruited as wives, they immediately acquired an independent economic role, and thus an independent relationship to society.[15]

Not only did new organizations have to be created for housewives after liberation, new methods had also to be evolved to deal with students and intellectuals. Here experience with the young intellectuals who had come over into the liberated areas during the previous decade was of use, though from them an active sympathy could have been presumed whereas in the new situation it had to be nurtured. An appeal to nationalism had been a basic means of rallying support amongst intellectuals whether men or women during the anti-Japanese War when so many communist organizational techniques were developed. It remained important in the new situation when the Party promised an end to the inefficiency and stagnation from which the country had suffered under the Kuomintang and urged people to make a personal contribution towards building China into a great country by working with it.

The early propaganda literature aimed at educated women

[14] See †Collection of documents from the national representative congress of the dependants of industrialists and merchants and female industrialists and merchants, and † Fully develop the activist role of women from the business world in socialist transformation.

[15] See chapter 5.

was nearly all based on this theme. It urged them to take jobs and to give of their best in their work in order to build up the country. In return it promised them equality of opportunity so that their talents, often wasted because of discrimination under the old regime, might be exploited to the full. For young intellectuals, the firm support for free-choice marriage offered by the communists also made the new regime attractive. The puritanism of the new moral code had appeal for some married women from wealthy families who had suffered emotional insecurity or unhappiness in the old society.[16] The Young Women's Christian Association and the Women's Christian Temperance Union of China were amongst the groups which affiliated to the Women's Federation from the moment of its foundation.[17] Thus, owing to various factors many middle-class women who might have been expected to be hostile to the communists came to welcome them with hope, or at least the wish to make the best of a bad job.

On 5 December 1948, the Preparatory Committee of the All-China Democratic Women's Federation issued an announcement to all the women's associations of the liberated areas, and to the democratic women's groups of the whole country. It stated that they intended to convene a national congress of women the next year to define the direction and tasks of the women's movement in the new situation, and to set up the All-China Democratic Women's Federation.[18] In later communiqués the Preparatory Committee declared that 360 delegates would attend the Congress, of whom 255 were to be elected from the liberated areas by county and district women's congresses, and about 100 from Kuomintang-occupied areas.[19] (According to the opening speech at the Congress, since it had not been possible to elect them openly, these delegates had been picked by 'all sorts of democratic methods'.)[20]

[16] Here I recall particularly the wife of a capitalist in Shanghai who spoke of her past unhappiness when her husband had taken a mistress and her old fear that he might leave her. In the new society she felt secure because she was sure he would never risk the criticism he would incur by deserting her.

[17] *Handbook on People's China* (1957), p.166.

[18] †*Chinese Women Stand Up*, p. 68.

[19] Ibid., p.70.

The siege of Peking was over by March 1949 when the Congress actually assembled, so it met in the ancient capital. The opening speeches set the tone for future congresses. They acknowledged the leadership of the Party, announced whole-hearted support for its policies and urged all women to unite behind it and work for the defeat of the Kuomintang, since only thus could they obtain liberation.

Like other mass organizations, the Women's Federation always included lengthy statements of support for current policies and campaigns of the Party in the literature it produced. These are remarked on in my brief description of the congresses only when they have a specific relevance to women as women, as in the case of land reform, the co-operatives, and the health campaign. Most of the reports and all of the discussion at the first Congress directly concerned woman-work. Among them were speeches on the mobilization of women in the north-east, on the women workers' movement in Shanghai, work with women in the newly liberated countryside and the women's movement in the Kuomintang areas.

The most important report was one made by Deng Yingchao on the immediate direction and tasks for the Women's Federation. She first reviewed the achievements of the women's movement in the liberated areas for the many delegates who had been living until very recently under Kuomintang rule and so had heard very little about them. She then spoke of consolidating these achievements and extending them to the newly liberated areas. In the countryside work should, she said, be based on the 1948 Central Committee directive. But while this rural work should not be despised, the main emphasis should be on the towns where production had to be restored as rapidly as possible and the Party faced huge tasks of which it had very little experience. Here she said women could join organizations and elect representative congresses on the basis of their own place of work, trade or study, or that of the family wage-earner. Where possible workers' dependants should be organized so that they became producers as well as consumers. When a good beginning had

---

[20] Congress documents 1, p.3. This collection is the basic source for the description of the Congress which follows.

been made, the whole town could set up an organization to lead woman-work — the Women's Federation. She talked at length of the great need for more women cadres and urged that working women, students, and intellectuals should be recruited to cadre training classes in large numbers. She accepted on behalf of the Federation the proposals for equal pay and maternity benefits put forward by the Sixth Labour Congress.[21] She ended with a few remarks about the international women's movement hoping that Chinese women would in future be able to play their full part in it.

The Congress passed the draft regulations of the All-China Democratic Women's Federation and the electoral law for the first session of the executive committee.[22] In these the formal structure of the Congress and its committees is described. The terms are very general, which seems to imply, not surprisingly, an uncertainty about future needs. For example, rule 12 (in Chapter IV) declares that the Congress should be convened about every two years, but adds that the convocation may be brought forward or delayed where necessary.

In fact, although there have been only three national congresses (they took place in 1949, 1953, and 1957), the Party continued to stress the importance of work amongst women throughout the 1950s. Discussion and statements on problems connected with women appeared in the press constantly and the work of women's associations in both town and village was frequently mentioned. (At the time of writing (1975) it has been announced that a fourth congress is in preparation.) The infrequency of the congresses does not therefore imply that the Party had lost interest in women's problems or that it believed them solved, but rather that such congresses were not necessarily central to the day-to-day execution of woman-work.

This impression is confirmed by the documents of the two later congresses. Those of the second, which was held in April 1953, were not even published in the form of a booklet, although they did appear in the official organ of the Women's Federation in May.[23] Formal speeches of greeting from the

[21] These were later codified in The Labour Insurance Regulations of the People's Republic of China, promulgated 26 Feb. 1951, published in *Important Labour Laws and Regulations of the People's Republic of China* (1961).
[22] Congress documents 1, p.94.
[23] Congress documents 2, *ZGFN*: No. 5 (1953).

Party and State organs took up much of the proceedings. Song Qingling and He Xiangning both spoke, but the first report of much interest was given by Deng Yingchao who again spoke of past experience and future tasks. Although the main emphasis of the report was on production, she also urged cadres to remember and make allowances for women's household responsibilities. She stressed that no woman should ever be forced to take an outside job. The last reports that the Congress heard, which were on women in the Chinese volunteer army in Korea and model women in agriculture and industry in China, were very similar to the type of reportage which appeared every month in the magazine *Chinese Women* (*ZGFN*). General themes of the congress were support for the war effort in Korea, the importance of learning from the USSR, and the development of women's organizations amongst the national minorities.

The third congress was held in September 1957. The official account of its proceedings named its three most important achievements.[24] The first was summing up the experience of the previous four years and agreeing on aims expressed in the slogan adopted by the Congress: 'Build up the country economically, manage the household thriftily, struggle for socialist construction'. The other two were the acceptance of a revised constitution for the Federation and the election of a new executive committee. The most obvious feature of the new regulations was the change of name from the All-China Democratic Women's Federation, to the All-China Women's Federation, which it was explained was felt to be more suitable in an era when socialism was already basically established.[25] The basic levels of the organization were clearly described and defined for the first time. The different levels of the Women's Federation were based on local government administrative units and each level had its own congress. Each congress elected the congress for the level above. This system extended from the fundamental level of the district (*xiang*) or street committee, up to the county, the province, and finally the

[24] Congress documents 3.

[25] This change was in line with what took place in other organizations which had played a part in the United Front at the end of what was known as the 'New Democratic' period. For example, the All-China Federation of Democratic Youth became the All-China Federation of Youth.

national congress. However, these regulations can be regarded as a formality in the sense that they laid down forms of organization which were probably not strictly adhered to. The recommended interval between sessions of the National Congress was raised from two to four years, a recognition of existing practice rather than a new idea, and the actual timing was again left to the decision of the National Executive Committee. Another administrative change was that the old standing committee was abolished and a praesidium was set up to take over its former tasks.

A striking feature of the documents of the 1957 Congress was the unprecedented emphasis on the importance of women's family and household duties brought in under the slogan 'Build up the country economically, manage the household thriftily.' At the 1953 Congress, Deng Yingchao had said that the Federation should get housewives to organize their housework and generally make themselves more capable so that when the possibility or the need arose for them to take jobs they would be able to do so. In 1957 efficient housekeeping was being promoted in quite a different way as the following extract from a speech by Zhang Yun will show:

Thrifty household management is of great and basic importance to the cause of our socialist construction. The family is a microcosm of society, all workers who are taking part in socialist construction live in families. If the family is well run those of its members who are taking part in socialist construction don't 'look back over their shoulders', but devote themselves whole-heartedly to raising production; if the house is badly run this will influence their production and thus the fulfilment of the state and the co-operatives' plans to raise output. A very large proportion of the articles needed in daily life produced in our country is consumed within the family and the degree of economy practised by families has a great influence on the national supply of consumer resources . . . Thus thrifty household management can greatly promote an increase in the national production and can further the national, collective, and family interests.[26]

Great changes had taken place at this time in the objectives of woman-work, and housework was being glorified at least to

[26] †'Build up the country economically, manage the household thriftily, struggle for socialist construction', Congress documents 3, p. 26.

some extent at the expense of women's independent econo. role. In later chapters I will detail the effects of these chang on women in both rural and urban areas, and attempt to explain the economic factors behind them. For the moment it is enough to note there were differences in the tone of policy statements from one congress to the next. Yet in studying these documents one gets very little sense of the Federation as a living movement. The arguments about the policies, aims, and methods of woman-work which must have taken place hardly find an echo here. The 1957 regulations had laid down as a task of the Federation that it should 'teach women to carry out the policies of the Chinese Communist Party and the People's Government'.[27] Congress reports seem always to have been written with that idea in mind. Too often they contain little to distinguish them from any other report at any other conference.

It was not until the time of the Cultural Revolution that any glimpse could be gained of disagreements which existed in the 1950s behind this rather dreary façade of the higher echelons of the Women's Federation, and the information which emerged at that time is difficult to evaluate. A women's Red Guard newspaper of 1966 was very critical of the way in which the slogan 'Build up the country economically, manage the household thriftily' had been used.[28] It claimed that though the slogan was based on a line from a 1957 speech by Mao Zedong in which he said that the country relied particularly on the women's organizations to promote household thrift, it had been taken out of context. In the same speech he had listed many other more explicitly political tasks for the women's movement, but the phrase 'manage the household thriftily' had been picked out and made to stand on its own as a slogan.

It is not my intention in this survey of the history of the Women's Federation to embark on the dangerous task of ascribing particular policy trends to certain individuals. However, it does seem worth while to point out that periods of radicalism and comparative conservatism in the women's movement can be quite clearly related to periods of radical or

[27] † Regulations of the Women's Federation of the People's Republic of China, 20 Sept. 1957, Congress documents 3, p.70.
[28] †'Red Women', *Combat Issue* No. 1 (19 May 1967).

conservative economic policy. Moreover, this is very much to be expected since radical economic policies generate rapid social change and conservative ones serve at least as a brake on it. These fluctuations in policy can be better understood through an examination of the general economic history of the period than through the documents of the national congresses.

A study of the work of the Women's Federation at grass-roots level is at once more interesting and more informative. Here one can trace the interaction of radical ideology, harsh and often limiting economic realities, and resilient social conservatism. At the national level most of what we can learn of the Women's Federation concerns its bureaucratic functioning; at the local level we can see that it did really act as a pressure group for women. In 1956 the Women's Federation of Zhongshan county, Kuangdong province, published a demand that of the cadres to be trained by the county in the following two years, 50 per cent of the technicians, 30 per cent of the tractor hands and veterinary personnel, and 60 per cent of the stockmen should be women.[29] The Women's Federation had a representative at every matrimonial case which came to court. Nor were such representatives just passive observers. In one case where a cadre had attempted to use his official position as a member of a county security bureau to force a girl to marry him, the provincial Women's Federation considered that the sentence passed by the court had been too light. It demanded and obtained a reassessment and increase in the sentence.[30]

Before 1949 there were many reports of local women's associations organizing beatings for husbands who persistently ill-treated their wives. Since such ill-treatment was regarded as 'a contradiction amongst the people', beatings in these cases were against official policy, and couples were asked rather to resolve their differences by discussion. Reports of such incidents almost ceased to appear after 1949, though it seems probable that they continued to occur. Among the less dramatic activities of the Federation were the support and encouragement of struggles for equal pay, the organization of

---

[29] † 'Zhongshan county draws up a woman-work plan for the next two years', *Southern Daily* (19 Mar. 1956).

[30] †*Compendium of reference materials on marriage problems*, pp. 36–7.

nurseries, and the promotion of study courses, health, hygiene, and literacy campaigns, natural childbirth classes, and production drives. Since by its nature woman-work touches on every aspect of the society in which it is performed, I have attempted to divide it into a few important sectors which I discuss in the succeeding chapters.

CHAPTER 3

MARRIAGE AND THE FAMILY

WOMEN'S low status in Chinese society as a whole was matched by their low status in the basic unit of that society, the family within whose confines their lives were largely lived.

It used to be customary to consider as typical of the Chinese family the Confucian ideal, in which the unmarried female descendants and all the male descendants of the family head, together with their wives and children, shared a common residence and a common budget. Age and sex were thought to be the only factors which determined the power of the individual within the hierarchical structure of the family.

Research has produced a considerably modified picture which is relevant to any consideration of the lives of ordinary women in China in the first half of the twentieth century. Although there was great variation in family size, very large families were in the minority.[1] Low life expectancy meant that many never lived to be grandparents while others did not enjoy the state for long. High infant mortality was a check on the number of children who survived to adulthood, and when two or more sons did, the pressure on the available land or a simple inability to live and work together made the joint family very difficult to preserve.

J. L. Buck's survey in the 1930s found that the average farm family in the north consisted of five and a half people as against only five in the south, while in the whole sample families of four persons were commoner than those of any other size, and families of three to six persons comprised nearly two-thirds the total.[2] Obviously, then, most women did not find themselves in the situation which has sometimes been described as if it were typical, where a team of daughters and

---

[1] For a detailed discussion of family size, and of definitions of 'the family', see Myron L. Cohen, 'Developmental Process in the Chinese Domestic Group', in Maurice Freedman (ed.), *Family and Kinship in Chinese Society.*

daughters-in-law performed the household work together under the direction of the matriarch. Though there were some gentry households organized like this, the average household was likely to contain only two women of working age, a mother and her young daughter-in-law, or, as one might view the same household a few years later, a grandmother, and the mother of two or three young children.

The old idea that age and sex were the only two factors governing an individual's place in the family has also been challenged. Though the eldest surviving male was normally named as the family head until the time of his death, this could be a mere matter of form. If a man lived long enough, the time might come when his son's superior strength and his own failing physical powers gave the younger man real power.[3] The change might begin with the son taking every-day decisions about the land since it was he who was mainly responsible for working it. Such decisions confer great authority in a peasant society where they can indeed be matters of life or death, and the one who takes them may in time gain the major say in the family affairs. Women very rarely attained this sort of authority, since even when they performed farm-work, they only implemented the decisions of others.

The birth of a girl was never as welcome as that of a boy, and might be felt as a tragedy in a poor family or in one with no sons. Since a daughter was normally married out of the family in her teens, just as she was becoming most useful, her upbringing was an expense which could not be recouped. Though in normal times a girl-child would be treated with the affectionate attention which Chinese typically lavish upon

[2] J. L. Buck, *Land Utilization in China*, p.369. Irene H. Tauber has shown convincingly that Buck's survey was biased towards prosperous villages which were free from natural disasters, see I. Tauber, 'The Families of Chinese Farmers', in Maurice Freedman (ed.), pp.64–5. Since there was a link between the prosperity and the size of the family, this implies that the average family size found by the survey would be an overestimate for China as a whole.

[3] An interesting description of this decline in status with age in Taiwan is found in Margery Wolf, 'Child Training and the Chinese Family', in Maurice Freedman (ed.), p.51. She observes that far from being the respected patriarch, the truly aged man may become the unprotected butt of children's teasing though outward forms of filial piety are maintained for the public eye.

small children, if, as happened quite often in an economy close to subsistence, times were hard and famine threatened, she would be left short of food before her brothers. In really desperate situations when infanticide was practised, it was again the girls who were the victims. Preferential treatment and infanticide were serious enough to give rise to a marked imbalance between the sexes commented on by observers in the first half of the twentieth century.[4]

Families so prosperous that they could educate some of their children would, as noted, normally choose the boys who would continue to belong to them, rather than girls who would soon be lost to them and who with their fixed destiny as housewives would not be able to put an education to practical use.[5]

Since parents were anxious to see their children settled and their posterity assured they arranged their marriages early if they could afford it. Buck, for example, found that 81 per cent of women marrying for the first time between 1929 and 1931 were under 20 years of age, as were over half their bridegrooms.[6]

The cost of marriage and its effect on the position of women is a complex matter in which class, period, and region are important variables. Certainly marriage was usually an expensive affair for both families. When a girl left her father's house, she took with her a dowry which was in theory her personal property. In the wealthy classes it was often in the form of jewellery, amongst the people it mostly consisted of clothing, bedding, and household items for the use of the newly married couple. Although it was a matter of pride to make the dowry as generous as possible, it frequently failed to match in value the gifts which the girl's in-laws sent to her parents, and amongst the poor was sometimes only symbolic. In such marriages there was clearly an element of purchase

[4] Buck, p.376. Sidney B. Gamble, *Peking: A Social Survey*, p.415. Fei Hsiao-tung, *Peasant Life in China*, p.22. For a detailed discussion of sex ratios in the Chinese population and differential mortality rates by sex and age, see John S. Aird, 'Population Growth', in Alexander Eckstein, Walter Galenson, and Liu Ta-chung (eds.), *Economic Trends in Communist China*, pp.265-70.

[5] For example Buck's survey showed that only 1% of females as against 30% of males had attended school for long enough to learn to read a common letter. Buck, p.373.

[6] Buck, p.381.

which served to strengthen the authority of the husband's family over the girl.[7] In other cases, however, the cost of the gifts which the bride's family had to send to the bridegroom's was much greater than those which it received; indeed this has sometimes been cited as a reason for the prevalence of female infanticide.[8] Presumably much hinged on the ratio between men and women in the local population, which must itself have been interdependent with these other factors, for where female infanticide was practised the bride-price would presumably have responded to the laws of supply and demand, and risen until it became less disadvantageous to bring up and marry off daughters.[9] Whatever the comparative costs of gifts and dowry, members of a household which had undergone much hardship to acquire a bride for a son were likely to be very critical of her performance.[10]

Another form of marriage, in which the future daughter-in-law was adopted as a small child into her in-laws' house, was common in many areas of rural China. This arrangement, which the anthropologist Arthur Wolf refers to as 'minor marriage' as opposed to more orthodox 'major marriage',[11] was once thought to have been a custom largely confined to the poor, since it made possible great economies in the marriage ceremony. The cost of bringing the child up, which was the responsibility of in-laws under this arrangement, was a minor disadvantage since it was spread over many years. However, it seems that poverty was not the only, and perhaps not the major reason for choosing this form of marriage. As Van der Valk pointed out, in some areas it seems to have existed amongst all classes, and in others to have been unknown.[12] Arthur Wolf, writing about Taiwan, suggests that it was

[7] Marion Levy, *The Family Revolution in Modern China*, p.46.
[8] See for example Ho Ping-ti, *Studies on the Population of China*, pp.60–1.
[9] The problem of the relationship between bride-price, dowry gift-exchange, adoption (of child daughters-in-law or of sons-in-law), and female infanticide is an important and interesting one. Since much work remains to be done on it, this discussion is brief and tentative.
[10] For an example of such attitudes in Taiwan see Margery Wolf, *Women and the Family in Rural Taiwan*, pp.144–5.
[11] Arthur Wolf, 'Adopt a Daughter-in-law, Marry a Sister: A Chinese Solution to the Problem of the Incest Taboo', *American Anthropologist*, 70.5. (Oct.1968).
[12] M. H. Van der Valk, *Conservatism in Modern Chinese Family Law*, p.49.

favoured by the parents-in-law, and especially by the mother-in-law, because it produced an amenable daughter-in-law who had strong ties of affection with them.[13] Though this seems very plausible, the uneven distribution of the institution in China has still to be explained. I would expect it, at least in origin, to be connected with two factors which were themselves related, the extent to which women participated in labour, and the degree of imbalance between the sexes in a given area. Since such an imbalance was usually created by the preferential treatment accorded to boys, it must to some extent have been a function of the comparative usefulness of boys and girls in the local economy. But it could also be aggravated by another factor—shortage of women. In areas where many women were lost to the marriage market because they were employed in sexual roles such as prostitution or concubinage, the adoption of a child daughter-in-law was clearly a good way to secure the future.

The system was hard on girls, who were thus separated from their families at an early age. Under the pressure of harsh economic reality, their adoptive parents could be more ruthless with them than with their own children, and such girls seem to have often grown up with a strong sense of personal misfortune.

Of course whether she had joined her husband's family as a child or more orthodoxly as a young adult, the life of a bride had many constant features. The primary function of marriage in traditional China was the production of male offspring to ensure the continuance of the family line. The way in which marriage was arranged reflected the way it was viewed. It was no capricious cruelty which prevented the senior members of a family from consulting the individuals concerned when they arranged a match, but rather the logic of the whole social system in which marriages were made in the interests of the family as a whole rather than on the basis of love or attraction between the couple. Necessary as marriage was to the family's posterity, in the short term it posed a threat to family cohesion. Any stranger brought into the household could upset the balance within it, and a wife was especially

---

[13] Arthur Wolf, 'Adopt a Daughter-in-law, Marry a Sister'.

dangerous since she could disrupt the most sacred of all relationships, that between parents and son. This danger was carefully guarded against.

The bride who came as a stranger to her husband's house had been brought up knowing that she would one day have to play this role, yet, since she was young and her previous horizons had been largely limited to her village, and her close acquaintance to her own family, she was hardly equipped by experience to deal with the new surroundings and relationships which marriage thrust upon her. Not only was she subordinate to all the senior members of the family, but, being without allies, she might even find herself dominated by younger members of the family who were formally junior to her. Her isolation was increased by the fact that she was cut off from her own family. Visits to them were discouraged except on certain specific ceremonial occasions. The husband–wife relationship was not stressed and even slight public demonstrations of affection were taboo. All these conventions reduced the danger that a bride would be able to cause any conflict between the members of her husband's family.

In daily life, because of the way in which work was divided between the sexes, the young wife's most important relationship was in fact with her mother-in-law who was both her forewoman and workmate. There were many sources of friction between them. The task of integrating the girl into the household and getting her to adapt to its ways fell mainly to the mother-in-law. Obedience was owed to both mother- and father-in-law, but it was to the mother-in-law that it was mostly given; a girl's relationship with her father-in-law was one of avoidance. A mother's affection for her son might be the strongest emotion of her life. Her marriage was unlikely to be an important emotional outlet, and she compensated for this in her devotion to her children and above all her sons who were her insurance for old age and who brought her an improvement in status in her married home. Obviously she was likely to feel jealous of her son's wife, and this was sometimes expressed in petty spite.

Not only did the daughter-in-law work under her husband's mother, she was expected to serve her at meals and to relieve her of the most unpleasant of the household chores. It was commonplace for a man or his mother to beat his young wife as a means of discipline, and this practice sometimes degenerated into a mere outlet for their frustrations.

Once she gave birth to a son, the roughest stage in a woman's life was over and she attained a position of some respect, though years might still pass before the death of her mother-in-law left her as the real mistress of the house. Even when she attained this position, she remained subject to her husband's authority, but the marital relationship usually became more one of partnership over the years and she could expect to be consulted in major family decisions. Usually the older woman in the house was in charge of the small-scale household expenditure, and, more important in a subsistence economy, she decided what the family should eat, and how much each member should receive. This gave her considerable power to reward and punish.

For those women fortunate enough both to bear sons and to survive to a fifth decade (which would be counted as old age in rural China[14]), there were compensations for past sufferings. They could supervise their households, hand the most arduous of the chores over to their daughters-in-law and enjoy the love and respect of their sons and grandchildren.

As a woman's life was characteristically lived within the confines of her family her contacts were normally limited to it or to the families of near neighbours. She spent most of her time with other women and children. Since she had never learnt to expect more, it was certainly not impossible for her to live a satisfied and contented life within these bounds. But the demands made on her were strict and inflexible and she had few outlets for frustrations. A bad relationship with a husband or a mother-in-law had simply to be endured, and in her claustrophobic world it could be a source of unbearable tensions. When a couple had no sons the wife was considered responsible for the misfortune. If he could afford it, it was the man's duty to take a concubine. A concubine would have been beyond the means of many families, however, and in such

---

[14] Buck stated that fewer than 60% of Chinese survived the 10th year. Life expectancy at birth was 34.85 for a man and 34.63 for a woman. Boys who lived to be ten might expect a further 47.5 years of life and girls a further 46. Buck, pp. 390-2.

situations the lot of a childless wife might have been harder still since she would have to endure both a sense of personal failure, and the reproaches of others for the rest of her life.

The only sanction that a woman had against ill-treatment by her husband's family was suicide or attempted suicide. Such incidents, if not hushed up, might bring an official investigation and would certainly incur both public disapproval and the hostility of the woman's family. Though the mere threat of all this could act as a deterrent, it was hardly satisfactory as the best institutional check provided by the traditional system on the ill-treatment to which women might be subject.[15]

Though the remarriage of widows was abhorrent to Confucian ethics and therefore not part of the 'ideal' of the Chinese family system, it was normal practice amongst peasants in many areas, at least in cases where the women were still young.[16] Only amongst the gentry was the ideal of the 'chaste widow' commonly realized. It was much more difficult

---

[15] Divorce was not the usual solution in these cases. The legal codes of the Chinese Empire followed the Confucian classics in recognizing 7 grounds on which a husband might divorce his wife: her adultery; her jealousy; her contraction of a loathsome disease; her garrulity; her disobedience to his parents; her failure to bear children; or theft committed by her. The grounds might not be invoked if the family, having been poor, had become wealthy during the marriage, if the wife had observed mourning for her parents-in-law, or if she had no family of her own to which she could return. These points are usually enumerated and discussed at length in descriptions of the Chinese marriage system. However, divorce was in fact rare, and they seem only of marginal importance to this brief and generalized picture of traditional marriage practice in China. See Olga Lang, *Chinese Family and Society*, pp. 40-1. For an analysis of women's suicide in Chinese society see Margery Wolf, 'Women and Suicide in China' in Roxanne Witke and Margery Wolf (eds.). *Women in Chinese Society*.

[16] There are somewhat conflicting views concerning the remarriage of widows under the traditional system. It was certainly condemned by Confucian ethics, but Marion Levy believes that most families would have been forced by economic pressures to arrange marriages for young widows. C. K. Yang accepts that a certain number of families were led by poverty to arrange remarriages for widows in exchange for a good price, but implies that such cases were exceptional. C. K. Yang drew his material from Guangdong where, since women often worked in the fields, a widow was not always an economic burden and might indeed, as he points out, support her parents-in-law. In other regions practice may have been more as Levy described it. William Hinton wrote on a curious state of affairs in Longbow village (Shanxi) where widows might openly have affairs, but their remarriage was unacceptable to the community. Marion Levy, *The Family Revolution in China*, p. 46; C. K. Yang, *The Chinese Family in the Communist Revolution*, p. 46; William Hinton, *Fanshen*, pp. 306-7.

for a poor family to resist the economic pressure to marry off a widowed daughter-in-law. The likelihood of having to undergo a second marriage arranged by people probably less concerned for her welfare than her original parents was of course quite different from the simple right to remarry at will. Custody of the children was vested not in the mother, but in the father's family, so that remarriage would mean separation from those she loved most.

Such, very generally, was woman's place in the traditional Chinese family. But in fact it is no more possible to make generalizations about the family which hold good for all areas and all classes than about any other aspect of Chinese society. In chapter four it will be shown that the status of women in the family was comparatively high in those areas where they took a greater part in productive labour. But even in such areas, girls were less valued than boys who would stay in the family; women were unable to inherit and therefore did not become owners of the land; they suffered the physical difficulties attendant on the bearing and rearing of children, which might prevent them working; and, though they had more part in family decisions, were ultimately subject, especially when young, to the authority of men.

The lives of women in richer families tended to be more restricted physically than those of the poor since only the rich could afford the space and the servants necessary to maintain the real seclusion of women. In literary families, however, indulged daughters might be taught to read and thus through books learn of worlds which were forever closed to them.

Poorer women were more active, they went to the river to wash clothes, to the well to fetch water, helped in the fields at busy times, and sometimes worked in the households of the rich. But though their lives were less circumscribed, poor women suffered special miseries. Poverty imposed particular burdens on women as the dependent sex. The anxieties of life lived just above subsistence level bred violence and cruelty within the family as it did within society, and it was the weakest members who suffered most. This goes far to explain the beatings which the daughter-in-law received, and the apparent harshness of even loving parents towards their daughters if they were driven by poverty to sell them for the sake of survival. Childbirth, already an ordeal in the countryside in insanitary conditions without modern medicine, was also aggravated by poverty since poor women were often undernourished and were unlikely to get sufficient rest before or after the birth. Both infant and maternal mortality were high and generally low life expectancy meant that many women were fated to widowhood.[17]

We have seen that the position of women in the traditional family structure of China came under systematic attack in the social, political, and intellectual movements of the first decades of the twentieth century, notably in the May Fourth Movement. By 1949, such attacks already had a history of several decades, but their impact was still limited largely to the towns or to people open to urban influence, such as the children of landlords who went to school in the towns, or peasant families whose sons and daughters worked in the mills and factories. Even amongst the urbanized and partly westernized groups, changes had not gone very far or deep, and they occurred unevenly.

Under Kuomintang family law, which in effect codified the practice of the most modern members of society, marriage was concluded by the couple at their wish, and in the presence of two witnesses, with the proviso that the man should have attained the minimum age of eighteen and the woman sixteen.[18]

Divorce by consent was permitted and a paper signed by two witnesses was the only formality required. The ten grounds on which one spouse might apply for judicial divorce were wide-ranging and made it technically easy to obtain. The law did not accord complete equality to the sexes. In the management of property and the custody of children it still favoured men. However, it did improve considerably the legal position of women. The law on inheritance gave daughters and sons equality and women were allowed to hold property in their own right.

The Kuomintang law thus attempted to establish the conjugal family stemming from a voluntary marriage. Had it

[17] For an indication of high female mortality during the reproductive years and for data on life expectancy generally, see Buck, pp.390-2.
[18] M. H. Van der Valk, *An Outline of Modern Chinese Family Law*, pp.61-2.

been enforced, it would have entailed great changes in the status of women. In the towns it both reflected and stimulated new trends, but in the countryside, tradition continued largely undisturbed. If the laws on inheritance and marriage had been implemented there, they would have destroyed the old family structure. But it was impossible to graft the sort of reforms embodied in the law on to rural society as it was, and the government did not want the sort of profound social changes for which it would have been necessary to work in order to enforce the law in the villages.

The towns presented a more confused picture. At one extreme some families functioned in an almost completely traditional way; at the other some young intellectuals, out of touch with their families, married at will and divorced almost as easily.

Within the same class, practice varied from one family to another. It was not unusual for working-class women to contribute to the family income by working outside the home both before and after marriage. In some industries, such as textile manufacture, their labour was preferred since it was cheaper and the work required dexterity. Such girls enjoyed a measure of economic independence, their lives were not centred on the home, and they might even live in factory dormitories. Yet even if they did not accept a traditional arranged marriage, as many still did, they did not necessarily choose a husband for themselves from their limited male acquaintance. It was very common for a friend or an older woman to introduce a suitable young man to a girl, or a suitor might be selected by the family who would then seek her approval. The significant change with all these arrangements was that the girl's interests as an individual were usually given precedence over those of the family.[19]

The young married woman in the town was less likely to live with her mother-in-law, and those who did often kept their factory jobs, which created a very different relationship with less contact and consequently less friction between them. But factory girls paid a heavy price for their improved status at

[19] Detailed information on changes of this sort may be found in Olga Lang, *Chinese Family and Society*, Part II.

home. Working hours were long, conditions bad, and pay poor. And for married women workers, there was cleaning and cooking in cramped, ill-equipped, sordid slum homes to be faced at the end of the day. Yet living conditions in the fast-growing industrial areas were so bad[20] that for the full-time housewife to endure them throughout the day must in itself have been a hardship, and one for which she was not paid.

In the middle and upper classes a few parents still refused their daughters schooling or allowed them only a few years of it, preferring to invest their money in their sons. Such parents often arranged their daughters' marriages according to tradition. A few brave girls from this sort of background fought convention and won themselves an education and independence, but many more did not fight or failed.[21] If they were not educated, girls of this class were completely dependent on men to maintain them at the standard of living they had been taught to expect.

Nevertheless, in the middle and upper classes girls had a good chance of receiving at least a limited education, and some even enjoyed equal educational opportunities with boys. Girl students, like girl workers, saw enough of the outside world to give them wider perspectives and to lead them to wish for greater freedom. A few enlightened parents allowed their daughters to choose their own partners, while others came to compromise arrangements. Many, however, continued to arrange marriages in the old way, and this frequently gave rise to bitter conflicts because the girls had acquired Western ideas about love and marriage in the course of their studies. Probably educated girls did have the best chance of being allowed at least some say in their marriages, but those who were forced to accept their parents' choice would have found it all the harder to come to terms with a fate which they had not

---

[20] See Jean Chesneaux, *The Chinese Labor Movement*, pp. 88-105.

[21] Several such women have written autobiographies from which one can learn of the struggles they went through to obtain an education, and the effects that this had on their relations with their families. Wei Cheng Yu-hsui, (Mme Wei Tao-ming), *My Revolutionary Years*; Chow Chang-cheng, *The Lotus Pool of Memory*; Buwei Yang Chao, *Autobiography of a Chinese Woman*; Xie Bingying, † *Autobiography of a woman soldier* (published in an abridged English version as *Autobiography of a Chinese Girl*).

been conditioned to accept. A few educated girls from this class became independent because they could earn enough to support themselves. They might have to struggle against both family opposition and employers' discrimination, but would not suffer from overwork as women workers did, since their hours were shorter, and they could employ servants to cook and clean.

A feature of this transitional period in the towns was a decline in family stability. The towns were expanding rapidly and their working-class population was composed largely of first-generation migrants from the countryside. These were often illiterate and found it hard to maintain close contact with their families left behind in the villages. This could be to the advantage of the woman who accompanied her husband or went to join him. Away from the more senior members of his family, she had no longer to endure the domination of a mother-in-law, and might even gain a more equal voice in family affairs. On the other hand, freed from the discipline and the institutional checks which had formerly governed their behaviour, migrants easily became the victims of city vices like drink, opium, or gambling. These, being economically ruinous, could cause the break-up of families. Even more important, high unemployment, the weakness of organized labour, the high degree of exploitation, the instability of the economy, and the lack of welfare measures for the sick made financial disaster a common experience for workers' families. In these circumstances a family might simply be deserted by its wage-earner, or he might migrate to another area in search of work and be prevented by the political situation or by poor communications from maintaining contact.

Women were the main sufferers in such situations since they were economically weak. Even for those who worked, life would be difficult if they were left with children on their hands; because family links were weakened by the move to the town, they could not so easily enlist the support of relatives, the insurance system of the old society. For those who had always been economically dependent, the situation would have been more difficult still.

Broken families could also be a problem in the middle and

upper classes. Here, economic factors were less important: the main cause was the breakdown of traditional moral sanctions and the bankruptcy of attempts like the New Life Movement to put something in their place. In these classes separation was more often formalized by divorce than amongst the poor, but even if this were accompanied by maintenance arrangements, the wife depended on the husband's good will since the machinery for getting them honoured rarely functioned.

A survey made by Olga Lang in 1936-7 showed that many boy students were potential bigamists, feeling that they should accept the wives chosen for them by their parents, but that at the same time they had a right to live with the girl of their choice whom they would regard as their wife.[22] It is hard to decide which is the more pathetic figure, the deserted village girl or the abandoned companion of the young man's city life. The village girl would be left to live out her days alone with her husband's family, unable to understand why she had not satisfied the man she considered as her husband, and despised or pitied by all who knew her. The town girl, on the other hand, could find herself completely alone, betrayed by the boy, often a fellow-student, with whom she believed she shared everything including even the ideals upon which they had based their life together. The boy's predicament was also a hard one. His village wife might have been brought to his parents' house without his consent or knowledge. Even if this were not so, it would be difficult for him to accept that romantic love and the freedom to form his own relationships, which were part of the wonderful new world his education had opened for him, were never to be his to enjoy. Yet if he repudiated his village wife, it would be a disgrace from which she could never recover.

Of course there were many stable families in the towns, some of them based on modern views of marital love and equality. Nevertheless some loss of the security afforded to women under the traditional system was certainly a negative influence on their position in the transitional period, though the strength of the traditional bond between father and children seems to have prevented the real breakdown of the

[22] Olga Lang, p.225.

marriage institution which has occurred in many impoverished urban cultures where the traditional order has been upset.

The Marriage Law of the People's Republic of China has been the basis of family law since 1949.[23] The fundamental principles of the new Marriage Law, like those of the liberated areas and the Jiangxi Soviet Republic, were that marriage should be based on the free choice of both partners, on monogamy, and on equal rights for both sexes.[24] The law expressly prohibited bigamy, concubinage, child betrothal, interference with the remarriage of widows, and the exaction of money or gifts in connection with marriage. It set the minimum ages for marriage at twenty for men and eighteen for women. Medical conditions were laid down for marriage, and the state's interest in what had formerly been a family affair was further expressed in a clause which made the registration of marriage with the local government a condition for its validity.

The equality of man and wife was asserted in a declaration of their freedom to choose their own occupations and social activities, their equal status in the home, their equal right to the possession and management of family property and their joint duty of striving for the welfare of the family and the construction of the new society. The responsibility for rearing and educating children lay with the parents. Children out of wedlock were given the same rights as other children.

Divorce by mutual consent was recognized although like all forms of divorce it had to be registered with the local government. *Ex-parte* divorce could be granted by the county or municipal governments, though only after mediation both at that level and at district level had failed. Men were not allowed to apply for divorce when their wives were pregnant or for a year after the birth. *Ex-parte* divorce was not permitted to the spouse of a member of the armed forces still in touch

[23] *The Marriage Law of the People's Republic of China.*
[24] In this brief description of the Marriage Law I examine the law as an instrument for social reform and family revolution. For a detailed discussion of the law from a lawyer's point of view see M. J. Meijer, *Marriage Law and Policy in the Chinese People's Republic.*

with his (her) family. Each party had the duty of rendering the other economic assistance should he (she) get into economic difficulties after divorce. The articles on custody made the interests of the children the guiding principle for decisions. The father was to be at least partly responsible for maintenance if the mother was given custody, but there was no such regulation for the cases in which the father had custody. The husband was held responsible for debts incurred jointly during marriage if there was no property acquired jointly with which they could be discharged. The wife retained the property which had belonged to her prior to the marriage. If any dispute arose over other properties, it was to be settled by the People's Court upon consideration of the state of family property, the interests of the wife and the children, and the principle of benefiting the development of production.

The importance that the communists attached to the Marriage Law in their struggle to revolutionize society is indicated by the fact that its drafting, which took several months, was done while the Civil War was still raging.[25] They knew from their experience in Jiangxi and in the liberated areas that the promulgation of such a law was only a beginning, and that it was extremely difficult to implement new social legislation. They attacked the problem by trying to change the whole way in which law functioned in China. Under the imperial administration the lowest representative of the Central Government was the magistrate at the county seat. Law and legal procedures impinged little on the lives of ordinary people although they were regarded with a vague dread. For thirty years after the 1911 revolution, under the Kuomintang and the warlord regimes, law and the courts remained something remote and incomprehensible to country people, and the legal system, when it functioned at all, was often very corrupt.

When the new Marriage Law was promulgated, it was not the responsibility of the court alone to get it implemented; the whole population was asked to live by it, publicize it and to

[25] Deng Yingchao, 'On the Marriage Law of the People's Republic of China, Part 1, How the Marriage Law was Drafted', published with the English edition of *The Marriage Law of the People's Republic of China*.

support anyone who tried personally to benefit by it. Though obviously members and cadres of the Women's Federation were particularly deeply involved, cadres at all levels, officers of the Peasants' Associations, and of course members of the Party and the Youth League were constantly urged to check up on the observance of the law.[26] Disputes so difficult that they had to be settled by litigation were taken to the District People's Court, or to the local government if no such court existed. But many more cases were settled locally with patient reasoning and argument or at times a firm ruling from responsible cadres. As many reports of injustices show, these cadres were sometimes governed more by their old prejudices than by the law, but in general it was the authority of the marriage law that they invoked in their decisions, and thus such decisions differed from locally mediated settlements in pre-liberation China which had merely followed custom.

After the promulgation of the law, tremendous campaigns were launched to publicize and enforce it. With land reform it became a major theme of all propaganda for social reform. The old system was condemned and the new advocated in newspapers, magazines, special booklets and comic strips, stories, posters, and leaflets. To ensure that word of the new law reached the illiterate, thousands of drama troupes were organized to take plays and skits about it to the villages,[27] the radio carried material on it, and on a local scale, literacy classes and newspaper-reading groups concentrated on it. Though much of this material was intended for use on a national scale, propaganda for local use which took account of special local conditions was also produced. For example, a book published in Canton in 1951, with contrasting illustrations of life before and after the marriage law, showed a woman farm labourer being sacked because she was

---

[26] As, for example, †*Points to which Youth League members should give attention in carrying out the Marriage Law.*

[27] I touch rather incidentally on the use of fiction to give women a positive activist image. It has been pointed out elsewhere that this is a feature of modern Chinese films (John Weakland, 'Chinese Film Images of Invasion and Resistance'). In the 1950s the story of the White-Haired Girl and the exploits of women fighters of Hainan island gained a place on the Chinese stage which was to prove lasting, and Sun Yü's play *The Women's Representative* had a great success.

pregnant, and a girl escaping an unwelcome betrothal by entering a 'home for those who have decided to remain single'.[28] The woman hired labourer was a familiar figure for Cantonese women and one with whom many could identify, but she would have seemed alien to the women of many other provinces. Completely peculiar to the extreme south, the 'home for those who have decided to remain single' was an institution abhorrent to Confucian values, yet well known in silk-producing areas of Guangdong where it was possible for women to live together in small self-supporting communities because they could work in the silk industry.[29] Such meticulous attention to detail is typical of Marriage Law publicity.

The most publicized examples of women oppressed by the old system to whom the new law brought relief were nationally known, but many towns and villages had their own stories which were written up in the local press or on the blackboards which served small communities as newspapers.

Yet despite such activities the implementation of the Marriage Law remained unsatisfactory. Investigation revealed that many arranged marriages still took place and that, worse still, many cadres intervened for the parents rather than their children when young people demanded freedom of choice in marriage, and for the husbands of women who unilaterally demanded divorce. In 1951 10,000 women were said to have suffered death by suicide or homicide in Central and South China alone after family disputes about questions of marriage and divorce, and in 1955 it was estimated that 70,000-80,000 women were dying annually because of such disputes.[30] The accuracy of such statistics is obviously open to question: the genuine concern of the government authorities at the frequency of violent deaths amongst women is not; the problem was not after all a very good propaganda point for the new law, and yet it was much discussed.

[28] †Comparative illustrations of old and new marriage.

[29] See Marjorie Topley, 'Women's Liberation in Traditional China: The anti-marriage movement of Kwangtung', in Witke and Wolf, Women in Chinese Society.

[30] Directive printed in XHYB (Sept. 1951) and quoted in C. K. Yang, Chinese Communist Society, p. 108. Other figures on murders and suicides arising from the Marriage Law are cited in †Important documents of the movement to implement the Marriage Law thoroughly, p. 12.

As early as 1950, Deng Yingchao had identified the shortage of able local cadres as a crucial difficulty in the administration of the Marriage Law,[31] and in the years that followed the press regularly carried rebukes to cadres who opposed the Marriage Law and exhortations to administer it better. The tone of these got more urgent as it became clear that cadres were often at least partially culpable for the deaths of women who had claimed their rights under the new law, only to meet with opposition from those who were meant to be carrying it out.

This concern culminated in the campaign of 1953, the greatest of the implementation campaigns, in which the main target was cadres rather than feudal-minded parents, parents-in-law, and husbands. The campaign was inaugurated on 1 February 1953 by a directive signed by Zhou Enlai (Chou En-lai).[32] The emphasis was laid more strongly than ever on the gradual process of education as the main weapon, and indeed the Central Committee's directive on the campaign expressly ruled that except in the case of serious offenders persuasion should be limited to propaganda. But it was firm that violent deaths of women had to be thoroughly investigated and the culprits properly punished.

Even more publicity and effort were devoted to the Marriage Law than it had first received in 1950. The public was deluged with information about it through every possible channel, and directives went out to Party and Government cadres at all levels to study the law again, to correct their own attitudes towards it, and to improve its implementation in their own areas. Tens of thousands of people, many of them village cadres in the Women's Federation, travelled to their local county seats to do training courses of a few days' duration. They returned to their villages with a clearer knowledge of, and perhaps a firmer belief in, the Marriage Law, and were thus better able to explain its principles or to assist people to claim their rights under it.

The campaign uncovered many cases where cadres had been apathetic about enforcing the law for fear that it might

[31] †'Comrade Deng Yingchao reports on the Marriage Law', *RMRB* (26 May 1950).
[32] For this and other documents of the campaign see †*Important documents of the movement to implement the Marriage Law thoroughly.*

cause trouble, and others where they had actually been opposed to it, and had hindered its implementation wherever they had had the power to do so.[33]

As in the original campaign at the time of the promulgation of the law, many cases of tragically unhappy arranged marriages being dissolved and followed by happy unions based on free choice were publicized. This time, however, there were also numerous stories told about cadres who had not supported young people and had even punished them when they tried to marry the partner of their choice. The campaign is said to have encouraged many unhappy people to seek divorce, and to have reformed cadres with feudal attitudes to marriage and divorce.

Since 1953 the effort to enforce the Marriage Law has been steady but less spectacular. Surprisingly, two new books of questions and answers on the Marriage Law published as late as 1964 indicate that even then there was still a feeling that the provisions of the law were insufficiently understood.[34]

Among the standard complaints about the Marriage Law, sometimes voiced even by cadres, was that it was really a divorce law (*hunyinfa shi lihunfa*), and that marriage freedom would be followed by chaos everywhere (*hunyin ziyoule, tianxia yao daluan*).[35] Though Marriage Law publicity indignantly rejected such allegations, in a sense they were confirmed by innumerable stories, articles, and news items. A striking feature of these is that very few describe a simple case of young unattached people meeting, falling in love and deciding of their own free will to marry, whether or not they will have to face parental opposition. Those which do are atypical in that they are often set in the town. Although it was

[33] In the State Council directives which introduced the 1953 Marriage Law implementation campaign, Zhou Enlai claimed that some cadres called the law a 'woman's law for oppressing men' and accused them of ignoring suicides and murders of women, and even themselves interfering in free-choice marriages (ibid., p. 3).
[34] †*Questions and answers on the Marriage Law* and Zhou Jiaqing, †*Talks on the Marriage Law*. Although in keeping with family policy at the time of their publication, these manuals are more conservative than those of the early 1950s, and go over many basic points as if they still needed explaining.
[35] †'Resolutely enforce the Marriage Law and guarantee women's rights', *RMRB* (29 Sept. 1951).

this very type of marriage which was advocated, and although the Marriage Law has a section entitled 'free-choice marriage', the themes of the stories were young people, and especially girls, struggling to free themselves from long-standing betrothals, rejecting the matches their parents made for them, or demanding divorce.

This will be easily understood if it is recalled that the minimum ages at which marriage was permitted under the Marriage Law (eighteen for a woman, and twenty for a man), were about the same as the normal age at marriage in pre-liberation China.[36] Of course many would still have been single at this age, but few would have been completely free of the necessity of dissolving some sort of marriage arrangement made by their families for the future before becoming involved with someone of their own choice.

Many of the stories do illustrate free-choice marriage positively, in that as soon as the girl is free of the man chosen by her parents she marries somebody else; but very few represent the girl's primary motive in rejecting the arranged match as her love for another man. In those which do, the girl is normally only betrothed, and she still lives in her own home. The stories of child daughters-in-law and of wives who want a divorce are usually more circumspect. These are lengthy accounts of the unhappiness and ill-treatment suffered by these girls in their in-laws' homes, to explain what has driven them to divorce. Occasionally 'the other man' is mentioned and even described as having admirable qualities such as industry, thrift, and enthusiasm for the new order. But he is not allowed to appear to break up the existing marriage, and the close relationship between him and the girl cannot be developed until after the divorce. It is impossible to prove, but it seems likely that the literature of the Marriage Law here betrays more caution about probable public reaction than concern for realism.

A story typical of those used to propagate the law was that of Liu Fuhuai who lived in Bishan county, Sichuan province.[37]

---

[36] Figures for age at marriage in the countryside can be found in Buck, p. 381.
[37] 'How I succeeded in marrying of my own free choice', in †*Emulate the most advanced people in implementing the Marriage Law*, p. 25.

Her father was a poor peasant who had betrothed her very early to a boy three years her junior to whom she was married at the age of sixteen. Her mother-in-law was cruel and she was very unhappy, but when she begged her mother to allow her to come home, the older woman was horrified. Four years later, in 1951, Liu Fuhuai was elected village head in place of a cadre who had been transferred to work elsewhere. At the same time a boy a year younger than her who had been a childhood friend became chairman of the Peasants' Association. In the same year the Women's Federation in the village held a meeting to discuss a case of wife murder with reference to the Marriage Law. This meeting made Liu think about her own unhappy marriage and she resolved to ask for a divorce. However, when she spoke to the district head (who was also a woman), she met with firm opposition. The senior woman pointed out that the old people of the village were already opposed to young women attending meetings and that such a scandal would undoubtedly lead to their being forbidden to do so. She also hinted that it might affect Liu's application to join the Youth League.

When she consulted the chairman of the District Peasants' Association he took a very similar line. He argued that old-style marriages were very numerous and that if Liu asked for a divorce it would set an example which could lead to chaos. Poor Liu dropped the matter for a time, but when she joined the Youth League, its secretary took a more progressive line and urged her to persist. A cadre from the County People's Court came to hear some divorce cases at a public meeting, so Liu took the chance to raise her case. She was granted a divorce and the cadres who had opposed her application were themselves criticized, so that the whole story became known throughout the village. The story illustrates well the weight of conservatism. Both the girl and the village must have been exceptional, or she would never have become village head. If such an important local figure, in a village which had shown itself to be progressive about women by accepting one as its head, met these obstacles in her fight for a divorce, things must have been still more difficult for ordinary women. Eventually Liu married her childhood friend, though we are told that a girlfriend acted as an 'introducer', a detail which shows how difficult it was to abolish the indirectness imposed by decorum in traditional marriage.

After the Marriage Law was first promulgated, some surveys of marriages made in the old liberated areas divided them into three types: those in which the couple married of their own volition, arranged marriages when the couple met and agreed to the match before the wedding, and marriages arranged by the parents without any consultation with the couple.[38] The figures given indicate rather different trends, not surprisingly, since not only would conditions have varied anyway from one locality to another, but the areas surveyed had been liberated for different periods of time. Nor can we have any idea how uniformly the rather vague definitions of the survey were applied. Clearly it could not always have been easy to decide how to categorize a particular marriage. Nevertheless it is interesting to note that in areas where the majority of the marriages fell into the second, 'semi-voluntary' (*banzizhude*) category, a minority were completely voluntary (*zizhude*), and a smaller minority were completely arranged, the situation was considered good.

Later practice was simply to publish a percentage figure for marriages freely entered into.[39] This figure is always very high. However, as an indication of social change it is really valueless, since it could presumably include not only all voluntary and semi-voluntary marriages, but even in some circumstances a number of wholly arranged marriages.

It seems significant that in a booklet published in 1964 it was still thought necessary to urge young people to struggle for the right to choose their own spouse, although the same booklet stated that the old system of arranged marriage had already been destroyed.[40] This apparent contradiction probably indicated that the author was thinking only of the system in which arranged marriage could be completely coercive, for he goes on to warn that some young people made unhappy marriages because they allowed themselves to be

[38] Dong Bian, 'Changes in rural marriage in the old liberated areas', in †*Compendium of reference materials on marriage problems*, p. 37.

[39] As for example in †*Selected essays on divorce problems*, p. 26.

[40] Zhou Jiaqing, †*Talks on the Marriage Law*, pp. 9 and 31.

bullied into them through 'filial piety' and a fear of offending. Another booklet, published in the same year, stated that marriage freedom did not imply that the marriage of children should not be the concern of their parents, and that on the contrary parents could give advice, or make introductions.[41] It even counselled young people to seek the advice of their parents since they were superior in age and experience, and to give weight to it, although advice could of course be disregarded if it masked an attempt to interfere, or if it were ideologically incorrect.

These two booklets strengthen the impression given by much of the literature of the 1950s that the compromise 'semi-voluntary' marriages were common, in the countryside at least, and were accepted by the Party. Further evidence may be found in a description of Henan village life as late as 1970 which shows that the initiative in arranging a marriage was always taken by the parents, although the young people normally met and approved each other before the wedding.[42]

This does not of course necessarily conflict with the claim that there was a fundamental change in the whole basis of marriage. The compulsory registration of marriage, when properly carried out, eliminated absolute coercion in marriage since the cadre in charge had the responsibility of checking that the union was voluntary. In 1955, as part of a campaign to enforce the law on marriage registration more strictly, the district office in the countryside and the street committee office in the town were made responsible for it.[43] The basic-level cadres in these offices would have been in a better position to discover any element of compulsion in agreement to marriage, and to hear of marriages where registration procedure had been omitted.

Of course strong moral or economic pressure might still be put on young people to produce the necessary verbal consent to marriage. The moral pressure could only be weakened gradually by a changing climate of opinion; the economic pressure which could be mounted was gradually reduced by

[41] †Questions and answers on the Marriage Law, p. 8.
[42] Jack Chen, A Year in Upper Felicity, pp. 72-82.
[43] †How to do marriage registration work well

reform, the participation of women in production, and ally by collectivization, which all helped to undermine the basis for an authoritarian family structure and made young people's independence a more practical possibility. At the same time, the support of local cadres, and of organizations like the Women's Federation and the Youth League increased as the popularity of the law grew and the cadres' own doubts about it waned. Finally, if, in spite of all this, young people were forced into an unhappy marriage, the threat of a divorce on terms which were likely to be economically disadvantageous to the boy's family would moderate its members' behaviour towards the girl. Thus even new marriages initiated mainly by the parents might be based more on the interests of the boy and the girl.

The persistence of 'semi-voluntary' marriage is only difficult to understand if it is considered in isolation from the society in which it evolved. As has already been observed, at the time of liberation, the marriages of most of the single people near marriageable age would already have been planned for them by their parents. Some such arrangements were cancelled, but there were probably many more cases where the consent of the young people was sought and the marriage was recorded as semi-voluntary.

A less transitory factor was that although the relationship between the husband and wife was given far more importance under the new system, the importance of the relationship between the bride and her in-laws could not be ignored when, as was still normal in the countryside, she was to join their household. Parents continued to play quite a strong role in their sons' marriages, because their relationship with the girl would be of real importance. Moreover in traditional Chinese society, there had been very little opportunity for young people to acquire friends of the opposite sex, and this situation changed only slowly, at least in the countryside.

It is true that women's lives were much less enclosed and they attended meetings and literacy classes and worked outside their homes far more often than before. But many of these were women's meetings not attended by men, and in any case meetings were not social occasions. When women worked on the land it was at first with members of their own families, and later, after the start of mutual aid, they were often in all-women teams. Of course contact between the sexes did gradually increase, especially among young activists, but they normally met in groups, and for a specific purpose. The inhibitions of the old society remained strong, and even a boy and girl who saw each other regularly in the course of political activity and were attracted to each other might find it hard to speak to each other of love. It is common to read of young people being attracted to each other on sight, and asking a friend for an introduction, or, when they felt they knew no one eligible, asking a friend to suggest someone. If marriage resulted from such a meeting it was considered to have been arranged by the young people themselves (*zizhude*).

Freer courtship and marriage were established in the towns more quickly and firmly. Opportunities for meeting on a social basis were greater and a young person's range of acquaintance amongst the opposite sex was likely to be wider. Almost all secondary schools in China are mixed and it is normal to stay in touch with classmates after graduation.[44] After school, work or college brought fresh contacts. Social occasions, and in the 1950s even dances, were organized by trade unions in factories and government offices and by student committees in colleges. Mixed parties of young people could visit parks, cinemas, and theatres together and it became more normal for unmarried couples to do so. Social attitudes remained extremely puritanical, so that for a couple to hold hands in public would be considered ill-mannered. Pre-marital sex, though not theoretically illegal, met with strong social disapproval, and when classed as seduction has occasionally joined adultery in being treated as a crime punishable in the courts.[45] Though it was usually less severely

[44] Most of the information in this passage is based on my observations in Peking (1963-5). Ballroom dancing was one of the most curious products of Sino-Soviet friendship. It began in Yanan where dances were held regularly and were attended by such figures as Zhu De and Zhou Enlai (Agnes Smedley, *Battle Hymn of China*, p. 123). Dancing was advocated as a valuable weapon in the struggle against feudalism since it necessitated social contact between men and women. However, in the early 1960s factories and offices ceased to hold dances.
[45] The Shanghai Court even went so far as to assert that intercourse between unmarried people was an offence (Pang Dunzhi,†*Basic knowledge of the new Marriage Law*, p.68), but this was not usually maintained. Adultery, however, was

dealt with, it was generally treated as such an unmentionable subject that we cannot get even the sort of inexact, generalized idea of its incidence that we are able to form of other social practices in China today.

Nevertheless, in spite of limitations, courtship has become unrestricted enough for free-choice marriage to be a real possibility in towns. Moreover, a young couple who had asked friends to provide introductions would be expected to see each other alone several times before committing themselves to marriage. When we read of young people meeting and falling in love in the course of routine contacts, affection develops and the marriage decisions are made on the basis of what seem very few meetings and very superficial communication. Though the impression may have been exaggerated by the reserve exercised by those who write about this subject, it was probably anyway quite a realistic representation of the situation in a society afflicted both by feudal inhibitions and by revolutionary puritanism.

To summarize, it seems that partner-selection has undergone very great changes and is now primarily based on the interests of the young people, but that 'western-style' courtship is still limited, and the help of a third party who may be a member of the family or a friend is frequently enlisted when marriage is being considered.

Where widows had traditionally not been allowed to remarry it took much persuasion to establish their right to do so. Surprisingly, even in those areas where poor families had always arranged a second marriage for widows, problems now arose over the implementation of the new law. Whatever the custom in the old society, it was based on the idea that a woman belonged to her husband's family, bound by links

---

illegal: 'The act of both parties is wrong (cuowude), and if one or both are married it is against the law (weifade)' (†Questions and Answers on the Marriage Law, p. 35). If a plaint was brought by the 'wronged partner' offenders occasionally got a prison sentence. See for example a letter from a woman who had actually decided to accept that her marriage was at an end and applied for divorce. She expressed her satisfaction that her husband's girl friend (and future wife) must serve eight months.(†Selected essays on divorce problems, p. 16).

which did not dissolve with his death and which she could not break of her own volition. This idea was as strong in communities where families had formerly disposed of widows for their own gain as it was where they had kept them for life as daughters-in-law, and the fact that a widow was free to get married when she wished and to the man of her own choice was equally unacceptable to both.

Under the new law, not only would her first husband's family cease to receive a price for her, but she was entitled in her own right to a share of the household property including even land (until collectivization) if the family had received any land in land reform. Even more controversial, she had the right to take her children with her if she wished to do so. Obviously all this would have caused deep conflict even where the old taboos on remarriage were no longer effective.

The clash of new and old ideas led in extreme cases to tragedy. One case which received much publicity in 1950 was that of the Widow Chen, a Henan peasant woman who was murdered because she wished to remarry.[46] Those involved in the killing included even her own brothers who felt that she was disgracing their family, and some of her husband's relatives who would no longer have been her heirs had she remarried. The ringleader was Peilian, the former boss of the village, who was jealous and angry because the widow's suitor, Yang, had been elected village head. Such was the strength of feudal feeling, that not only was Peilian able to make the whole village hostile to the couple, he even persuaded the District Head to imprison Yang on some trumped-up corruption charges. This official took the view that since the widow was an 'immoral woman' (because she was considering remarriage), Yang who was associating with her was probably guilty of the charges. The true facts came out months after Yang's imprisonment and the widow's murder.

A case with a happier ending was that of the Widow Zhang who lived in the Taihang mountains.[47] This woman had been

---

[46] †*Compendium of reference materials on marriage problems*, p. 12.
[47] The case of the widow's 'illegitimate' child in Fang Ming, †*How the women of Beiguan village, Lincheng, are struggling free from the bonds of feudal tradition*, pp. 28-31.

widowed before liberation and left with small children, so a cousin of her husband's came to stay in the house and farm the land for her. In time they began to sleep together and she bore two babies but killed them for fear of public opinion. A woman cadre who was in the village to organize land reform heard this sad story and, realizing that the widow was again pregnant, began to fear that the tragedy would be compounded. She talked to many of the villagers separately about the case and then held a public meeting to discuss it. The older people, including even some village cadres, said that the couple were making the village lose face and that they should be punished or driven away. Some of the young people, especially the young women, said that they should have been allowed to marry long ago, and that the solution now was to let them marry and keep the child, but it was many months before the majority was persuaded of this. It is an interesting case because it shows that the villagers were prepared to ignore the fact that a widow was living with a man. They felt obliged to act only when the birth of a child forced the matter on their attention. However, they would not accept a marriage which they felt would be immoral and would bring disgrace on them as a community.

A report of 1950 states: 'Amongst the masses and the village cadres there are those who accept the idea of free-choice marriage but not that of freedom to divorce for they regard divorce as disruptive to the family.'[48] Yet in the China of 1950, the possibility of divorce was necessary to many young people before they could enjoy free-choice marriage. Even in the long run it was a necessary safety valve in a society where the marriage relationship was supposed to be based primarily on the wishes of the individuals directly concerned.

Divorce was of course unacceptable to the traditionalists, and the fact that after liberation it was commonly initiated by the woman did not make it less so.[49] Male opposition to divorce increased after land reform because if a family had

---

[48] †*Compendium of reference materials on marriage problems*, p. 12.
[49] Ibid., p. 38. Figures based on returns from 'several counties and districts' in the old liberated areas indicate that 60%-90% of cases were initiated by women. Similar figures appear in many reports on divorce.

obtained land, a woman leaving it through divorce had the right to take her share with her. One early report complained that in areas where land reform had not yet been carried out, women who got divorces were left without the means of support, while where it was already complete men obstructed divorce because they did not want to lose land.[50]

Considerable efforts were made to make divorce more acceptable to public opinion. Pleas for divorce in cases where the wife's misery was evident, as when she had been treated with exceptional cruelty or married to a simpleton or an infant, were given great publicity because they won sympathy. Cases where divorce was granted were not the only ones publicized. It was stressed that the freedom to divorce did not mean divorce at will, and examples were given where divorce demanded on unreasonable grounds such as the poverty of the husband had been refused.[51] The court's functions as a mediator were extensive. For example, in one case the court investigator found out that in the opinion of the neighbours the couple had originally got on well, and it was the bullying behaviour of the mother-in-law which had driven the wife to apply for a divorce. The investigator then sought out the mother-in-law, had a long talk with her and asked the couple to try again.[52]

Nevertheless early reports from divorce courts give the impression that divorces were usually demanded on what were considered anti-feudal grounds, and were fairly easily granted. Later in the 1950s, divorce seems to have become more difficult to obtain, at least where only one partner really wanted it. Investigations became more searching, and couples were sometimes flatly advised that an emotional basis for marriage did still exist between them and that they should try again.[53]

A report of 1950 on divorce based on returns from a number of people's courts claimed that of those applying for divorce, 50 per cent were between 25 and 45 years old, 40 per cent were

[50] †'Implement the new democratic marriage system', *RMRB* (16 Apr. 1950).
[51] Luo Yijun, †*New Words on the Marriage Law*, p. 43.
[52] Ibid., p. 23.
[53] † *Selected essays on divorce problems*, p. 10.

under 25, and 10 per cent were minors or old people.[54] These figures seem to imply that divorce was mainly used by young people as a means of freeing themselves from an unhappy marriage. This being the case, a falling divorce rate might have been expected in the mid-1950s, by which time the dissolution of 'feudal marriages' should have been a less important factor in divorce. The problem of the continuing occurrence of divorce and its rate was dealt with in a collection of essays expressing various views on divorce.[55] Although this pamphlet was published in 1958, several of the articles included in it first appeared in the Chinese press during the Hundred Flowers Movement in 1957. They indicate that considerable differences existed, even amongst the sort of educated people who might be expected to write to the press, about how easily divorce should be granted. Some appeared to regret the increasing difficulty of getting a divorce. Others complained of the tendency to use 'complete breakdown of the relationship' as a criterion. Any determinedly selfish partner could, they pointed out, manufacture a 'complete breakdown', and under such a system would be rewarded for his (her) deceit and ruthlessness by getting what he (she) wanted.

Though the authoritative writing in the pamphlet rejects the more punitive implications of such opinions it nevertheless reflects the growing ambivalence of official attitudes to divorce. It condemned as unrealistic the idea that divorce, as a rational way to end a marriage which has become a source of unhappiness to all, would ever disappear. Things could go wrong even with a relationship which was originally healthy and based on love if the contradictions which normally arise in everyday life were not satisfactorily solved. On the other hand figures were quoted to refute the allegation of a rising divorce rate and to show that a high proportion of contemporary divorces were products of the feudal marriage system, which seemed to imply that divorce was considered an undesirable social phenomenon.

Unfortunately the figures given (see below) were only for divorce cases heard by the courts. They must therefore have

---

[54] Chen Shaoyu, †*Marriage Law of the PRC: report on the course and reasoning of its drafting*, p. 42.

[55] †*Selected essays on divorce problems.*

omitted both the undisputed cases (which had only to be registered in the appropriate government office in the presence of both partners), and divorces which took place in the countryside before the judicial system was fully established; these also seem to have been dealt with by local cadres. The figures are therefore of doubtful significance, themselves, but their use in an attempt to disprove the proposition that the divorce rate had risen rapidly is itself of interest.

1950–June 1951	99,300
July 1950–Dec. 1952	not available
1953	1,170,000
1954	710,000
1955	610,000
1956	510,000[56]

In the detailed discussion of the reasons for divorce in China the pamphlet says that since most divorces were brought by young women, some people wrongly believed that the commonest reason for divorce after co-operativization, especially after the transition to higher co-operatives when women became economically independent, was financial discontent. Others believed that the prevalence of bourgeois thought was giving rise to divorce. The article challenges both these ideas, using figures from investigation of divorces in various areas of ten provinces from June to December 1956, which revealed that about 50 per cent of the cases concerned marriages which had been arranged. (The highest figure, from Minhou county in Fujian, was 73 percent and the lowest, from 12 counties of Guilin province, was 41.3 per cent.) The article claims that in backward areas as many as 70 per cent of marriages were still arranged. It admitted a connection between divorce and the co-operatives only in as far as they had enabled women who really wished for a divorce to apply for one. Even cases of young people who married by choice and then quickly demanded divorce were said to be a natural consequence of the old society, for as the article rather quaintly explains, when young people start to make their own

[56] These figures and those in the paragraph which follows are from pp. 1–4 of the pamphlet.

decisions after thousands of years of feudalism, it is quite likely that they will not be very good at it at first.

Divorce, like free-choice marriage, was more easily accepted in the towns than in the countryside. In spite of this, the divorce rate in the towns for the first few years after the promulgation of the law was lower than that in the countryside, because the near impossibility of divorce in the countryside under the old regime had built up a great backlog of unhappy marriages. In the towns on the other hand, where divorce had for years been concluded with little or no legal formality, the new law actually made it more difficult to obtain. Anxious queries appeared in the press demanding to know if it were really true that the insertion of an announcement in a newspaper to the effect that a couple had decided to divorce was not now a valid way of ending a marriage.[57] However, it does not seem likely that the divorce rate in the towns would actually have fallen with the imposition of formalities since they were neither complicated nor expensive. Moreover, there must have been many urban families, especially in small towns out of reach of the strong Western influence in coastal China, which had preserved the traditional morality intact. For them, as for rural families, divorce was almost a new phenomenon and would take time to become acceptable.

The divorce of cadres received a lot of attention in the literature on divorce. According to the pamphlet, 'statistics from several district courts showed that less than 10 per cent of all divorces involved cadres'.[58] That estimate was probably too conservative since it was given in an attempt to show that the rate of divorce amongst cadres was not unduly high. Many factors made for a comparatively high divorce rate amongst cadres. They were the most 'modern' section of the population and were the most likely to regard divorce as a reasonable solution to an unhappy marriage. Socially, economically, and geographically they were the most mobile group in society. Old revolutionary cadres who had left their villages to join the

---

army or to do political work had often been separated from their families for many years. Even after liberation cadres were frequently taken away from their families by work. In most cases, especially in the early years, those who left were men, and they left behind them women to whom they had often been married by their parents.

The problem of 'village wives' was of great concern to progressives, even when Bertrand Russell was teaching in Peking in 1921, and the issue was still a live one in the 1950s.[59] With the experience and education they had gained in the outside world, young cadres of peasant origin tended to become alienated from the illiterate women they had left behind and to feel closer to the sophisticated women with whom they worked in the city. Having assimilated the idea of love marriage, they developed a sense of deprivation that they were never to enjoy it. They often fell to the temptation to cast off their 'village wives', to whom they might never have been very close, in favour of educated women with whom they had more in common.

This subject was raised very early in a paper aimed at educated young people.[60] Editorial advice to the young men was to be flexible and to try to find a solution which would suit both parties. It gave the following cases as those in which divorce could justifiably be insisted on:

1. If the family of the girl are reactionary and so is she.
2. If she is seriously unsound in body or mind (e.g. if she is mad, or has a loathsome disease).
3. If she or you already had a sweetheart before the betrothal or she was really opposed to the marriage.
4. If the age difference between you is too great.

In other cases the young man was told that he and the girl should pay great attention to each other, and try to develop a mutual affection. If the girl was backward politically he was

---

[59] Bertrand Russell, *The Autobiography of Bertrand Russell 1914-1944*, pp. 182-3. For treatment of the problem in the 1950s see †*Basic knowledge of the new Marriage Law* p. 56, †*Explanation of problems of matrimonial property*, p. 31, and the reminiscences 'Divorce?' ('Lihun?') and 'Let's go home' ('Huijia ba') in the reportage booklet, †*Our marital relationship*, pp. 31 and 49, and †'What attitude should one take to a backward wife?' *GRRB* 2 Dec. 1956.

[60] †'Some views on village wives', *Democratic Youth* (21 Mar. 1950).

urged to help her to study — 'reform is always possible'. If all this was unsuccessful the boy could ask for a divorce, but he should not insist on it. He was reminded that it was the old system that had been hateful, not the person of his wife, and that women had suffered most in the past. The expression 'village wife' was itself attacked as it was said to reveal an intellectual's contempt for peasants in general and women in particular. The article warned that romantic films create illusions about marriage, that in fact, like other things, it must be based on love, will, and a correct viewpoint. Finally the writer denied that he was advocating surrender to the feudal marriage system.

Essentially in these cases there was a conflict between the principle of freedom of choice in marriage and the interests of certain village women. If such men had been encouraged to break with their old fiancées or wives, the women, already the victims of the old system, would have become victims of the new, suffering from social disgrace, economic difficulties, and emotional disturbance. But the basic principles of the Marriage Law would have been contravened if the men in such cases had been ordered to accept their fate. The final answer, in which they were asked to try to compromise but were left the possibility of escape, clearly reflected this dilemma.

Such a cadre could be sympathetically viewed as a lonely, dedicated man seeking to escape a feudal relationship with a near-stranger whom he rarely saw, in order to marry a woman with whom he could enjoy a real partnership. Less sympathetically, he could be considered as a man who, having suffered and made good, now wished to exchange his peasant wife, perhaps aged by work and hardship, for a younger, prettier city woman. If the case of a cadre was judged according to the first analysis, his divorce application was seen as an anti-feudal act, whereas according to the second it was based on bourgeois ideas and would be treated with less sympathy. In fact, although a particular case might fit one interpretation much better than the other, most would have elements of both. In the early years the courts tended to grant this type of divorce easily, but as the danger of a high rate of cadre divorce discrediting the regime in an extremely puritanical society was recognized, and social stability was given a higher priority, policy changed. More effort was made to make cadres see the difficult position in which they would leave their wives, and to persuade the men to try to educate them to become more suitable companions rather than abandoning them.

Although the causes have changed a bit, the divorce rate amongst cadres probably remains comparatively high. In the new generation cadres have had the chance to arrange their own marriages. Those who come to the cities from the countryside to obtain an education leave their villages before the age of betrothal. However, state cadres remain a very mobile part of the population. A cadre may be sent to a post thousands of miles away at a few weeks' notice with no idea of when he or she will be able to see their family again. Accommodation difficulties, and the fact that in most cadres' families both the husband and the wife work, make it difficult to reunite such families and they often have to undergo lengthy separations. This phenomenon has its positive side. Women are not expected to give up their own jobs whenever their husbands are transferred, indeed if they would be hard to replace they are discouraged from doing so. This of course enhances the public consciousness of the value of their work. I knew one young woman who was so indignant when her fiancé demanded that she follow him to his new job in a big city that she broke off the engagement. In other cases, when the woman has a rare skill it may be her posting which decides their residence. But combined with the generally more loosely structured nature of city society this mobility makes cadres' marriages less stable.

There were two conflicting trends in divorce in China in the 1950s. As it became socially more acceptable, it was likely to be opposed less vehemently by the family, to meet with less obstruction from the cadres who were meant to administer it, and to occur more readily to people who were involved in unhappy marriages as a way out of the situation. But after the early years of the Marriage Law when easy divorce was felt to be a necessary part of the wholesale attack on the old system, the courts became more reluctant to grant it, especially if there were children of the marriage. The combination of these trends has made divorce a regular but minor feature of Chinese life.

The implementation of the Marriage Law has proved difficult and the attention devoted to it in the early years after its promulgation has not always been sustained. Even during the Cultural Revolution there was a spate of reports of feudal-style marriages, and of dowries still being asked and given.[61] In 1966 *Chinese Youth* carried an article praising three girls for persuading their parents not to take gifts, send them in sedan chairs, or force them to stay at home for six months, when they were getting married.[62] The implication of the item is that these were still common practices in that area, yet they all ran completely counter to the letter or at least to the spirit of the law. Such evidence of the tenacity of custom makes it clear that it would be wrong to claim absolute success for the Marriage Law in the 1950s. However, as far as we can judge from the available evidence, it did strike a death-blow at the old system. No new marriages, even when they were only a compromise between the old and the new, could wholly escape the influence of the law.

As land reform was the primary instrument in the overthrow of the old power structure in the villages, so the Marriage Law was the main factor in changing the old authority structure within the family. The subservience of women, a basic principle under the old system, was challenged by their rights under the new law, by land reform itself, and by measures which made it possible for them to work. The association between these changes was recognized if not accepted by the old peasant who said, 'This land reform is very good, the only trouble is we cannot beat our wives any more.'[63]

The Party has been conscious of the danger of alienating its supporters by over-radical policies on marriage and the family, so reforms have been brought about with patience and caution. Though the family has undergone great changes, no attempt has been made to destroy it; on the contrary, it has

---

[61] †'Be a revolutionary changing old habits and customs', *Guangming Daily* 12 Apr. 1966.
[62] Zhang Zhe, †'When getting married don't have betrothal gifts', *Chinese Youth* No. 2. (1966).
[63] Peter Townsend, *China Phoenix, The Revolution in China*, p. 161.

frequently been stressed that, in another form, the institution will survive into socialist and communist society. At present it forms the basic unit of both urban and rural society. Both the Marriage Law and the propaganda written for it advocate the 'new democratic family'. The basic relationship in this ideal structure was to be that between husband and wife who were to work together at home to bring up their children to be good members of society, while outside the home they were to contribute as much as possible to society. Other family relationships were considered subordinate to this central one.

Nevertheless the young wife's relationship with her mother-in-law remained extremely important to them both if, as was still common, they both belonged to the same household. It is very interesting that the tensions between the two women are a frequent theme in recent fiction and that they actually seem to receive more attention than marital difficulties in articles and advice columns on marriage and family problems. This is indicative of the depth of emotional turmoil to which the change in the women's relative positions gave rise. When marriages were made primarily as an agreement between the couple concerned, even if they used intermediaries, any exchange of presents was symbolic, and the young woman entered her new home of her own free will. As a strong young woman, she would normally be able to contribute to the family's income from production. From being her daughter-in-law's supervisor, the mother-in-law was now often relegated to the position of her helpmate. While the girl went out to work, the older woman might look after her grandchildren and do the menial tasks once done by the younger woman.

Some mothers-in-law took a permissible escape from this fate and began to work outside the home themselves. In such cases the women usually shared the housework. Others simply refused to take over any chores, or demonstrated their resentment in such ways as doing the cooking but refusing the daughter-in-law her food. If such squabbling went far enough it would come to the ears of a cadre who would normally deal with the old woman gently but firmly. However much he might understand her behaviour, she had to be persuaded that it must cease, for it could sabotage the work of her daughter-in-law and possibly of other members of the family too, thus affecting production. Sometimes in reportage on this theme the daughter-in-law is presented as performing a single act of service as if symbolically for the old woman, for example by making her a suit of clothes, which restores to her some sense of status. Thus the family revolution attacked not only the dominance of the male, but also the age hierarchy.

Industrialization and the collectivization of agriculture brought more women into productive labour, and this movement remained the keystone of policy on the family in the early 1950s. In official literature individual women were evaluated in terms of their contribution to society at large, and when they were praised for their role in the family it was usually for their success in combining it with an outside job.

All this changed completely towards the end of the first Five-Year Plan (1953–7). The press ran many articles on the 'new socialist housewife'. The women's magazine *Women of China* was filled with articles on love, marriage, family life, children, dress-making, and other such subjects. Far less was written on women with jobs. Discussion of housework in the early 1950s had been on redistributing it within the family and on minimizing what needed to be done. Now housewives were vaunted as workers who made an important contribution to society since, as wives and mothers, they gave the physical and moral support necessary to other members of the family who did or would take part in production.

All over the country, papers published letters and lent editorial support to women who complained that they were despised as mere housewives. Dependants' organizations held congresses and figured prominently in the news.[64] The *Peking Workers' Daily* published a letter in December 1956 from a man whose wife was too busy with their three young children to take a job.[65] Some of the leading cadres in his organization had criticized his domestic arrangements as feudal and had called his wife a parasite. She was upset and asked him to find a maid to care for the children so that she could work. But this

---

[64] Typical of this trend in 1957 were such publications as: †*Experience of work amongst the dependants of workers and employees,* †*Important documents of the national representative congress of the dependants of workers and employees,* and †*The new type of housewife.*

[65] †'Do housework and child-care count as work?', *GRRB* (16 Dec. 1956).

would have cost them more than they could afford refused to accept that someone who worked as hard as h did could be a parasite. The editor answered that althoug. the new society women were encouraged to work outside th home, housewives certainly did a job and made a contribution to society by enabling other members of their families to concentrate on their productive work. He also urged the cadre to help his wife to study so that if in future she was free to take a job she would be better qualified to do so. Nevertheless his acceptance and even approval of the woman's absorption in her domestic work would have seemed extraordinary a few years earlier.

Another new departure was the 'clothes reform' campaign of 1955.[66] The poverty of the liberated areas, the shortage of cloth there, the hard war-time conditions, and the wish of women cadres to identify with the peasants had produced the 'Yanan' style of dress. The need for thrift after liberation, combined with a strong tendency to social conformity and a movement among much of the professional middle class to take up with enthusiasm everything associated with the new order, meant that even the clothes of the well-to-do assumed the drabness and uniformity of the Chinese poor. This tendency was now reversed, and under the slogan 'Let's be pretty', women were urged to wear prettier clothes, flowered rather than plain cloth, skirts or dresses rather than trousers, and even to put on make-up. The official women's magazine began to feature regular fashion articles. This was an extraordinary campaign, unprecedented, and irreconcilable with the direction of the women's movement before or after 1955-6. It can perhaps be seen as a herald of the 'Hundred Flowers' movement which saw a reduction in many types of social conformity. But it must also surely be seen as part of a general presentation of conservative feminine models. Woman was being presented as a housewife and mother; the prettification campaign added to this emphasis on her nurturing role an emphasis on her decorative role.

Still, in 1956 there was not a complete reversal in the official

[66] See *ZGFN* for 1955, especially †'Clothes problems of women today', *ZGFN* No. 3 (1955).

attitude, and sharply differing attitudes on the role of women were reflected in the press. Women still received some praise for working outside the home; in propaganda the housewife took her place as a model beside the working woman, but did not replace her.[67] An article in July urged the expansion of nursery services, and rebuked factories which promised to open nurseries but did not do so, or opened bad ones.[68] The *Workers' Daily* published another letter in December by a woman who worked full-time although she had five children.[69] This letter stood in sharp contrast to articles which idolized women who ran their homes efficiently and thriftily, cared for their children well, and saved money by making clothes and the shoes for the family at home. The campaign for thrift went so far that it soon became irreconcilable with the early beautification campaign. Clothes became plainer again, and by mid-1956 rather pathetic letters began to appear in the women's papers asking if it was not in fact wasteful to pack away clothes made last year which in the atmosphere of the economy drive people no longer dared wear.[70] They were followed by a spate of articles giving instructions on cutting down dresses or skirts into jackets or clothes for children.

The glorification of the housewife, however, continued, and as we will see in chapter five, by 1957 even the right of women to employment at that stage in China's economic development was under challenge. The explanation of this change in writing on and for women in 1956–7 is not absolutely clear. It seems probable that the state of the economy was a factor in the change. In these final years of the Five Year Plan, the last individual farmers entered the co-operatives. There followed an influx of peasants into the cities seeking to better themselves. Industry could not absorb so many, and there was a sufficiently serious increase in the urban unemployed to warrant very strict measures to force people back to the villages. In the cities therefore there was probably a feeling

[67] Among the books about women workers which appeared in 1956 were: †*Women on the industrial front;* Xu Fang. †*Women on the iron and steel battlefront.* †*Wherever my country needs me.*

[68] †'They need help', *ZGFN*, 7 July 1957.

[69] †'Is it domestic slavery to be considerate to your wife?', *GRRB* (8 Dec. 1956).

[70] †'Frugality and clothes beautification'. *Heilongjiang Daily*, 10 Feb. 1957

that it was <u>unrealistic to ask women to take jobs which did not</u> <u>exist, and that it would be better to encourage them to find</u> <u>satisfaction in their traditional roles.</u> As we will see in chapter four, the mobilization of women for field work on an un-precedented scale was a feature of the movement to form ad-vanced co-operatives in 1955–6. Although the effort to get <u>women to the fields</u> slackened off in 1957 they were certainly not discouraged from going. Decreasing returns to labour may have followed the all-out effort to get women to participate in agricultural work in some areas, but it seems to have been a less serious difficulty than the <u>unemployment in the towns.</u> Many articles appeared in this period about children who were neglected and had accidents while their mothers worked. This could be seen as an attempt to discourage mothers from working, but could also be taken at face value as the con-sequence of the over-energetic campaign of 1955–6. Other articles appeared demanding improved nursery facilities to ease the problems of working mothers.[71]

It is interesting to view the fluctuations in policy on women in the context of a general tendency in Chinese communist history for great intensive campaigns to be followed by periods of lull or even retrenchment. During the Cultural Revolution, the housewife-orientated campaign of these years was fiercely attacked as part of the whole structure of Liu-ist policies.[72]

In 1958 the Great Leap Forward brought back more familiar themes with the expansion of industry and the establishment of the communes. Once more labour shortages appeared in both town and country, and enormous efforts were made to get women into productive jobs. Unprecedented attempts were made to get the work of child-minding, cook-ing, and sewing performed on a community basis, and

---

[71] †'Can women workers and employees who have children continue to make progress?', *GRRB*, 26 June 1956.

[72] The big attack on Dong Bian, the former editor of *ZGFN*, came in *ZGFN* No. 7 (1966). It was followed up by communications from branches of the Women's Federation in a pattern characteristic in such campaigns. Further supporting attacks whose titles are listed below were published in *ZGFN* No. 8 (1966) and continued in Nos. 9 and .11. †'Denounce the crimes of black gang element Dong Bian', by the revolutionary personnel of this press, *ZGFN* No. 7 (1966); †'Women of Lankao denounce the criinal acts of the black gang element Dong Bian', and †'The great plot of false discussion and real poisoning', *ZGFN* No. 8 (1966).

nearly all praise of women was again for contributions made to society in their own right.

The commune movement, especially in its early days, has often been presented as an attack on the family. It is true that it attempted to communalize some of the practical functions of the family such as the day-care of children and the feeding of its members. Nor, even when with the closure of some communal facilities many tasks reverted to the housewife, was there a return to the glorification of her role.

Yet after a decade of change in its structure, Chinese society remained firmly based on the family. In the countryside official figures for population and income are still normally quoted in terms of households rather than individuals. Members of village families live and eat together and usually work in the same team. In the towns, the family is more often a simple nuclear one and it may not be so unified economically. Members of the same family, though they may sometimes be employed by the same enterprise, will more often be separated for the working day. Work assignments may split families for months or even years. There are more crèches, and since city work does not follow the seasonal pattern of the countryside, they are permanent crèches. But even in the town the majority of people live in family groups. Separations are regarded as unfortunate and temporary. If young people work in the same town as their parents they are expected to live with them at least until marriage and probably afterwards too if there is room. If they work away from home they live in dormitories for single people until they marry. Since the single state is regarded as a transitory stage in a society in which almost everyone marries, these dormitories are considered a temporary measure.

The continuing value of the family in a socialist society was consistently stressed, while family reform was seen as a necessity. The position of women within the family certainly changed in the 1950s as the practice of ancestor-worship declined and girls' productive role increased. Men and women had equal legal responsibility for their parents' support. Myrdal found a woman who contributed 20 yuan a month to her mother's support just as her brothers did.[73] As women's

[73] Jan Myrdal, *Report from a Chinese Village*, p. 206.

economic independence increases, this presumably becomes commoner. Nevertheless, there can be little doubt that the preference for sons remained. As late as 1970 Mao Zedong, speaking of the conservatism of the peasants, said that if a woman in the countryside had girls as her first children she would keep on trying . . . [74]

Part of the remaining rationale for this preference is the fact that marriage in the countryside remains patrilocal. Sometimes work took a couple away from both sets of parents, and occasional instances can be found of men who went to live with their wives' families, but they were usually outsiders who had no family of their own in the area where they were working. The old practice whereby a couple with no sons could bring a son-in-law into the house to marry their daughter, though now encouraged, was condemned as feudal in several districts of Fujian as recently as the early 1960s, [75] but this may have been because the cases considered were obviously cases of arranged marriages or because money passed from the girl's to the boy's family. In law, it is true, children could take the family name of their mother rather than their father, if they wished, though in practice few did so, and most of these were probably the children of cadres. As long as daughters married out, it was to their sons and their sons' children that the mass of the population would look for the continuation of their line and, perhaps of more importance, for support, care, and company in their old age.

Not only did the institution of patrilocal marriage continue to incline parents to value their sons over their daughters, it also disadvantaged women when they married, in relation both to their work[76] and to their new family. Though the increasing stress on affectionate, co-operative, and equal marriage relationships eased the fate of a bride, and though she was better educated and less enclosed in the family and able to count on more outside help if ill-treated, she had still to make far more adjustments in her life, her work, and her personal relationships than had her husband. In neighbouring

---

[74] Edgar Snow, *The Long Revolution*, p. 171.

[75] C. S. Chen and C. P. Ridley, *Rural People's Communes in Lien-chang*, p. 183.

[76] For a detailed analysis of the way in which patrilocal marriage disadvantaged women at work see chapter 4.

south east Asian countries, people explain the custom of matrilocal residence as better for the bride, who can co-operate more easily both in the house and over the children with her own mother.[77] In rural China she must learn to do so with her mother-in-law. Presumably a change in this custom would have been too disruptive. Marriage reform at least united young people, whether male or female. Any challenge to patrilocal marriage might have upset young men as deeply as it would certainly have disturbed the older generation. Significantly there was no attempt to vary the practice until the 1970s, and even then it was not condemned as disadvantaging women. Peasant bridegrooms were encouraged to 'marry in' only where their fiancées had no brothers. This arrangement would assure the woman's parents of support in their old age, and if established, might dissuade couples from persistently trying for a son, regardless of China's efforts to limit her population growth.

Children, especially sons, are still greatly valued, and women still gain status by bearing children. It appears that many women now wish to limit their fertility, but that at least two children are still necessary to establish them in their families. The mass popularity of family planning only developed in the 1960s; earlier the status which constant child-bearing brought a woman in the family was in sharp conflict with the social status that productive labour might otherwise have conferred on her. It is interesting that in 1962 in Liu Ling village in Shaanxi, peasant women had most praise for those housewives who successfully combined the roles of mother and commune member.[78]

As a result of marriage reform, greater economic independence, better education, increased contacts with society, and a heavy commitment to sexual equality by the prevailing ideology, women's position within the family has undergone a marked improvement. However, many problems remain, and since these are related to complex general socio-economic problems they are unlikely to be quickly resolved. In the following chapters, I will examine these relationships first in rural and then in urban society.

[77] Lucien M. Hanks and Jane Richardson Hanks, 'Thailand: equality between the sexes', in Barbara Ward (ed.), *Women in New Asia*, p. 447.

[78] Jan Myrdal, *Report from a Chinese Village*, pp. 203 and 229.

CHAPTER 4

WOMEN IN THE COUNTRYSIDE

After 1949 work among rural women at first received less attention than woman-work in the town because it could continue on the basis of policies and techniques which had already been developed in the liberated areas. But obviously it would be wrong to impute a static nature to work which extended to the whole countryside of the Chinese mainland the revolution that had already engulfed the lives of a few million peasant women. Conditions in the newly liberated areas were often different from those in the old, and policies were adapted to meet them. However, it was a process of adaptation, not one of innovation, and cadres who worked with rural women were recommended, even in the early fifties, to take as their guideline the resolution passed by the Central Committee in September 1948.[1]

In the countryside then, as opposed to the towns, 1949 did not mark any great watershed for the women's movement. By this year, long before land reform with its momentous impact on women had even begun in the south, in some of the older liberated areas in the north it was complete, and here there were sometimes to be found mutual-aid teams, and even producers' co-operatives, forerunners of institutions which became nation-wide during the 1950s. According to the Party's analysis, the key to the position of rural women was their relationship to production and to the ownership of what in the rural areas was the main means of production: the land. It is on this that I will now focus.

The role played by women in agriculture varied from one area to another and from one class to another. But as a rule, in traditional China they did not own land. Inheritance went from father to sons or to other male relations. Occasionally widows held land on behalf of their infant sons, though it was usual to entrust it to a male relative of the dead father so that it could be worked by a man. Neither as wives nor as daughters

---

[1] CC decisions (1948), see appendix 2.

were women themselves able to inherit it.[2] Only in the odd situation when the family had no male offspring, and chose to fill the gap in the line of descent by keeping their daughter at home and arranging an uxorilocal marriage for her was the land passed through the female line.[3] This still held good for most of China at the time of liberation, although in the liberated areas it had long been different.[4] Land reform, which overthrew the landlord system, also upset the male monopoly of land ownership. As we have seen, the Agrarian Law, like the 1948 resolution on women, ruled that men and women should receive equal shares of the land, and directed that separate property deeds should be issued where necessary. Unfortunately there is not sufficient evidence for an exact assessment of how far the ruling was implemented, though it is mentioned frequently enough (not only in official documents and reports, but also in local reportage and in fiction) to justify the assumption that it was at least widely known. When put into effect, this measure would presumably have been a stimulus to get women working on the land, but it would have benefited only women from the families of labourers, poor peasants, and lower middle peasants, since it was to these families that land was distributed. It should be noted, however, that the concept of women's separate right to land could be confused with the practice of allocating more land to those households with more mouths to feed, as the following quotation from Chou Li-po's novel *Hurricane*, based on his observation of land reform, seems to imply: 'Every peasant was entitled to 5 mou, but he, being a bachelor, had a right to 10 mou for himself and his future wife.'[5]

The campaign to get village women to involve themselves directly in production cannot of course be considered apart from the various stages of the transition from individual to

[2] This is one of the many instances where custom triumphed over law in Nationalist China. Legislation of 1931 gave sons and daughters equal rights of inheritance and made the wife her husband's legal heir, but it remained ineffective and probably largely unknown outside the cities: a situation which has changed little even today in Taiwan. For a description of the law see M. H. Van der Valk, *Modern Chinese Family Law*, pp. 123–41. For the situation in contemporary Taiwan, see Margery Wolf, *Women and the Family in Rural Taiwan*, pp. 203–4.

[3] Interesting material in this can also be found in Margery Wolf, cited above.

[4] †*Regulations on women's property and rights of inheritance.*

[5] Chou Li-po, *The Hurricane*, p. 377.

collective farming. Before examining these stages in detail, I will briefly describe women's traditional relationship to production in the countryside. In doing this I have mainly to rely on data gathered for Professor Buck's surveys in the 1920s and 1930s which, despite the problems involved, are the most useful available for my purpose.[6] The bias of the surveys towards more prosperous areas accessible to roads and free both from natural disaster and civil war has already been mentioned.[7] A further problem arises from the nature of the data, which is in fact information gathered from villagers by local investigators. Answers to questions about the percentage of work performed by women must therefore be assumed to have been influenced by cultural bias, for example a strong feeling against women working in the fields in a given region would presumably have led to low estimates of their participation for that region. It is not clear how the work was measured, that is how one job was weighted against another, but in the absence of evidence to the contrary I would assume a tendency to evaluate a day spent on a heavy job of the sort done by men far higher than a day spent on the sort of job which women might do, especially if, as seems likely, most of the informants were men.

In spite of these difficulties Buck's figures remain important to my argument, for they represent, whatever their relationship to reality, the perceived contribution of women to agriculture and the handicraft industries. It is precisely this, the contribution which women are seen by their community as making, which is so vital as a determinant of their status.

It is often said that women did not work on the land in traditional China. This statement requires considerable qualification. There were villages in the north where it was most exceptional for women to do farm work; on the other hand, there were others in the south where they played a leading part in agriculture. From his surveys Buck estimated that in terms of work accomplished, men performed 80 per cent of all the farm labour in China, women 13 per cent and children 7 per cent. His figures show a general difference

[6] The date in the discussion which follows is taken from J. L. Buck, *Land Utilization in China*, p. 293, and its accompanying Statistical Volume.

[7] See above p. 71 note 2.

between north and south, with 16 per cent of farm work being performed by women in the rice-growing areas as a whole as opposed to only 9 per cent in the wheat region. A breakdown of the figures within these areas shows further great contrasts, more extreme for the rice areas: in the double-cropping rice area for example (mainly Guangdong province, south Jiangxi, and south Fujian), 29 per cent of the labour was performed by women, whereas in the neighbouring rice-tea area, directly to the north (north Fujian, Zhejiang, Jiangxi, and Hunan), their share was only 5 per cent. Between the two extremes, the women's share was 22 per cent in the south-western rice area, 19 per cent in the Yangtze rice-wheat area, and 11 per cent in the Sichuan rice area. North of the Yangtze the differences were far less. Women performed 14 per cent of the farm work in the spring wheat area, 8 per cent in the winter wheat-kaoliang area and 5 per cent in the winter wheat-millet area.

It seems significant that the double-cropping rice area was the only one (apart from the national minority areas) where foot-binding had never been generally adopted, and that Fujian and Jiangxi, the two provinces divided between the rice-tea area and the double-cropping rice area, are also bisected by the 'foot-binding line' (see map). However, I would not wish to advance the absence of foot-binding as a *cause* of women's major role in agriculture in the double-cropping rice area; it seems more probable that it was an effect, in which case we have still to look for an explanation. Even if one accepted foot-binding (or its absence) as the determining factor, we would be left with the problem of explaining the great variation in women's participation between different areas north of the foot-binding line.

Here it may be useful to apply the economist Ester Boserup's analysis of male and female farming systems of which she has made this excellent summary.[8]

The sex roles in farming can be briefly described as follows: in very sparsely populated regions, where shifting cultivation is used, men do little farmwork, the women doing most. In somewhat more densely populated regions, where the agricultural system is that of extensive plough cultivation women do little farmwork and men do much more. Finally, in regions of intensive cultivation of irrigated land,

[8] Ester Boserup, *Women's Role in Economic Development*, p. 35.

both men and women must put hard work into agriculture in order to earn enough to support a family on a small piece of land.

If we attempt to fit China into this framework, we can see that all of north China and a considerable part of south China belong to the second category of extensive plough cultivation. In such areas women's contribution to agriculture was small and was probably made mostly in the busy seasons of the farming year. In the far south and the south-west where several crops were grown each year and much of the land was irrigated, the demand for labour was high for most of the year and many women performed farm work as part of their normal routine. The busy periods of planting, transplanting and harvesting occurred several times a year in the multi-crop system. During these periods even women who were unable or unwilling to go daily to the fields tended to be drawn into the work. The cultivation of rice being especially labour-intensive, women's participation rate was highest in the double-cropping rice area.

This is a satisfactory general explanation for the greatest regional differences, but there remain intra-regional differences which cannot be explained by the differing intensity of cultivation.

The spring wheat area of the far north which showed the comparatively high female participation rate of 14 per cent was the most sparsely populated area with a short growing season, low productivity per acre, and correspondingly extensive agriculture. Buck, who suggested that the greater prevalence of woman labour in the rice regions was partly due to an association between the amount of work done by women and the extent to which foot-binding was practised, was also troubled by this high figure of 14 per cent, since foot-binding was not only still widespread in the spring wheat area, it was done so tightly that women could not stand for any length of time and were compelled to work in the fields on their knees. Other factors are significant here. In this region the growing season was so short and the winter so bitter that only one crop could be produced. Labour demand peaks were therefore concentrated on the spring sowing and autumn harvest periods, and must have been even more pressing than the four peaks which occurred in the winter wheat with kaoliang or winter wheat with millet regions. The adverse climate and soil conditions, and, Buck postulated, high opium addiction of the region gave rise to the lowest labour productivity in China. It was therefore presumably simply impossible for a man to support so many dependants as he could do elsewhere in China. Climate and productivity thus combined to raise women's participation in farm work, although their role was still a minor one.

The comparatively low intensity of cultivation may have been a factor in the exceptional region of the south, the rice–tea region where women did only 5 per cent of the farm work. The accuracy of this figure is particularly questionable because the investigators must have been excluded from a very large part of the area which was communist-held, or affected by the fighting between the Kuomintang and the communists. However, various factors could have produced a low figure. Here the grain crop yield index was only 86 per cent of the China average.[9] The main crops, rice, tea, and rape seed, all had high labour requirements, and as much land was double-cropped as in the Yangtze rice region. A lot of the land was irrigated, but since mountain streams could be utilized, the irrigation was less labour-intensive than in the Yangtze plains. Very little land had to be artificially drained. Low labour demand for water control may thus partly explain women's absence from the fields. Much of the region consisted of barren hills, and there was less cultivated land per person than in the Yangtze area.

It may be, however, that the low figure for women's participation was due to the factor of perception. Women seem always to play an important role in tea-cultivation, especially in picking, and this work, which was probably seen as 'light', may have been under-assessed. This difficulty is basic to the comparative use of these figures; they must contain distortions due to differences in perception which we cannot now determine.

Subsidiary work, like pig and poultry rearing, spinning, weaving, basket-making, and other handicrafts, brought extra income to peasants and occupied time when other work was slack. But Buck's figures do not show a consistent relationship

[9] Buck. p. 76.

between the proportion of subsidiary work done by women and the amount they did on the farm.[10] For example, though in the wheat-millet area, where they rarely went to the fields, they were responsible for 25 per cent of the subsidiary work, in the rice-tea area, where they did equally little of the farm work, they performed only 13 per cent of the subsidiary work. These occupations provided 15 per cent of the income of farms in the former area and 13 per cent in the latter, so their importance to the economies of the two areas was not very different.

In some prosperous areas women may have been too busy at home because the meals to be prepared were more elaborate, or because there were far more clothes to be made, while in others the gain from extra labour contributed may have been so great as to tempt them out to work. While it is hard to know to what extent decreasing marginal returns to labour discouraged women from working, it is obvious that in so labour-intensive an agriculture this must sometimes have been a factor. Certainly in the 1950s steeply decreasing returns to labour were often an obstacle in the campaign to get women to work in the fields.

Women's participation in agriculture was thus part of a complex pattern. Some local variations cannot be explained by the factors examined and might be better understood in terms of the local history or local sub-ethnic differences. Any village with a significant proportion of Hakka residents would, for example, certainly produce quite different figures from villages without Hakkas, since Hakka women did not have bound feet and normally worked in the fields. In villages whose cultivated land was at some distance, women may have been discouraged from going there to work since it would increase their problems with children, especially if it was deep in the hills, as in tea-growing districts.

For China as a whole only a very broad generalization can be made. This is that though women did more work in the south than in the north, their agricultural role in all but a few localities was rather a minor one. Moreover, when women did do field work it was often on a very seasonal basis. They helped with the harvest especially in those areas where it coincided

---

[10] Buck, p. 297.

with the planting of another crop, and did secondary chores such as weeding, whch carried no prestige. Except in a few areas in the south, it remained the ideal that women should not do agricultural work, and an adage from I-liang, Yunnan, quoted by Buck, probably expresses the reluctant acceptance of women in the fields at rush periods which was general in China:

> In the two busy seasons
> Maidens may leave their chambers.[11]

Raymon Myers, in his detailed study of north China in the 1930s,[12] clearly indicates the seasonal and auxiliary basis on which women worked in the areas which he studied. Of the early summer in a Hebei village where cotton and millet had to be thinned at the time of the wheat harvest he says, 'the demand for labour was so great, even women came to the fields to help the men'. Again, in a Shandong village, a seasonal shortage was met by women, but only from the poorer households. 'During the wheat harvest when the spring crop was also being planted, women and children in poor households with only 10–30 mou even worked in the fields because so much labour was needed.' In the richer households this need was satisfied by temporary hired labour.

In China as a whole, Buck found that subsidiary occ-upations provided 14 per cent of the income of farm families.[13] It was thus an important though minor source of income. But the contribution of women was quite a small one here too: they provided only 16 per cent of the labour. This figure masks wide regional variations (from 25 per cent in the winter wheat–millet region, to as little as 7 per cent in the spring wheat region), but it confirms the implication of the data we have on agricultural production: that women played an unquestionably minor part in rural production. This had its bearing on their status, since in traditional China, as land ownership conferred power and prestige within the village, productive labour did so within the family.

---

[11] 'Er ji nong mang
    Guinü dou yao chu xiufang.' Buck, p. 307.
[12] Raymon Myers, *The Chinese Peasant Economy*, pp. 75 and 110.
[13] Buck, p. 297.

If women's participation in directly productive work was traditionally minor, their share of work was not. The household work for which they were responsible was demanding and often arduous, and it made an indispensable contribution to family welfare. Providing meals, for example, did not simply mean cooking; it could include the gathering of fuel, the drawing and fetching of water, the husking and grinding or polishing of grain, and the preserving of glut vegetables and fruits. The processing of grain was often spoken of by women as the heaviest of their tasks. Rudolf Hommel, writing of China in 1937, said: 'In almost every village in the rice-growing districts of Chekiang (Zhejiang) province there is a rice-husking mill, the property of the community . . . Every farmer owning a draft animal can use it, the others have to be content to use their hand mill.'[14] In the north, too, descriptions of villages also mention both large animal-powered equipment for husking and grinding grain, and household querns. So presumably, north or south, it was the poorer women (whose incentive to work outside the house was the greatest) who would be compelled to give the most time to one of the very basic household tasks. In some households the women made bean curd, fermented alcoholic drinks, and prepared tobacco leaves for pipe-smoking at home. Clothes were usually made at home, and so sometimes were the cloth and the thread which went into them. Cloth shoes stitched by women took two days to make but lasted only five or six months. In the poverty stricken and backward conditions of the Chinese countryside, where even water and soap for washing were costly in terms of effort, housework and child-care were more burdensome than in advanced societies. In the slack seasons men might sometimes help by carrying firewood or fetching water; but in general domestic tasks were the responsibility of women.[15] It was therefore clear that to increase their share in productive work was impossible, or at least would make their lives still harder unless household work

---

[14] Rudolf Hommel, *China at Work*, p. 96.
[15] Jan Myrdal, *Report from a Chinese Village*, p. 237.
An interesting exception was observed by Jan Myrdal in north Shaanxi, where men did the family knitting in the slack season. This was a very practical arrangement since the long northern winter brings more leisure to men than it does to women, whose busy household routine continues. *Report from a Chinese Village*, p. 237.

and child-care could be reorganized. Otherwise they would suffer from the double burden of which the Russian Bolshevik, Alexandra Kollontai, had warned.[16]

Arduous though housework was, much agricultural work could be heavier still. This was a factor in the traditional divison of labour and had to be considered if that division were to be changed. Many women were permanently handicapped by bound feet which precluded them from carrying heavy loads or walking any distance. Moreover, until recently, a woman might expect that for many of the years which would otherwise have been her prime, she would be almost continuously pregnant or nursing, her health and strength gradually undermined by child-bearing in primitive conditions. The surveys made by J. L. Buck in the 1930s indicated that Chinese women who completed their fertile period bore an average of between five and six children.[17] High infant mortality and the tendency to omit female births probably led to under-reporting, and this figure is likely to be too low. Moreover, since a large number of pregnancies no doubt ended in miscarriages brought on by hardship, poor nutrition, and heavy work, women must have undergone many months of pregnancy which did not result in births.

Where it was not customary for women to work on the land, they had not developed the many skills and techniques that they needed in order to do so. They were therefore thought incapable, so that a lack of trust on the part of men, and of self-confidence on the part of women were serious obstacles. A further prejudice was the one against women leaving their homes at all, especially if it meant being in the company of men. When women began to break this convention, it was often regarded as a disgrace both to them and to their families. They were sometimes criticized by other peasants for 'immorality', beaten by their husbands, or refused food by their mothers-in-law, who attacked them just as fiercely as did the men.

The mobilization of women for farm work could not take place evenly everywhere in any case, because labour shortages made it imperative in some areas, while surpluses made it

---

[16] Alexandra Kollontai, *Communism and the Family*, p. 13.
[17] Buck, *Land Utilization in China*, p. 386.

impractical in others. When these problems could be solved at all it was only in a gradual and piecemeal way. At each stage of the collectivization of agriculture one finds the same claims made about the great numbers of women becoming involved in agricultural work. The repetitive nature of these claims unfortunately tends to make the reader feel much effort is being expended for little progress, and this is aggravated when, by claiming 'unprecedented' successes at every stage of the campaign, the Party publicity machine constantly devalues all earlier and previously much vaunted achievements. For a historical perspective I think it is better to stress the continuous and gradual nature of the mobilization. Since throughout the campaign the essence of the problems did not change, it is possible to discuss the general approach to them, before going into any detail on the particular way each stage of the transformation of agriculture affected them.

The conflict between domestic and outside work was dealt with by exchange of labour, improved amenities, the products of the consumer industry, and the provision of communal child-care and eating facilities. The bulk of housework and child-care in traditional society had fallen on the younger women. As mothers grew older, their elder chidren helped by caring for the younger ones; on the marriage of sons, the new daughters-in-law took over the worst of the burden; and though the older women remained in charge of the the house, their role was not such an active one. But once the younger women began to work outside the house, this balance was changed, and a greater share of the chores fell to the mother-in-law. While her son's wife was out at work, the older woman would look after her grandchildren and do menial tasks which would once have been the special duties of the younger woman. She cooked for the family, including the daughter-in-law, who would formerly have had to serve her. The symbolism of this reversal of roles was certainly not lost on a people who lived in a society loaded with symbolism. The older women were, not surprisingly, often resentful. In the 1950s, publications for women carried much that was clearly directed at this unlucky generation of middle-aged women, reminding them that in enabling their daughters-in-law to work, they were themselves making a contribution to the welfare of society and to that of the family. Judging from this material, the care of children was a far more popular task than housework, and there are even reports of grandfathers taking it on.

When no member of the family was available to take care of the children, an arrangement might be made with a neighbour. In such cases the household was effectively purchasing services from outside. The payment for minding a child was indeed sometimes even settled as a proportion of the mother's earnings, an indication that the care of the child was still firmly regarded as the mother's responsibility, although it was permissible for her to find a substitute when it was economic for her to do so.

Crèches and nurseries were a natural extension of such arrangements, especially when the formation of mutual-aid teams and co-operatives provided organizations on which they could be based. At their simplest they were informal and temporary, formed so that mothers could help with a rush harvest. Such *ad hoc* groups were usually housed in a borrowed building such as a temple and were put in the charge of old ladies or small-footed women who could not do heavier work. Later, after the formation of co-operatives, the best nurseries were sometimes quite well-equipped establishments managed by women who had trained for a few weeks in the county town. Communal child-care facilities were usually subsidized to a greater or lesser degree,[18] an important principle, for as long as the mother is considered responsible for the cost of looking after her children, the value of her earnings is reduced in her family's eyes by the amount that must be paid for their care.

A report from Lankang district, Chu county, Anhui province, in 1955, which I summarize below, gave much interesting detail on the care of the children of working mothers in that particular area.[19]

In this district (xiang) there are 24 co-operatives and three mutual-aid teams. In 581 households there are 455 children under six

[18] †*The experience of Dongyan agricultural producers' co-operative in getting women to work in the fields,* in †*Work experience in the countryside of Zhejiang (Chekiang) in 1955,* pp. 213-15.
[19] †*High tide of socialism in the Chinese countryside,* p. 581.

needing care. Some mothers get grandparents or elder children to care for them, and others make exchange agreements with neighbours. This has taken care of 332 of the children. Eight old ladies between them care for 28 more of the children. Thus, 216 mothers go to work with easy minds.

For 95 other children there was no solution; either their mothers did not work or they worked and worried that their child would get up to mischief and have accidents. The district Women's Federation organized exchange of care for the busy seasons to help these mothers and prevent the loss of their labour, but this was not at first very successful. Investigation showed that some mothers still worried if they left their children with others, especially if an only son was involved. Others merely used their children as an excuse because they did not want to work. Some did not like parting with their wages in order to pay for the care of the children. The women who had charge of the children found the work and the responsibility overwhelming, and feared critical mothers. The co-operative chairmen were not interested, and the women's representative was unable to cope with all these problems.

A meeting was held for the mothers, the child-minders, and the cadres (both men and women) of the district. It was pointed out that women constituted 42 per cent of the local labour force, and that if they worked it would be possible to increase yields, thus enriching both their families and the child-minders.

A nursery set up earlier for busy periods was chosen to be the model for the district. Its rules were as follows:

> Keep children away from matches and streams.
> Have things ready to give the children to eat and stop them quarrelling.
> Change nappies often and don't let chickens or older children scratch the faces of babies.

Vegetable leaves, clay and empty match boxes were recommended as economical and versatile play materials.

The nursery was to be in the charge of old ladies and children over 10 if possible, otherwise a rota of mothers was to be drawn up. Charges for the nursery were decided according to the age of the child and according to how difficult it was to look after. Thus the care of a baby was valued at a half work-point per day, against a whole work-point for a toddler. Children who needed continuous attention were charged for at the rate of $1\frac{1}{2}$ points, but there was no charge at all for children over seven.

Such measures were said to have solved the problems of working mothers in the district.

In the countryside, communal eating facilities have not attained the importance of nurseries. In 1953, at the Second National Congress of the Women's Federation, Deng Yingchao even spoke against sewing groups and canteens as attempts to relieve country women of their housework completely, which 'were not feasible and therefore mistaken and harmful'.[20] This line was of course reversed during the Great Leap Forward (1958–9), but the new policy was not very successful, and today in most of rural China, canteens function on a large scale only at the rush periods of the agricultural year.

Canteens had been expected to bring other advantages besides the obvious one of freeing more women for productive labour. One of the problems of collective farming was that it required a more exact sense of time than existed generally among peasants accustomed to planning their own work-day. If everyone ate together in a canteen, it was hoped that they would find it easier to report for work promptly. It was also argued that canteens would yield great economies of scale.

A complaint mentioned in almost every report of commune canteens was 'You can't eat when you like.'[21] Dissatisfaction with the quality and quantity of the food was aggravated by the food shortages of 1959–62. Even under ideal conditions it is of course difficult to cater for individual tastes in cooking on a large scale, and conditions were far from ideal.

The expected economies of scale were not always achieved. During the years before the establishment of the canteens, the job of cooking at home had increasingly been undertaken by women who were too old or too weak for outside work. Work in the canteens was heavy, and hours long, so that it was necessary to employ able-bodied workers who might otherwise have been in the fields, while the old ladies were left idle. If public trust was to be preserved, the canteens had to keep accurate accounts, but collectivization had already caused more demand than could be satisfied for people who could

[20] Deng Yingchao, 'Report on the present orientation and tasks of the Chinese women's movement', ZGFN No. 5 (1953).

[21] I. and D. Crook, The First Years of Yangyi Commune, p. 68.

keep books. The big stoves used in canteens did not warm the peasants' homes as private cooking stoves had done, and in the colder areas where some sort of house heating is needed, this separation of cooking and heating functions tended to increase fuel consumption. In the end most communes closed their big canteens, opening them temporarily at the busiest times of year when all available labour was needed.

Improved amenities and consumer goods, although still inconsiderable by Western standards, have helped to lighten household work. Running tap water in the home remains rare in the countryside, but new taps and pumps have made it easier to draw, and for many have brought a source nearer to the house. Thermos flasks, which are proudly displayed in most peasant houses, have made it possible for people to take the ordinary country drink of hot water without always having first to kindle a fire to heat it. Soap, and more recently detergents, have become cheaper and more available, making all cleaning jobs easier. Husking and grinding by hand is less usual since many brigades[22] have set up small mills to which their members take their grain.

Jan Myrdal described how the installation of an electric mill set up by the brigade in Liu Ling, northern Shaanxi, in 1969 had affected one woman's life:

Li Yangqing's household consisted of seven persons. They consumed about 1,500 kilos of grain a year. Formerly she used to grind all this herself, by hand. Now it was being ground for her in the brigade mill. The brigade charges at cost for this service. The prices vary slightly for different sorts of grain. On an average it is 0.66 yuan per 100 kilos of grain. Last year Li Yangqing paid about 10 yuan. This is deducted from the money she gets for her work. But since the mill has freed her — as it has the other women — from the hardest and most time-consuming part of her household work, and this has given her more time for agriculture, so has her working income risen.[23]

Products of the machine textile industry have gradually replaced the old handicraft industry, and peasants have even begun to buy some ready-made clothes. More popular were factory-made cotton shoes with hard-wearing plastic soles which have saved millions of housewives the old time-consuming job

[22] A brigade is a sub-division of the agricultural commune.
[23] Jan Myrdal and Gun Kessle, *China: the Revolution Continued*, pp. 10-12.

of stitching cloth soles. 'Sewing stations' were set up in some communes. These stations were provided with sewing machines, and employed people who became highly skilled at making clothes. Through them women could save an enormous amount of time which could then be given to remunerative labour. To take an example from Liu Ling village in Shaanxi again, women paid 2.5 work-points to have a child's jacket and trousers made at the sewing stations. Formerly, working by hand, this job had taken them three days, the equivalent of 18 work-points.[24] These institutions are also important because they put work formerly done by women on an individual basis through a public measuring process and get it priced. It thus enters the work-point system.

Although men were occasionally urged in the mass media to assist their wives with housework, it has only lately been implied that they should divide it equally. Such persuasion as there was earlier seems to have been directed at urban men whose wives worked. All the young women of Liu Ling village expressed pride or gratitude when they mentioned that their husbands helped in the house or with the children. They clearly recognized it as a difference between their generation and that of their parents, but did not yet take it for granted even for themselves. Women took more time off from field work than men, because they needed it for their housework. In the words of one peasant housewife, Li Yangqing:

It isn't easy being a woman. My husband brings up four buckets of water a day from the well. I myself go down to the river to wash clothes once or twice a week. We often go down, a lot of us together. We do that when we have our day off. Or we do it during the midday rest when our husbands are asleep. When we have our rest out in the field, we take out clothes to make or shoes to sew. The men either sleep then or walk about collecting fuel.[25]

By 1969, women in Liu Ling were in a more militant mood. They had been demanding that men should care for the children sometimes so that their wives could go to meetings. Nevertheless, pay rate norms for an adult woman still stood at 6–7 work-points a day, as compared with 7–9 points for a man

[24] Ibid., p. 136.
[25] Myrdal, *Report from a Chinese Village*, p. 238.

since the woman's working day was shorter to allow time for household duties, which did not of course carry work points.[26]

The official line was that eventually the drudgery of housework would be eliminated, but in the meantime it was primarily the responsibility of the women. No effort was made to explain or justify this assumption; presumably because in the traditionalist countryside none was required. In unmechanized agriculture productivity is still often closely related to strength and stamina, and the continuation in a less sharp form of the old division of labour seems really to be a tacit acknowledgement that a man's time in the fields may be more productive than a woman's.

Women's capacity for farm labour, even for the lighter tasks like hoeing, picking, and transplanting which occupied so much of the peasants' time, was of course affected by the state of their health. The abolition of foot-binding, which in the most backward rural areas had continued into the 1940s, meant that in future women would cease altogether to suffer from what had once been their worst physical handicap, though it continued until the end of their days to hamper those unfortunates for whom unbinding would have been too late.

The damage previously inflicted during childbirth has been mitigated by improved knowledge of and facilities for pre- and post-natal care. Immediately after liberation a huge programme was initiated to train midwives for the countryside.[27] Many of the 'students' were former village midwives who, though they had infected countless women by probing with unwashed hands and long finger-nails, had practical experience, which when combined with a little theoretical knowledge turned them into useful medical workers. Basic precautions against septicaemia, such as scrubbed hands, and instruments sterilized in locally distilled spirits, drove maternal and infant mortality down. Later, 'maternity stations' were built in some villages, so that many women, especially those for whom complications were feared, could have their babies in better conditions than their homes

---

[26] Myrdal and Kessle, pp. 133-5.

[27] 'Vigorous reform of old delivery and child-rearing methods', in †*Experience of Welfare work amongst women and children.*

could furnish; and at these, better medical help was available. But this was a much slower development than the crash programme to train midwives, and even by the late 1950s medical care in countryside remote from large towns was still far from adequate.

The problem was not simply one of a shortage of personnel. Childbirth in China as in so many societies was associated with feelings of shame and fear, and tended to be shrouded in myth and superstition. The retrained midwives of the early 1950s were taught that the old Chinese customs of making a newly delivered mother sit up in bed for three days and of sealing her room to protect her from draughts were not only unnecessary, but could be harmful. And the barefoot doctors twenty years later still preached the same message.[28] Even when maternal mortality began to fall, many women still suffered from ill-health. A survey taken over the period of a year in one county of Jiangsu province showed that 20 per cent of the 151 women investigated were unable to take part in physical labour, and 50 per cent suffered from some ailment.[29]

A great deal of effort was put into the maternal health campaigns from the earliest years, though the results were not completely satisfactory. Both women's magazines and papers intended for the general public carried articles on feminine hygiene, pregnancy, childbirth and post-natal care, and other such subjects, which were reproduced in primers for adult literacy classes.[30] They also became the subject of propaganda posters and radio talks. The real problem, both with propaganda and with facilities, was one of reaching the remote countryside.

Early efforts to popularize birth control were less sustained and effective. Its advocates were always vulnerable to and were sometimes attacked with accusations of Malthusian heresy, and although sporadic efforts were made in the 1950s, it was not until the early 1960s that there were really successful large-scale birth-control campaigns, urging later marriages and smaller, spaced families. Moreover, when these did come, they met with considerable opposition in the countryside, where the

---

[28] Norman Webster, in *International Herald Tribune* (13-14 Mar. 1971), quoting information gathered in China.
[29] Ibid.
[30] See for example † *Women's reading primer.*

longing to have many sons was still strong. In the Shaanxi village of Liu Ling, much of the resistance was put up by men: women were more easily persuaded of the advantages of planned pregnancies.[31] Of course throughout the period contraceptives were legal and, in the big towns at least, quite available. But without propaganda for smaller, spaced families, and the instruction in techniques which was to be so widely promoted in the 1960s, modern birth-control had little impact outside the towns and the countryside just around them.

Although the ability to do any job was much praised in the model workers held up for emulation (and indeed one occasionally meets rather worrying stories whose heroines insist on working almost up to the time of their delivery),[32] women were usually allocated the lighter jobs, and there are frequent references to the importance of giving special consideration to older women or pregnant and nursing mothers in job allocation. Such rational division of labour was facilitated by the formation of mutual-aid teams and the co-operatives.

But perhaps through over-enthusiasm, serious mistakes were sometimes made in job allocation. Occasional references to them can be found in the press throughout the 1950s. For example in 1953 the *Fujian Daily* reported three miscarriages among women who had participated in the spring ploughing and irrigation work, and complained that even after the first accident, cadres had continued to press other women to overwork.[33] The same article told of a four-year old boy who was drowned when playing alone because his whole family were at work. Cadres were urged to take more notice of women's special situation when mobilizing them for field work.

In 1956 and early 1957 there was a spate of similar reports, in the aftermath of the 'High Tide of Socialism' when co-operatives were established all over China. This gave rise to many articles in which work-team leaders were urged to pay more attention to women's state of health when allocating

[31] Myrdal, *Report from a Chinese Village*, pp. 226-7.
[32] †*The High Tide of Socialism in the Chinese Countryside*, p. 357.
[33] †'Some special problems of women at work which need attention', *Fujian (Fukien) Daily*, 30 Mar. 1953.

work. Co-operatives which arranged for women to have days off, or to be given very light work during periods and pregnancies, were praised. To facilitate this, mixed work-teams were asked to appoint women deputy leaders if their leaders were men since women found it difficult to discuss such matters with men.[34] Although the commune movement was characterized by the sort of sweeping enthusiasm which produced strong social pressures on everybody to work harder, and some peasant women have harmed their health by overwork, these articles urging care continued to appear in the press and probably had some moderating influence. This was also a time when medical services were greatly extended in the countryside, and many new nurseries were set up. But a negative feature of the period was that the family planning campaign, which had gained a little impetus in 1957, temporarily lapsed again. It was not positively condemned, though the theory that population control was necessary to the economy was fiercely attacked. The use of contraception to safeguard the health of mothers and children was advocated, but at the same time large families were encouraged.[35]

The health of women in the countryside certainly benefited in general, and above all during pregnancy and childbirth, from the increased medical care which became available to them in the first decade after liberation, but improvements were nevertheless limited by scarce resources and personnel. The same difficulties existed in the field of birth control, with further problems, in particular the conservatism of the people, and in the 1950s at least, a certain ambivalence and vacillation in official attitudes. Knowledge of and access to scientific methods of birth control, essential though they are to the health of women and to their liberation from heavy domestic burdens, were not widespread in the villages until the 1960s.

The prejudice against women doing farm work was attacked on many fronts. It was most easily eliminated where there was a serious shortage of manpower. In other areas. husbands and families were won over by the realization that women's earnings

---

[34] †'Attend to the special problems which women have at work'. *Nanfang Daily,* 20 July 1957.

[35] †*Battling against nature on many fronts,* p. 134.

brought the family greater prosperity. Everywhere convention was usually first defied by a few women activists, often office-holders in the local Women's Federation. They put enormous effort into learning how to do the work and, being young and highly motivated, they were often spectacularly successful. Their achievements were then widely praised and publicized, and other women were urged to follow suit. At district, county, provincial, and national levels the campaign was backed by the election of a whole hierarchy of women 'labour models' selected for their enthusiasm and their achievements. They were also given enormous publicity in the mass media, and were rewarded with prizes of money, cloth, and farm implements.

Many of the heroines of this campaign were from the north-east where the problems of organizing and assimilating large areas of the countryside within a short space of time were first tackled. Fairly typical of them was Deng Yulan of Fuan village, Rehe (Jehol).[36] The first time she was sent to the district seat as a model worker she was given six feet of cloth and a towel. The next time she came back with a towel, a garden fork, a spade, and a laudatory banner. Her parents-in-law exclaimed, 'What good fortune we have been granted in getting such a daughter-in-law.' She continued to win one honour after another until finally as a national labour heroine she saw Chairman Mao in Peking. Her fellow villagers were said to have been most impressed when, unspoilt by this great experience, she returned to work side by side with them in the fields.

The report gives some information about her background. We are told that she got on well with everyone, was a willing worker and often sought advice from the cadres. The key to her success seems to have lain in her childhood, when she had started to work on the land with her two sisters since her parents were poor peasants and had no sons. Her father and mother also became labour models. A long, detailed description is given of all the different sorts of farm work she could do, and the article adds, perhaps to reassure traditionalists, that she was also an excellent needlewoman. She was an active member of the Women's Federation and organized the women of her

[36] †*Agricultural production heroines of the north-east*, pp. 1-10.

village for production so successfully that women in neighbouring villages began to follow their example. When the mother-in-law of one girl objected to her working, Yulan got other old ladies to talk her round by telling her how glad they were that their own girls worked, and how much their families were prospering as a result. When some of the women in her group had difficulties in working because of their children, she involved them in such subsidiary occupations as pig and chicken rearing which allowed them to stay close to their homes.[37]

One interesting aspect of this report and others like it, is that it was above all the poor peasant women who emerged as the women's leaders in this campaign, because of their skill in agricultural work which their hard lives had forced them to acquire.[38] This gave them an advantage over other women, and most labour heroines originated from this class.

In the effort to overcome the problem of women's lack of skills, the Women's Federation organized classes for them. The teachers, like the labour heroines, usually came from the poorest families. Through the classes they began to learn a pride in abilities which they had once been ashamed to possess. This gave them the courage to overcome the other obstacles which were still in their way. For example, Guo Shuqin, a labour model from Heilongjiang, still faced problems when she organized women in her village into a team to do the hoeing: the men were afraid they might damage the young wheat shoots, and would not let them try. She persuaded her father-in-law to allow them to give a demonstration on his land, and after careful instruction, the women did it so well, that the men changed their minds.

Even in those families where land reform brought women the ownership of land in their own right, they might, in the areas where the men themselves were underemployed, lack the incentive to work.[39] Buck found that the proportion of able bodied men over 15 and under 60 engaged in full time work was

---

[37] Ibid., pp. 10–20.

[38] Among the men, the situation was quite different. Their agricultural skills were not confined to one class. Indeed the more prosperous farmers were often also more skilful and enterprising. Thus the Party had at times to struggle against a tendency for the old leadership of the village to regain all its old power under the new regime.

[39] Buck, *Land Utilization in China*, p. 294.

35 per cent, 58 per cent worked only part-time. The seasonal unemployment characteristic of agriculture in temperate zones is aggravated in China by the lack of a sizeable livestock industry. This was a particularly serious problem in the north, which has a much shorter growing season than the south. From this it might appear that women's labour was not needed on the land. In fact, even in the areas where men were very much underemployed for most of the year, there could be labour shortages resulting in lost production at rush periods like harvest time.[40] As the Chinese economist Ma Yin-ch'u put it:

The key problem at present in rural areas is that of uneven busy and slack periods, as in south China where the double rice crop is being extended. In the fifteen days which witness the cutting of early rice and the planting of the late rice, peasants have more work than can be accomplished. The future key to rich increases in rural production is in mechanical assistance during the excessively busy period.[41]

In such areas, when women did not work on the land, the men's labour had to produce enough surplus over their own needs to feed the women and the other non-productive members of the community throughout the year. Double rice-cropping was extended to all areas where it was feasible in the 1950s,[42] and the work requirements of this type of cultivation absorbed the labour of women entering the work force.

But in the areas where the land is untillable for much of the year and in other areas where the marginal return on labour input fell very rapidly, the mobilization of women could not be carried out in the same way as in the lush south. Attempts were made to introduce new side occupations and handicrafts in these areas to provide women with an alternative productive role. The Women's Federation or marketing co-operatives were usually responsible for the organization of such ventures, most of which produced traditional objects like mats, sacks, baskets, and brooms for which there was a steady local

[40] For a detailed discussion of this problem see Dwight Perkins, *Agricultural Development in China, 1368–1968*, chapter 4.
[41] Ma Yin-ch'u, 'My Philosophical Thoughts and Economic Theory', quoted in Kenneth Walker, 'Ma Yin-ch'u: A Chinese Discussion on Planning for Balanced Growth', p. 182.
[42] Perkins, p. 189.

demand.[43] Less commonly, their wares would be sold much farther afield; some groups for example picked medicinal herbs which would be sold all over China. As these groups became better capitalized, some of them acquired machinery and made buckets, cheap plastic goods and other such products for local consumption.

The great irrigation and flood prevention works were also a rich source of extra employment for both men and women during the traditional idle months. These projects sometimes involved people living away from home for weeks on end, enough in traditional eyes to make them completely unsuitable for young women, even if the working conditions had not been tough and exhausting. But to girl activists the work, however arduous, had a touch of glamour: it symbolized revolution in its most romantic form in the rapid changes which it brought to the countryside. Of course they had to fight for the right to participate, but it was a battle which many won: for example, of the 220 volunteers working on the Min river dam in Yangyi commune in Hebei during 1959, 80 were women.[44] And in other cases all the students of middle schools, boys and girls alike, would go to work on great irrigation projects. No doubt, such experience did give young women all over rural China more independence from their families, wider horizons and greater self-confidence.

Except in the older liberated areas where great advances towards equality had already been made, the real revolution in the position of women in rural China began with another revolutionary process — land reform. The relationship between the two movements received a lot of attention. In 1947 Deng Yingchao wrote that mobilizing the masses of labouring women was an urgent and indispensable part of land reform.[45] She criticized the inadequate attention given by the Party to women in most areas, and recalled the declaration of the National Land Reform Conference earlier in the year, that to carry out land reform properly and to abolish feudalism, all levels of the Party should improve and revitalize woman-work. To achieve this it urged all cadres:

[43] See for example Sun Yü, *The Women's Representative* (a play about women's lives).
[44] I. and D. Crook, p. 80.
[45] Deng Yingchao, †*Land Reform and the new tasks of woman-work*.

With land reform as the focus, co-ordinate work among women with the Peasants' Movement, for when the two are thoroughly integrated, they will stimulate each other and interact favourably together. Village women of the labouring classes have suffered the exploitation and oppression of the landlord class just like other peasants, and have the same demands, the same fierceness. Therefore, whenever land reform is going ahead, when the peasants are being mobilized, the labouring women must be mobilized at the same time. There must be no division with, 'men first, then women', or worse still, scrappiness and irregularity in the work. Nor must the work of going deeper among and mobilizing the hired hand and poor peasant woman be abandoned or held back with excuses such that they are backward, gossipers, bothersome, or irritating so that the work with them is left to take care of itself.[46]

It was resolved at the conference that hired and poor peasant women be treated as the core and united with middle peasant women. Cadres were told that they themselves should unite with peasant women, teach them to 'speak bitterness', distinguish classes and look for the causes of their poverty in order to make them class-conscious. In fact, typically, it was the poor peasant woman who came to the fore in land reform, because it was they who stood to gain most from the movement. And among them, widows and other women who were the economic mainstays of their families were especially prominent.

The start of land reform in a particular village was marked by the arrival of the land reform team. The team's first task was to find out as much as possible about the village by observation as they lived and ate with the peasants and helped with their daily work, but above all through conversations which they had with everyone. Frequently the team included a woman whose freedom and independence served as an example of what was possible to the village women. Even if the team consisted only of men, by their willingness to listen to the opinions of village women and the respect they showed them, they began the long task of undermining the general contempt with which women were regarded. During the land reform women were most active in those villages where many of the men were away fighting in either the Civil war, or later the Korean War. Yet they played

[46] Ibid.

..eir part in other villages too. The Peasant Associations, through which the movement was run, were expected to have a minimum of 30–40 per cent women members.[47] They had also to found either a Women's Department, or a village branch of the Women's Association. Women who spoke out at the fierce, harsh meetings which were a feature of land reform could not but be affected by the experience. Having taken a part in public life, learned to express opinions and to argue in front of crowds, and been stirred by the heady feeling of controlling their own destinies, they were not likely to settle back easily into their former lives, upon which they looked with new and more critical eyes. Now when they saw a way of improving their lot, they might muster the courage to try to carry it out, even if it meant facing bitter opposition. Their old fatalism began to crack. The prestige enjoyed by the Party was a weapon in this struggle. Partly this was so because it made the people more receptive to new ideas introduced by the Party. It also operated at the more subtle level of association. For example in the new vocabulary spread by the workers in the land reform teams, 'feudal' was an adjective applied to the landlords and the old system of land ownership. So for the poorer peasant it acquired pejorative connotations, and he was uneasy at being accused of 'feudalism' in his attitude to his wife or to women in general.

In China, as elsewhere, peasants tend to exchange help at harvest-time. In the liberated areas such help was sometimes formalized by a system of temporary and eventually permanent mutual-aid, or work-exchange teams. These made possible a more economical use of labour and eased the labour shortage usual at rush periods, which was often aggravated by the absence of men at the front. Since such teams were commonly first organized in areas where women replaced their soldier husbands in the fields, they had a large number of women members.

The development of mutual-aid teams tended to follow very closely on land reform; for though all peasants now had land, the ownership of animals and tools could not be so easily divided. Although these were also distributed they were too

[47] †*Experience in mobilizing women during the land reform movement in Beiyue district.*

scarce to go round. Few peasant households owned a complete set of tools, and many gloried in the acquisition of 'one leg of an ox', as a quarter share was picturesquely known. Families who shared an animal had to come to an agreement about its use and its care; and when the means of production was shared this way, it could seem natural to share labour power too.

Mutual-aid teams, like co-operatives, raised the problem of the valuation of labour, and its reward. Work was measured in terms of work-points since the variety of jobs to be done and the different levels of skill and effort required to perform them made simple exchange unsuitable. But as people work at different tempos and to different standards it is difficult to allocate work-points either simply on hours or on a piece-rate basis. In some villages it was done by discussion. For example, women in Nanhe village, Hebei, were first given five points to a man's ten, but then had them doubled when it was found that they were working as fast as the men.[48]

A Women's Federation leader Luo Qiong, in an article of 1948, reported that not only were women demanding the same number of work-points as men when they did the same amount of work, but they were raising the slogan 'Points of men and women in the same family should be recorded separately.'[49] She supported this demand as a justified attack on the old monopolistic authority of men who should not, she said, be allowed to grab their wives' work-points and thus to control their earnings.

She described the methods of recording work-points which were in use at the time. The first was to consider all women as 'half-labour-powers', and to give them five points where men got ten. The second was to grade workers, male and female, once and for all, allowing good workers to be awarded far more points than poor workers for a day's work. The third was to assess points for each job done separately on the day that it was done, giving points according to how well the job had been done, and how long it had taken. She recommended the third method, which she claimed was the one most commonly

---

[48] Er Dong, †Women and children do important work.
[49] Luo Qiong, †Production by rural women in the past year. Both after co-operativization, and under the communes, it has been the rule that points should be recorded separately.

used, because it gave women the best incentive to go to the
fields and to work hard. However, the struggle for equal pay
for the same work was still being waged twenty-five years later;
and general arguments over the merits of different systems of
work evaluation continue.

Producer co-operatives existed on a small scale even in the
pre-1949 liberated areas, but their main development came in
two stages in the 1950s. In the first stage, several mutual-aid
teams pooled their land, tools, animals and labour, and the
unit so formed came under unified management. The income
of these co-operatives was divided partly on the basis of the
work performed by members, but also partly depended on the
ownership of the means of production, which continued to be
vested in the individual. They were therefore considered to be
'semi-socialist'. Full socialization came in 1955–6, the period
dubbed the 'High Tide of Socialism', when all over the
country, lower co-operatives and mutual-aid teams merged
into larger units known as advanced co-operatives. In these,
the dividend based on the former ownership of the means of
production was abolished, and income was henceforth
awarded purely on the basis of work performed. The lower co-
operatives enlarged the unit under one management, thereby
further rationalizing the division of labour, which of course
affected women. Small nurseries could be set up within
the co-operatives and women's work teams became quite
commonplace since most co-operatives included enough able-
bodied women to make them practicable.

The changes brought about by the formation of advanced
co-operatives were more profound. Now that the division of
the collective's income depended solely on labour, everybody
had the maximum incentive to work. Ownership of the
means of production ceased to be a factor in women's
economic strength, all now depended on productive labour.

The question of equal pay for equal work, which from the
time of the first mutual-aid teams had been raised periodically
in the press, began to receive a great deal of attention. Like
every other big campaign, the High Tide was accompanied by
an enormous surge of directives, reports, and propaganda
stories, many of which concerned the way in which individual
co-operatives functioned. These often contained accounts of

the role being played by women in which the subject of equal pay was nearly always raised.

The policy of the Party had consistently been one of equal pay for equal work. Peasant men put up a tenacious opposition to the principle and it seems probable that male cadres, most of whom were themselves peasants, were not always very particular about getting it applied.

Where equal pay was achieved it was usually after women had proved that they merited it. Sometimes this was actually done in a production competition with men. In the Unity Co-operative of Dali county, Shaanxi province, a man objected when his wife's two mornings of cotton picking were given the same value as his own two mornings of ploughing.[50] He demanded to be put on to cotton-picking, which he considered a pleasanter job, if the remuneration was to remain the same. The management committee decided to make this a test case and allowed him to pick. He exhausted himself but failed to keep pace with the women. He was thus convinced that equal pay between these jobs was fair.

Such miraculous conversions were presumably rare and the issue was usually a difficult one to settle. Yet where equal pay did not exist women felt they were being inadequately rewarded for their efforts and were unwilling to work. Their exasperation with the situation was reflected in the expression 'Those old five points' (lao wu fen), by which women's half-pay was familiarly known.[51]

In 1952 in a village of Kouxi district, Fuyang county in Anhui, the men of a mutual-aid team almost always got ten points, while women normally received only five or six and even the strongest never got more than eight.[52] Once, when they were hoeing together, the women's team did as much as the men's. At the end of the day when points were being allocated, the men asked the women how many they thought they should get. The women replied, 'It's up to you, but we

[50] †*Socialist Construction in Rural Shaanxi,* pp. 61-70.
[51] See the story of the women of Ximan village, Pingshun county, Shaanxi, who fought for and gained equal pay through production competitions against men after their woman deputy co-operative head had arranged training courses for them. Shen Jilan, 'Women models on the agricultural production front', in †*Women in co operativization.*
[52] †*Outstanding examples of women taking part in production and construction* p. 43.

did as much as you did.' The men then felt there was nothing for it but to give equal points though there were some grumbles that the women should try their hands at carrying loads or pulling carts. The women retorted that men should try making clothes and looking after children.

In other areas differential rates continued. In June 1957, the *Shenyang Daily* published an article about discrimination against women in which it alleged that many co-operatives automatically gave women seven points to do jobs for which men would have been paid ten, and that piece-work rates which men sometimes worked under were never applied to women as it was feared that their earnings might then rise too high.[53]

In September 1956 the *People's Daily* published an article on pay.[54] It condemned both the idea that 'equal work' should be defined as 'the same work' so that men and women would only be paid equally where their jobs were identical, and the idea that if a man gets ten points for a day's work, a woman should too, no matter what the nature of their jobs. It urged instead that both quality and quantity be considered, so that women would earn more if they did more or worked better than men, and less if they did less or worked to lower standards. In spite of such articles, some co-operatives went on classifying workers quite rigidly according to sex and age. Table 1 illustrates this sytem under which days worked (work-days) were converted into the 'labour-day', an abstract unit of measure valued at ten work-points according to a fixed ratio based on age and sex.

This problem, so complex, and so central to the whole practice of collective agriculture, continued to be a difficult one, even under the communes. Table 2 shows how men and women workers in a certain production brigade were distributed among seven 'skill' grades. The distribution pattern of women is significantly different from that of men. This system, while it militated less absolutely against women since it was at least possible for them to get into the higher grades, obviously did not allow many of them to achieve equal pay. Little guidance was given on the evaluation of jobs which

---

[53] 'Oppose contempt of women, housework is glorious too', *Shenyang Daily* (5 June 1957).

[54] 'How to deal correctly with equal pay for men and women', *RMRB* (9 Sept. 1956).

TABLE 1
*Labour-day equivalents of peasant work-days
Xin Kuangsan Agricultural Production Co-operative*

Category	Age group	Equivalent of one labour-day
Male, full labour force member	18–50	0·88
Male, half labour force member	16–17, 51–60	0·80
Female, full labour force member	18–45	0·77
Female, half labour force member	16–17, 46–55	0·48

Source: Peter Schran, *The Development of Chinese Agriculture 1850–1959*, p. 31. Unfortunately no date is given, nor are we told the whereabouts of the co-operative. I have not been able to consult the original source which is given by Mr Schran, *Rural Work Bulletin*, (*Nongcun gongzuotongxun*), No. 3 (1958), p. 26.

TABLE 2
Distribution of the 1,453 male and female agricultural workers by wage grades. Sun Yan production brigade, Guangming People's Commune, Runan county, Henan province, 1958

Wage grade	Distrib. in each grade			Proportion in each grade	
	total	men	women	men	women
1	12·4	5·8	18·4	22·2	77·8
2	16·0	12·7	18·9	38·0	62·0
3	26·4	21·2	31·2	38·3	61·7
4	23·4	23·1	23·7	47·0	53·0
5	9·5	14·1	5·3	71·0	29·0
6	7.5	13.4	2.1	85.3	14.7
7	4·8	9·7	0·4	95·7	4·3

1 = lowest; 7 = highest.
Source: Charles Hoffman, *Work Incentives, Practices and Policies in the People's Republic of China, 1953–1965*, p. 49.

really lies at the heart of this problem. Reports indicate that it was based primàrily on physical strength and to a lesser extent on skill. Both criteria tended to favour men over women, though at least as time went on and women learned more they were less disadvantaged.

In 1958, the Central Committee added to its consistent line that men and women should receive equal pay for equal work, a policy statement which was very relevant to job evaluation and work-point allocation: 'Existing differences in skill in rural areas are not such as to warrant wide pay differentials.'[55] Nevertheless, we find that in Yangyi Commune, in Hebei, in 1960, the tradition of giving women a low assessment in terms of work-points still prevailed. When it was challenged by record-breaking women, men began to fight to get some jobs assigned to women only at women's rates, and others to men at men's rates so that it could never be established whether men and women did 'equal work', for no direct comparison could be made. Yet women did make a major advance in this commune when the administration began to issue pay directly into the hands of the person who earned it, regardless of age or sex. Although the women's demand that work-points should be recorded and remunerated separately dated back to the beginnings of co-operativization, it was at times ignored in favour of tradition which decreed that the head of the household controlled its budget.[56]

The formation of co-operatives helped certain groups of women who had benefited very little from mutual-aid teams. Article 7 of the Model Regulations for Co-operatives stated that all labouring peasants, both men and women, who had reached the age of sixteen and were capable of performing labour in the co-operatives might join them.[57] It went on to specify dependants of revolutionary martyrs and servicemen, as well as the aged, the weak, widows, widowers, and the disabled, as also eligible for membership.

[55] Central Committee of the CCP, *Resolutions on some questions concerning the People's Communes, 6th plenary session of the 8th CC of the CCP.*
[56] I. and D. Crook, *Yangyi Commune*, pp. 127 and 244. There had been a similar development under the collectives in the Soviet Union. One observer wrote: 'The separate wage is of immense importance. . . A man said he had one complaint to make of the collective: he no longer received his daughter's wages. Female labour is very extensively used on the farms, and the women's dividend is one reason why there has been acquiescence in collectivization; because it has put women on the side of the Soviets.' (Sir John Maynard. *The Russian Peasant and other studies*, p. 399). The principle of separate income does not, however, seem to have been maintained consistently since, on the Viriatino Collective at least, payment in the 1950s was by household, though there, as indeed in the whole of the Soviet Union, separate records must have been continued since statistics exist to show the total proportion of agricultural work performed by women. (Sula Benet (ed.), *The Village of Viriatino*, p. 251, and Norton Dodge, *Women in the Soviet Economy*, p. 164.)
[57] †*Draft decisions of the standing committee of the National People's Congress on model regulations for the agricultural producer co-operatives*, 9 Nov. 1955.

Mutual-aid teams had largely been organized by friends and relatives coming together on a basis of choice. They were often formed by groups of the many peasants who had received a little land but no animal or only a share of one in land reform and who had to share their draught power in order to get their ploughing done. Often they had to pull the ploughs themselves, and naturally such groups tended to try to recruit strong members whom they expected to be of most use. The new, less personal co-operative organizations had to accept more people from groups which were poor in labour power like those mentioned above. Of these it was the women, whose handicap was more often one of social convention than one of physical disability, who could most easily become more economically productive, and a minor campaign to persuade them to do so was one of the themes of the women's movement during the formation of the co-operatives.

In collective agriculture women sometimes worked in the same teams as men but were often organized into special women's teams. This helped to reduce the suspicions, which had made difficulties for many young women when they first went into the fields, that women who left the confines of their homes to work were usually just looking for love affairs. All-women teams made it easier to allocate suitable jobs to women. This continued to be important because with a low level of mechanization, much of the farm work still consisted of jobs such as heavy portering.[58] A well-known rhyme expressed concern with the allocation of appropriate work to women:

When pregnant they must be given light work not heavy.
When nursing, work must be close-by not far away,
During their periods, their work must be dry not wet.[59]

Obviously in mixed teams this sort of policy was more difficult to implement.

Small manufacturing co-operatives also played an important part in women's lives, often being run exclusively

[58] One source estimates that a third of all agricultural labour is used in carrying manure to the fields and bringing grain from them. (Cao Ding and Liu Kuangbai, 'The role of communications and transport in our national economy' (Jingji Yanjiu, 20 Feb. 1965), quoted in Dwight Perkins, p. 58.)
[59] I. and D. Crook, *Yangyi Commune*, p. 126.

for women and occasionally even coming under the local women's organization. In the liberated areas these were often the earliest organized work-groups because they were usually started to increase the income and self-sufficiency of an area or to supply the needs of the army. Thus, they were not only new as groups, they were often producing new things rather than reorganizing existing work. They were supplied with raw materials by a credit co-operative backed by the People's Bank, which also undertook the collection and marketing of the finished products. In the early 1950s such enterprises were set up in village after village, and they accounted for an important part of the income earned by women. Often the work was done on a 'putting-out' basis in the homes of co-operative members, and so posed less of a problem to women with children.

The original purpose of these co-operatives had been to beat the economic blockade of the liberated areas. Obviously, after the acquisition of the great manufacturing centres and the restoration of industrial production, the pattern of these small-scale handicraft industries changed. The handicraft textile industry, for example, contracted again, though in some cases new mills were set up in the same area which could take advantage of the pool of skilled labour developed in handicraft production. But many small consumer goods continued to be made on a workshop scale by women in rural areas. In time the old handicraft co-operatives were absorbed into the Advanced Agricultural Producer Co-operatives and finally into the communes, under which they were developed still further in the campaign to increase the range of goods which could be produced locally in each area.

If the success of Party policy towards women in rural China is to be judged on its own terms it is necessary to consider to what extent its aim of involving women in productive labour was achieved. Then one must try to analyse the effect that the achievement had on the women concerned.

The data available on women working in the countryside are inadequate, and do not really admit of comparison over time. Definitions vary or are not stated, and figures are not given consistently for one area. In 1949, Deng Yingchao estimated that 50-70 per cent of women in the liberated areas (and 80 per cent in the best-organized parts) were engaged in agriculture.[60] For areas not liberated until 1949, figures of the same order were being suggested ten years later.[61] We know that local variations could be considerable: in Ten-Mile Inn in Yangyi commune, Hebei, two-thirds of the women between the ages of 16 and 45 turned out regularly for field work in 1960, whereas in Bailin brigade in the same commune, the figure was 95 per cent.[62] But it seems that 'regularly', in this context, could mean anything from a work-record of 70 days a year to one of 200 or more. Much more significant is the figure of 25 per cent given as the percentage of total work-points allocated by the co-operatives all over China which were earned by women in 1956.[63]

Women undoubtedly still continued to work fewer days than men each year, and they often did lighter, less well-remunerated jobs. Where work-points were allocated on a piece-work basis women probably earned less than men if the job was a heavy one such as shifting manure, and since pay discrimination persisted in many co-operatives, they would sometimes have had to do more than a man to earn the same number of work-points. All these factors make it remarkable that women should have earned a quarter of the total work-points in 1956, and it is clear that the figure indicates a very high level of participation in production by peasant women. Under the communes, which even in their modified form after 1962 seem to have provided more communal child-care, especially at the rush periods, the percentage of work-points earned by women must also have increased.

Although it is impossible to quantify the change, it is safe to say that until 1949 in most areas of China it was exceptional for women to work much in the fields. But by the late 1950s it was quite normal, and most able-bodied women did so, though to an extent which varied greatly with local conditions.

[60] Deng Yingchao, 'Chinese Women Help to build a New China', *People's China* No. 6 (1950).
[61] Neither her reports nor the later ones attempt to quantify the work done, which makes it impossible to assess their real significance, or to make any confident comparisons.
[62] I. and D. Crook, *Yangyi Commune*, p. 247.
[63] see Zhang Yun, †*Build the country and keep house thriftily, struggle for socialist construction*, in Congress Documents 3. p. 13.

A greater proportion of work performed by women now enters a formal accounting system and so has a value set on it publicly. Such work confers more prestige than household tasks, however endless!

With the change brought about in their economic status by their involvement in productive work came great changes in the peasant women's place in society and in the family. The majority of teams and brigades had a woman as head or deputy head,[64] so that even those peasants who were not themselves in an organization with a woman leader would at least know of one which had one. Even ordinary women became used to expressing their opinions in meetings at least at work-team level, and to participating in the making of important decisions such as work-point allocation.

Within the family, women's increased earning power began to change their position. Girl children were no longer regarded as liabilities for whom the family must make the most profitable match possible. Young women found it far easier to delay their marriages until they wished for them, and to persuade parents at least to consider their view on the choice of a partner. When they did marry they were treated with more respect, since they would no longer be viewed by their in-laws as a drain on the family's resources or savings, and they made their own contribution to the family income. Consultation between husband and wife on family decisions was more natural in households where the woman earned. These changes were clearly recognized by a young peasant woman from Liu Ling village, north Shaanxi, who said in an interview in 1962:

In the older families, it is the husband alone who decides [what to grow in the private plot], but my husband and I discuss everything together because we're a young family. Sometimes he gives in, and sometimes I give in.[65]

Another young woman from the same village said:

It has now become quite usual with our generation for husband and wife to discuss the family's problems and decide about them together. Women no longer work just in the house; they also work in

[64] Ibid.
[65] J. Myrdal, *Report from a Chinese Village*, p. 213.

the fields and earn their own money. But the men of the older generation still say: 'What does a woman know? Women know nothing!' In such families the men decide everything and their wives say: 'We are just women. We are not allowed to say anything.'[66]

These achievements were gained quite slowly over many years. For example, the second young woman quoted above recalled that women had first taken part in open discussion at a meeting in 1956 when the higher co-operative was founded. Even at that late date, their right to put forward opinions was challenged quite fiercely though Liu Ling village had been part of an early liberated area.

Undeniably women pay a price for all they have gained. Even if there were a sufficient number of crèches and nurseries, and if the canteens had been a complete success, a certain amount of housework would remain. As it is, the surviving domestic burden is a heavy one, and it falls most heavily on women.

In 1953, an article on getting women to participate in field work listed the three main obstacles to their doing so: the need to care for children during the day, to find time to weave cloth for the family's clothes, and to cook at the end of a long day's work.[67] The solution urged by the article, which it claimed had been put into practice in the area described, was that older women should help out whenever possible with the children, and that husbands should assist wives. When the older women take on an extra household burden, young women participate in production to some extent at the expense of their elders. However, in Yangyi commune in 1960, it was still the younger women who did most of the work in the house.[68] Nor did it seem usual, in that commune at least, for men to give more than occasional help in the house.

Women were certainly aware of their double burden. A young mother in Liu Ling explained:

Women work harder than men. We have two jobs: we work both in the fields and in our caves. I know my husband helps me, we're a young family of course, but he isn't as particular about housework as a woman is. Life is a lot of hard work. I don't take part in any kind of women's activities, political or otherwise.[69]

[66] Ibid., p. 221.
[67] †Outstanding examples of women taking part in production and construction p.43.
[68] I. and D. Crook, Yangyi Commune, p. 245.
[69] J. Myrdal, p. 238.

The tendency of the early 1950s to disparage housework was reversed in the 'Five Goods' *(wu-hao)* movement of the mid 1950s. As we have seen, this was an attempt in both town and countryside to counter the contempt for the housewife which had tended to develop during the intensive campaigns to get women to take part in productive activity, and to restore some self-respect to the millions of women who by choice or necessity continued to devote their lives to their families. In the countryside the general slogan 'wu hao'—'five things to be done well'—was applied to the following tasks:

Be patriotic, love the co-operative, do productive labour.
Run the home thriftily, and manage money and food,
Unite your family and neighbours so they help each other.
Lead the old, care for the young, teach the children.
Study and help loved ones to work and study.[70]

Housewives were praised for their thrift and hard work. Articles appeared everywhere on the social value of housework, which was said to make a great contribution to socialist construction by increasing the satisfaction of the individual within the family, and thus enabling him to do his job better. This rather tortuous attempt to give housework some justification in terms of production, the great status-giver of the new society, is understandable as an attempt to boost the drooping self-respect of the housewife, especially since it was economically impossible to supply all women with work in any case, but it was completely at odds with Marxist ideas on the oppression of women, the possibility of liberation, and indeed the nature of housework itself. It was a short-lived aberration, an early victim of the advent of the communes which again stressed the paramount importance of productive labour for women; their role as housewives has since then received only slight recognition.

Village life in China is still very tough. Survival requires hard work, and economic progress demands still more. Many women, with their dual role, work even harder than men. Some are no doubt held back by this from playing an active

[70] †'The Provincial Women's Federation calls an enlarged executive committee meeting to agree on future tasks for women in our province', *New Hunan paper* (7 Apr. 1957). For more detail on the movement see the book †*Popular Talks on the Five Goods Movement.*

part in politics and public affairs. Others, with great sacrifice of time and effort, become leaders in rural society. Women cannot yet be said to have won equality of opportunity in the affairs of rural society, but, in the sense that it is now possible for them to rise in it, they at least have *more* opportunity, and can continue the struggle.

Women of all ages now have a voice in decision-making in village, work team, and family affairs. Girls grow up expecting to make an economic contribution to the family, and no longer wait for others to determine the whole course of their lives. Emancipation is of course still far from complete, but women's place in rural China has undergone as tremendous a revolution as any other aspect of village society.

CHAPTER 5

WOMEN IN THE TOWNS[1]

THE task of organizing in the major urban areas of which the People's Liberation Army began to take control in the late 1940s presented problems which were new. True, women had been active in the great labour movement of the 1920s, and the Party had exercised influence on women workers through the unions, some general and some exclusively for women, to which they belonged.[2] Overt Party activity in the towns had, however, come to an end with the suppression of this movement in 1927. Thus in 1948-9, the Party faced the immediate and urgent task of building up its power within the towns from rather a small base. The organization of women, which was naturally a part of this task, received prompt attention.

Of course even during the anti-Japanese War when the rural basis of the Chinese revolution made it necessary to concentrate on the villages in all spheres of revolutionary work, some special attention was given to the women of the small towns of the communist-controlled border regions. As we have seen, women played quite an important part in the small handicraft enterprises that were set up to manufacture products which became scarce during the economic blockade of the border regions, and many of these were in such towns.[3]

[1] 'Countryside' and 'towns' are in fact oversimplified categories. If the material had allowed it I would have preferred to follow Professor Skinner in distinguishing between major and minor cities, market towns, and so on ('Marketing and Social structure in China, Part I', *Journal of Asian Studies* (Nov. 1966)). Unfortunately this has not proved possible, so I have merely followed the Chinese distinction between urban and rural woman-work. The bias of this chapter is largely towards the large industrial towns of which most was written. Conditions in the smaller towns which were essentially local trading centres were no doubt rather different. Changes in them probably occurred at a slower pace, and may indeed have resembled those of the countryside as much as those of the large towns.

[2] See Jean Chesneaux, *Les Syndicats chinois 1919-1927*, pp. 31 and 61. Two out of the four textile unions at Canton in the 1920s listed by Chesneaux were women's unions. See also Jean Chesneaux, *The Chinese Labor Movement*, p. 324.

[3] See for example †'Recollections of the struggle of past life', *GRRB* (3 July 1957).

The governments of the border regions were based on small towns and they were thus centres of employment for administrative and political cadres amongst whom of course there were some women.

The government of the Shanxi-Chahar-Hebei border region issued regulations on the care of women cadres and their children in 1943 which not only covered such general matters as maternity leave and the provision of kindergartens, but even ruled on such details as the extra rations to be given to a woman who had had a miscarriage, and the cloth allowance that was to be given before birth so that clothes and nappies could be provided.[4] In 1946, a new women's magazine, published in Zhanjiakou (Kalgan), carried articles on the life of women workers, on the women of Shijiazhuang, and on the reform of prostitutes in that town which had just been liberated. Similar articles were later to be carried by the national women's press about Peking and Shanghai, so this early magazine shows that concern with the welfare of workers and with the sexual exploitation of women, both characteristic preoccupations of urban woman-work after 1949, can be traced back to the liberated areas.[5]

However, it was not until the great campaigns of 1947–8 in which the communists gained control of the vast north-east that they had to deal with towns which were very much more than simple marketing and administrative centres. The problems which they faced then were enormous. Their new territory, the north-east of China, had undergone a Japanese occupation of fourteen years and had known little peace since the surrender. The war economy had made the last years under the Japanese particularly hard, and conditions had deteriorated as more and more productive capacity was pressed into the service of the military. Nor had the area benefited fully from the rapid growth of industrialization which the Japanese had promoted, for the Soviet forces which liberated it took much of the plant which could be removed back to the Soviet Union with them. This experience was

---

[4] †*Chinese Women stand up*, p. 30.
[5] For the liberated areas see *Contemporary Women (Shidai Funü)* No. 1 (Zhanjiakou, July 1940). For the post-liberation period see issues of *ZGFN* for 1949–50 or *Women of Peking (Beijing Funü)* (25 Jan. 1950).

followed by the disruption of the Civil War and looting by the fleeing Kuomintang armies.

Thus in 1948, industry in the north-east was almost at a standstill, unemployment was very high, and the housing and living conditions of the workers were miserable. Inflation was so bad that even middle-class people with salaries which had once made them prosperous found it hard to get enough to eat unless they were involved in corruption or black-market activities. The aspirations of the population were not very high. They craved a bare minimum of economic security and were ready to work hard for it. The communists had two somewhat contradictory priorities, manpower for the army whose ranks swelled from under one million to two million between 1945 and 1947,[6] and production: above all the production of military supplies.

In response to the Party's call to concentrate effort on organizing the urban population and on restoring industrial production, the women's organizations changed the focus of their attention from land reform to work in the towns, a development which was explained to a conference of cadres responsible for woman-work in September 1948 by the commander-in-chief of the communist armies, Zhu De. His speech was typically verbose, but the following quotation seems adequate to make his point:

. . . with the development of the revolutionary situation, the task of those who work amongst women has become more important than ever, especially now when many towns, large medium and small, have already set up revolutionary power, and the towns contain thousands upon thousands of women workers. This means there must be another change in woman-work.[7]

The new policy was formally adopted in 1949 by the First National Congress of the Women's Federation as point 3 of its 'Resolutions on Present Tasks',[8] which stated that work in the towns would henceforth be the core of work amongst women,

---

[6] Statement by Mao Zedong quoted in Edmund Clubb, *Twentieth Century China*, p. 285.

[7] Zhu De, †*Mobilize women for production and construction*, speech at a conference on woman-work, 20 July 1948, in LA documents 1, pp. 35-6.

[8] †*Resolutions on the present tasks of the Chinese women's movement*, in Congress documents 1, p. 88.

though rural work should not be despised, and that the most urgent need in the towns was the restoration of production. It advocated taking working-class women[9] as the base and getting the intellectual and professional women to unite with them.

The Women's Federation, in the towns as in the countryside, was the major means through which the Party was at once able to mobilize the support and energies of women, and to get an idea of their wishes and needs. It organized women on the basis of their occupation or residence, according to their circumstances. Dependants' associations set up within particular factories or enterprises were more specialist organizations whose membership consisted mostly of housewives from workers' families. They were directed by the relevant trade union.[10] Residents' committees or street associations differed from these in that their membership was recruited on the basis of residence. They were open to both sexes, but since in practice the great majority of their activists were women, and their work was so similar to that of the Women's Federation, the two bodies sometimes became indistinguishable. I will discuss both in some detail in this chapter.

Special provision was made for the representation of women within trade unions in all enterprises where women worked. Women workers and employees also held periodical congresses within each enterprise and area to discuss common problems.[11]

It is interesting that though student organizations were supposed to set up women's organizations, they did not receive the sort of attention in official literature which one would expect had they really existed. Probably since they were mostly without the ties of children, and, being away from home, suffered less from parental pressure over marriage, students were freer from discrimination and other special problems

---

[9] The term used is *laodong funü*. Since it is elsewhere specifically stated that this includes not only women workers, but housewives in workers' families, "working-class women" seems the best translation. See a report of the fourth meeting of the executive committee of the All-China Women's Federation, *RMRB*, 2 Jan. 1953.

[10] †*Regulations on the organization of trade unions*, p. 69.

[11] See 'Regulations on the organization of women workers' committees', in †*Regulations on the organization of trade unions*, p. 64.

than other women. Indeed at the First Congress the Harbin student representative reported with evident disapproval: 'Women students reckon that they are already liberated and have no interests particular to them as women, so they ask why they should have a women's section.'[12] Where they did meet with difficulties they could seek help from the Youth League.

Thus, in the newly liberated areas, the majority of women in the towns participated, even if superficially, in some organization which tried to involve them in the world outside their homes and to make them feel that they had some influence over the way their neighbourhood, factory, or office was run. The membership and to some extent the functions of the organizations responsible for this work amongst women sometimes overlapped. This was indeed acknowledged in a handbook of regulations for trade unions which criticized the disharmony and duplication of work that had occurred between the Women's Federation and the trade unions, and directed that the women's sections of the trade unions should in future maintain close contact with the Women's Federation over problems of common interest.[13] It ruled that the trade unions should have over-all charge of woman-work where workers' families were accommodated in factory-owned blocks but that the Women's Federation should be responsible for it in cases where they were scattered in different areas of the city.[14] Dependants' organizations could join the Women's Federation collectively if their delegate conferences voted for them to do so.

Nevertheless, though the distinction, as we will see, was sometimes blurred, the tendency was to organize working women and women not working for wages or salaries separately, and since this reflected very real differences in

---

[12] †*All the delegations discuss Deng Yingchao's report*, Congress documents 1, p. 38.
[13] †*Regulations on the organization of trade union work*, p. 64.
[14] In China, as in Japan, workers' accommodation is frequently provided in dormitory blocks by the factory for which they work. This makes possible a greater sense of solidarity between the families of the workers of a particular enterprise. Since much of the industry in the north-east was Japanese-owned, this type of accommodation was particularly common there, hence the frequent mentions of dependants' associations in documents which date from the end of the Liberation War. After liberation, new industrial enterprises in China tended to house their employees in the same way.

their lives and problems, it may be easier to consider the two groups separately here.

In view of the priority given in organizational work to the restoration of industrial production, it may seem surprising that political organizers should have started working amongst women dependants, immediately upon the takeover of the towns. The reasons quickly become clear on examination of the earliest organizations for dependants, for these concentrated on mobilizing their members for handicraft or even industrial production[15] more than on the welfare, hygiene, and literacy work which became typical of their activities a year or two later.[16] Moreover, an even greater proportion of working-class women in the north-east would have been dependants than in towns elsewhere since it was an area of heavy industry, offering few opportunities of employment for women as long as the traditional division of work in industry continued.

A degree of confusion about directives was evident in a speech by a delegate from the north-east to the First Congress of the Women's Federation.[17] She quoted Party instructions, 'The object of work in the towns should be to unite working-class women with intellectuals while giving women workers the leading role.' How, she asked, could this be applied in a town like Changchun, where in a population of 400,000 there were only 600 women workers and they were outnumbered even by women intellectuals? How could this minority play a leading role? Should not rather the intellectuals do so? She concluded by remarking that this was a problem which required further investigation. Her report on what her branch had done made it clear that they had in fact concentrated on working with women dependants, and judging from reports given by delegates from other areas, this was the normal practice.

For example, an article on the town of Benxi, in Liaoning province, stated that since it was a centre of heavy industry, almost all the women apart from cadres and students were

[15] See for example the speech †*Experience of woman-work in the towns*, **Congress documents 1**, pp. 46-7.

[16] †*Experience •of work amongst the dependants of workers and employees* and Zhang Xuewen, †*Hygiene in New China*.

[17] †*All the delegations discuss Deng Yingchao's report*, **Congress documents 1**, p. 36.

workers' dependants and it was necessarily with them that women's organizers had mainly to concern themselves.[18] In this town much effort had gone into setting up structures through which housewives could contribute directly to production. A glove factory is mentioned as a specific example. Housewives were frequently organized to produce clothes for the army, a relatively simple task since it involved only skills which the women had already acquired in making clothes for their families, and they could do the work together in groups or in their homes according to the circumstances. Such projects were limited by a lack of capital, by the narrow range of skills which the women possessed, and by the strength of conservatism in a society where a woman's right to work outside the home was still often contested. The efforts which were made to involve women in productive work may not at first sight seem very ambitious, but they were well adapted to the situation. Of course the same needs arose, and the same patterns were repeated as the armies fought their way south. In Kaifeng, in Hebei province, the Women's Federation organized 3,000 women to produce shoes for the army in units varying from a co-operative with its own premises to *ad hoc* groups whose members worked at home.[19]

One of the first issues of the new national women's magazine (*ZGFN*), which began to appear in 1949, carried a detailed article about organizing women to make clothes in the newly liberated towns.[20] Cadres had gone from house to house collecting the names of those who wished to join the sewing circles. Those who could leave their homes went to work in small sewing shops, but even those who could not took part at home. Group leaders were put in charge of allocating work to them, collecting it, and inspecting it. Occasionally meetings were held for members to point out bad work, exchange ideas, and suggest improvements.

After the liberation of the south, for a time less attention was given in most areas to involving housewives in production on this sort of basis, but they were encouraged to become active in other domains, notably in the work of the residents' committees. These took shape slowly in the early 1950s and

[18] †*Experience of city women taking part in production*, p. 30.
[19] Ibid., p. 52.
[20] *ZGFN* No. 1, (Sept. 1949).

most of the early information about them comes from Peking, Shanghai, and Tientsin. They were at first quite variable in form, function, and name, but in 1954 the National People's Congress laid down definite regulations for their organization.[21] Each committee's area was to consist of 100–600 households, which were to be subdivided into groups of between 15 and 40 households. Each sub-group elected a leader to keep in regular contact with the committee, attend its meetings, and report back to the residents on its plans. Committee members performed these duties in their spare time, and were unpaid, which of course was why they were so often housewives. Although the prominence of these committees has fluctuated according to circumstances both over time, and from one area to another, their activities, which under the guidance of the street office (the basic organ of government in China today) were multifarious, guaranteed them a certain importance in daily life.

Peter Townsend, writing of Peking early in the 1950s, related how the residents' committee in his area made house-to-house checks for rats, lice, bugs, flies, and dirt, giving advice on how to get rid of them, and persuaded people to get themselves vaccinated, to cover their privies, and to sweep their courtyards and the lane outside them daily.[22] In addition it administered unemployment relief, found jobs for people, organized evening classes, made presentations to soldiers' families on army day, and held discussions with the local police. Residents' committees were later also charged with marriage and divorce registration and counselling in the cities, frequently ran kindergartens, and played an important part in security work by reporting new arrivals or any suspicious activities in their area to the Security Bureau.

Little information is available about the work of residents' committees in the fields of marriage registration or security, though there are many casual references to the welfare and health work they performed, and several foreign writers give descriptions of it. It was at this level that the residents'

---

[21] Schurmann, *Ideology and Organization in Communist China*, p. 377; for additional information on residents' committees see Janet W. Salaff, 'Urban Communities after the Cultural Revolution', in John W. Lewis (ed.), *The City in Communist China*.

[22] Peter Townsend, *China Phoenix*, p. 214.

committees' work was most important as a means of transforming the lives of city women. The attacks on vermin and on disease-carrying insects, the cleaning-up of the streets, and the promotion of elementary hygiene obviously had a great effect on the lives of all city dwellers though not one which can be measured. Housewives, who spent more time in their homes than others, who bore children and nursed the sick, were in the best position to appreciate improvements in health and the environment, as well as the removal of threats to the safety of young children such as pools of filthy stagnant water.

The most revolutionary effect of residents' committees on housewives was that they enabled them to relate directly to society as individuals rather than through their families, and provided them with a vehicle through which they could alter their own environment. The work was not at first at all easy for women whose lives had been so restricted and who had been discouraged since infancy from advocating or even expressing an opinion. Peter Townsend observed that the women who came to his compound to search for vermin and check sanitation were very timid. Shirley Wood's detailed account of life in a Shanghai lane soon after liberation shows that women were at first very reluctant to act as lane representatives out of a fear of making themselves conspicuous.[23] They doubted their ability to do the work, especially if it involved contact with men. But within a few years, the women had grown immensely in confidence. The symbolic culmination of this was their victory over a landlord whom they forced to make various improvements in the property he let out, and to cease operating a coal-briquette yard which constituted a fire hazard. When they had first broached these problems with him, he had told them if they wished to talk business they had better send their husbands.

Even when the major hygiene and sanitation movements had achieved their objectives, residential areas had been made cleaner and more orderly, and many of the early activists in the residents' committees had taken up full-time productive work in other spheres, the committees continued to fulfil important functions, providing a means of caring for and

[23] Shirley Wood, *A Street in China*, pp. 99-101.

organizing socially and politically the old, the sick, and the unemployed in a very cohesive society where great efforts were made to see that nobody was forgotten and nobody dropped out. They played an educational role by forming literacy and newspaper-reading groups, and helped working women by setting up low-cost child-care groups.

Much of this work continued to be shouldered by housewives who, because of a lack of suitable work, family commitments, or reluctance to take a job, remained quite numerous. As a means through which women might liberate themselves, residents' committees always remained a sort of compromise between theory and practical realities. At the theoretical level, the Chinese Party continued to accept the orthodox Marxist view that economic dependence was the basis of women's subordination, yet it had increasingly to accept that it would not be possible, except in the very long term, to offer all women an independent economic role. The activities of the residents' committees, which absorbed so much of women's time, were never primarily economic, and indeed they had been forbidden by the 1954 regulations to control productive enterprises.[24] So though they did give women a real social function outside their homes, they did not usually involve them in production.

However, the implications of residents' committees for the standing of women in the family and the community were complex. Though the widespread glorification of industrial labour in the 1950s probably did rather devalue other types of work, efforts were made to set up a new system of values in which earning power would count for less, and selfless service to the people more. The social worth of the work done by housewives in residents' committees was anyway more obvious than that of housework, so that though unpaid it certainly conferred some prestige.

Attempts to increase the employment of women outside the home did continue though they varied greatly in their intensity. Moreover, though increasing numbers of women were recruited as industrial workers throughout the 1950s, the most forceful campaigns to involve them in productive work concentrated on small-scale ventures in the tradition of the

[24] Schurmann, *Ideology and Organization*, p. 380.

garment-sewing groups. Thus under the urban communes of 1958, and again with the advent of the neighbourhood factories of the late 1960s, large numbers of housewives started work using labour-intensive handicraft methods. They produced simple consumer goods, and performed single processes or did finishing work for large factories on a sort of putting-out basis. In obedience to normal economic laws, work in such under-capitalized units was not very productive and tended to be poorly remunerated. They were too small to be covered by labour insurance laws, and so offered no welfare benefits.

Such workshops had some advantages for women. Since they recruited labour on a very local basis, they did make it easier for women with family responsibilities to work. However, the income of women working in them would have been of marginal importance in the family budget, with implications for equality which we will consider later. Moreover, such enterprises were very vulnerable to the economic climate. Like the small workshops of Japan and Hongkong, they gave the economy a useful ability to expand and contract the production of certain types of items rapidly. The corollary to this was that they could offer neither secure employment nor generous long-term welfare benefits. Many of the workshops set up in 1958 proved uneconomic and were closed down with the withering away of the urban communes.

Estimates of female non-agricultural employment in the 1950s are subject to all the usual difficulties which attach to Chinese statistics. Problems of definition, interpretation, and method, and the inadequacy of the infant statistical machine in China, leave grave doubts as to their accuracy, and the validity of using them to make comparisons over time. However, I will use some selected figures to try to indicate broad trends.

The data for 1949–58 were issued by the State Statistical Bureau.[25] Unfortunately no comparable information exists for subsequent years. These figures are anyway inadequate for our purposes since the classification 'workers and employees' did not normally include people employed in the street factories (*minbangong*) or contract labour on construction sites. In

[25] State Statistical Bureau, *Ten Great Years*, p. 82.

April 1960, the Minister of Labour, Ma Wenrui (Ma Wen-jui) said that if street industries and businesses were included there were more than 12 million women workers and employees throughout the country.[26] If we use the 1959 figure of 8.25 million for the number of 'regular' women workers and employees, we may deduce that between 3.75 and 4 million women were employed in street factories in 1960. Unfortunately we do not know how many of these lost their occupation in the closure of these enterprises and how many continued in the reorganized handicrafts co-operatives. Since the tendency to underestimate the numbers employed in workshop and putting-out industry is universal, this figure may not in any case be reliable. Emerson estimates female non-agricultural employment (a wider concept than the worker-employee one used above) at 17 per cent of the total for 1957, and 17.7 per cent for 1958.[27]

In a detailed monograph on employment in Shanghai,[28] Christopher Howe has shown that though the proportion of Shanghai's factory labour force which was female remained very high, at 45 per cent, it was lower than the 1931 figure of 51 per cent.[29] The figure for women as a proportion of Shanghai's total employed labour force was much lower; 21 per cent in 1957 which Howe believes probably represents a fall. If this is so, trends in Shanghai have not been typical of national trends, presumably because its industry was so dominated by textiles.

The national figures for female employees in the 1950s, then, show a twelve-fold increase over ten years, a far more rapid increase than that of the total non-agricultural work

[26] Quoted in John Philip Emerson, *Non-agricultural employment in Mainland China 1949-1958*, pp. 50-1.

[27] J. P. Emerson, 'Employment in Mainland China, Problems and Prospects', in Joint Economic Committee, Congress of the United States, *An Economic Profile of Mainland China*, p. 465.

[28] Christopher Howe, *Employment and Economic Growth in China*, pp. 62-3.

[29] This fall probably reflects the diversification of Shanghai's industry which had once been so dominated by textiles that a Bureau of Public Safety census for 1928, which found that 58.7 per cent of all factory workers were women, also showed that female workers in the textile industry were 52 per cent of all factory workers in Shanghai (*Standard of Living of Shanghai Laborers*, Bureau of Social Affairs, City Government of Greater Shanghai, 1934, pp. 86-7, quoted in Nym Wales, *The Chinese Labour Movement*, pp. 16-17).

TABLE 3
Female workers and employees[a] *in Communist China by year 1948–1960*

YEAR	Total workers and employees in 1,000s	Female workers and employees in 1,000s	Females as % of total workers and employees
1949	8,004	600	7.5
1950	10,239	b	b
1951	12,815	b	b
1952	15,804	1,848	11·7
1953	18,256	2,132	11·7
1954	18,809	2,435	12·8
1955	19,076	2,473	13·0
1956	24,230	3,266	13·5
1957	24,506	3,286	13·4
1958	45,323	7,000	15·4
1959	44,156	8,286	18·8
1960	b	8,000	b

a Employees = government and administrative personnel etc.
b Data not available.
Source: Cheng Chu-yuan, *Scientific and Engineering Manpower in Communist China 1949–1963* p. 145. His source for 1949–58 is State Statistical Bureau, *Ten Great Years*, pp. 180 and 182, and for 1959 and 1960 *Zhongguo Xinwen (China News Service)*, 22 Feb. 1960, p. 11.

force.[30] The trend was to continue into the 1960s. In his study of thirty-five Chinese industrial enterprises in 1966 Barry Richman estimated female employment at 25–30 per cent of the total. This is consistent with the figure of 25 per cent he was given for females as a percentage of total employed personnel in industry, commerce, education, and culture in China's major cities in 1962.[31]

What does emerge clearly from the figures is that though the percentage of women in the non-agricultural labour force rose considerably, women were still very far from achieving equality in employment. Nor was their share of non-agricultural employment commensurate with their share in the population from which it was drawn. 47.8 per cent of

[30] Cheng Chu-yuan, *Scientific and Engineering Manpower in Communist China, 1949–1963*, p. 144.

[31] Barry M. Richman, *Industrial Society in Communist China*, pp. 303–6. The same figure is quoted by Cheng Chu-yuan for Shanghai, Peking, Tientsin, and Chungking for 1963 (p. 144).

the non-agricultural population between the ages of 14 and 64 were female in 1950, and this did not vary by more than 0.1 or 0.2 per cent in the decade which followed.[32] Under the provisions of the labour code women retire when they are 50 while men continue until they are 55;[33] a discriminatory arrangement would obviously reduce women's possible share of employment, but this again would be a factor of minor importance.

The level of regular employment of women in the late 1950s still lagged far behind that in the Soviet Union and most advanced industrialized nations, though it compared quite favourably with that of some underdeveloped countries.[34]

In view of the frequently expressed commitment of the Party to encourage the full participation of women in the labour force, this gradualism, the fluctuations in the rate of increase of women's employment, and the attempt to satisfy women with 'marginal employment' in neighbourhood workshops, require an explanation. It lies of course in the general economic context of the 1950s.

[32] These percentages have been calculated from estimates of the male and female non-agricultural population in Hou Chi-ming, 'Manpower, Employment and Unemployment' in Eckstein, Galenson, and Liu (eds.), *Economic Trends in Communist China*, p. 346.

[33] 'Provisional Regulations of the State Council Governing Retirement of Workers and Employees', 16 Nov. 1957, NCNA handout, Peking, 10 Feb. 1958.

[34] The following figures of the percentage of women amongst personnel in modern occupations (employees in industry and trade, and all personnel in clerical, administrative, and professional occupations) are presumably roughly comparable to those for women workers and employees in China (Table 3):

Country	%				
Sierra Leone	10	(1963)	Cambodia	11	(1962)
Syria	5	(1960)	Malaya	12	(1957)
Pakistan	3	(1961)	Singapore	13	(1957)
India	9	(1961)	Philippines	29	(1960)
Ceylon	14	(1963)	Hongkong	26	(1966)
Burma	22	(1953)	Korea (S)	9	(1955)
Thailand	26	(1960)			

In most Latin American countries the comparable figure was 25 per cent or more. Percentages of over 20 per cent are normally only achieved in those developing countries where women traditionally took an important part in home industries, bazaar, and service occupations. (Ester Boserup, pp. 176-7.) In Britain in 1970, 37 per cent of the work-force was female (Leonora Lloyd, *Women Workers in Britain*). In the USSR in 1959, 44.2 per cent of non-agricultural workers and employees were female (Norton Dodge, *Women in the Soviet Economy*, p. 44).

Unemployment was endemic in Chinese cities in the 1950s.[35] It was present at the beginning of the decade, and continued because the enormous growth of the urban population (brought about both by natural increase and by migration from rural areas) was greater than the expansion of employment. Expectations of an increase in employment to be generated during the Five Year Plan were unrealistically high. Moreover residual unemployment was aggravated sporadically by further waves of temporary unemployment. These resulted from periodic falls in the level of general economic activity, which not only followed the fluctuations in agricultural production in a way characteristic of an underdeveloped economy, but also arose from the loss of confidence in the private sector which occurred during the big political campaigns of the 1950s.

Numerical estimates of this unemployment are so varied that it seems pointless to quote them. However, we can trace changes in policy towards women which seem to match changes in the employment situation quite closely. The need to restore production, and perhaps the economic innocence of the Party in 1949–51, produced much propaganda urging women out to work. The first note of caution was sounded in 1952 when, partly because of the crisis in business confidence which followed the anti-corruption movement, unemployment soared.

The State Council issued a document which divided the unemployed into various categories, of which housewives who wished to work were acknowledged to be one.[36] The Women's Federation was urged to seek out such women, make inquiries as to their degree of need, qualification, and experience, and, in suitable cases, help them to find jobs. However, it was made quite clear that for the moment there was no hope of jobs for all who wanted them, and the document pointed out that housework was not to be despised since it had now a far greater significance than in the old society. Six days later, the

[35] This discussion on unemployment is based primarily on Christopher Howe, *Employment and Economic Growth in China*, p. 149.
[36] †'Decisions of the State Council of the Central People's Government on employment problems', *RMRB* 4 Aug. 1952.

Women's Federation issued a directive, couched in very much the same terms, directing all its branches to implement the decision of the State Council.[37] Both documents pointed out that the Women's Federation could do educational work amongst women which would be useful in case of their eventual employment.

The year 1955 saw a similar mood of conservatism, this time manifested in the 'wu-hao' (five good things for a housewife to do) movement which attempted to politicize housework by giving it a declared revolutionary worth. The housewife's role as a sort of (unpaid) service worker for those who participated directly in production was glorified. Representative of much of the reportage of this period was a series of articles on housewives which appeared in the official women's magazine in 1955. It was later reprinted as a booklet entitled *The New-Style Housewife*. An upswing in both the industrial and construction sectors of the urban economy saw some reversal of this trend in 1956, permitting the publication of such books and articles as:

> *Women on the iron and steel production front* (by Xu Fang).
> *Women on the industrial front.*
> *Wherever my country needs me* (stories of women workers).
> 'Mobilize women's energies and develop their active role'.[38]

Before the end of the year a rise in unemployment which resulted from heavy migration from the countryside after co-operativization, a net outflow from the army, and a reduction of the proportion of young people in full-time education, produced an abrupt change of mood signalled by articles like:

> 'The problem of female employment can only be

---

[37] †'Directive of the All-China Democratic Women's Federation to all levels of the organization to co-operate in the implementation of the decisions on employment of the State Council of the Central People's Government' *RMRB* (10 Aug. 1952).
[38] See bibliography.

met gradually.'
'Doesn't doing the housework and caring for the children count as work?'[39]

In an attempt to get housewives to see themselves as contributing to society through their husbands, their status as dependants was stressed; the word itself was used more often, and dependants' conferences were held at which women discussed how best they could maintain their husbands' morale and preserve their strength for their jobs, protecting them from any problems at home.[40]

By early 1958, pressure was even being mounted to make working women retire. In a long article in the women's magazine (*ZGFN*), An Ziwen (An Tzu-wen), the director of the Chinese Communist Party organization department, paid a long tribute to the achievements of women cadres, many of whom he said were doing the same work as men, and doing it as well.[41] However, he went on to claim that a small number of women cadres, because of bad attitudes, lack of qualifications, poor health, or problems of combining a job with the care of a family, were doing their jobs badly. He pointed out that the second Five Year Plan envisaged a considerable pruning of cadres, and that already some had

[39] †'The problem of female employment can only be met gradually'. *Liberation Daily*, 13 Dec. 1956, and †'Doesn't housework and caring for children count as work?' *GRRB* 13 Dec. 1956.

[40] see †*Important Documents of the national representative congress of workers' and employees' dependants*. Dependants' organizations in Guangxi, Shenyang, Datong, Qingdao, Jilin, Heilongjiang, Sichuan, Harbin, Shanghai, Anshan, Henan, Peking, and Jiangxi are mentioned in the book.

[41] An Ziwen, †'A correct approach to the problem of retirement of women cadres', *ZGFN* (Feb. 1958). An Ziwen was formerly (1950-4) Minister of Personnel. In 1950 he wrote that in Marriage Law implementation, the first task was to wipe out feudal thought amongst Party members. This sort of thought was manifested in a belief that women were inferior. Such members did not understand that women's weak points were a consequence of physiology and the old society. In 20 years of revolutionary history women had always been outnumbered by men and had made slower progress for which the leading Party organizations were very much to blame since they had not helped or educated women cadres enough. Criticizing some husbands, he said that they treated their wives as appendages instead of equal partners who should progress with them. He condemned some women who, instead of studying to make themselves good, independent cadres, concentrated on getting a husband on whom they could lean. (An Ziwen, 'Carry out the Marriage Law and destroy the remnants of feudal thinking', in †*The Marriage Law and related documents*.) An Ziwen fell from power during the Cultural Revolution.

gone to the shop-floor and to the countryside.[42] Just as the sick and the old should now retire so he said should women of this sort withdraw from their jobs. He even cited the example of an acquaintance who had found great contentment in retirement since she was now able to give her attention to her family. Her husband was happy and she was better able to bring up her children. He condemned women who tried to resist returning to housework with the excuse that it was not glorious: on the contrary, in such circumstances, it was work of national importance which would benefit both self and state. Furthermore, as housewives women would have time to take part in hygiene campaigns and other social affairs.

He did qualify this by saying that only a small minority of those who worked should retire, that it should always be done voluntarily, and that he was neither casting aspersions on the abilities of women nor implying that useful women cadres should withdraw. Nevertheless, the tone of the article is pressurizing; it does not question woman's total responsibility for household chores, and the joy he attributes to the performance of housework contrasts sharply with Lenin's condemnation of its unproductive, stultifying drudgery.[43] The article's emphasis on the advantages accruing to the husband and children of a full-time housewife must also have worried

---

[42] This was not just an excuse. Figures given for the organizational retrenchment of cadres are amazingly high.

Retrenchment of State Cadres in selected cities 1957

Date of report	City		Number retrenched	No. as % of all cadres
Sept. 1957	Guangzhou	(Canton)	20,000	33
Oct. 1957	Jinan	(Tsinan)		40–50
Nov. 1957	Xian	(Sian)	2,425	41
Nov. 1957	Beijing	(Peking)	21,000	30–50
Dec. 1957	Zhengzhou	(Chengchow)	9,100	30–40
Dec. 1957	Datong	(Tatung)	10,000	40
	Wuhan		32,900	33

Source: Kan Ying-mao, 'Recruitment and Mobility of Urban Cadres', in John Wilson Lewis (ed.), *The City in Communist China*, p. 116.

[43] V. I. Lenin, 'International Working Women's Day', *Pravda* (March 1920). reprinted in Lenin, *Women and Society*, pp. 26–7.

those working women who had not yet developed a full confidence in their right to work.

The whole period from the end of 1954 when the 'wu-hao' movement began was one of debate about the relative value of outside employment and housework and, although the ratio of publications praising housewives and women workers changed, neither stream ever completely dried up. Some women strongly resisted confinement to the domestic sphere. When the *People's Daily* published an article called, 'What should you do when you can't manage a job on top of your housework?'[44] a reader wrote in to express opposition to its line that women with considerable family responsibilities should give up work.[45] She herself had four children: the eldest at primary school, two at her organization's kindergarten, and the baby with a child-minder. They ate in canteens except on Sundays when they cooked at home. She did worry about the children's eating habits, but that could not be helped, and she believed it was good for them to be toughened. The figures she quoted showed that most of her wages went on child-care, but her answer to the suggestion that she stop work was that she had certain abilities which she wished to use for society and that to recognize this was not to despise housework.

Fortunately the campaign to induce women to retire was not sustained: it was swept away in the optimistic, expansionist mood of the Great Leap Forward.

Success in bringing women into the urban work force in the 1950s was of course limited by their lack of skills, by family burdens, and by socio-cultural attitudes towards their role to which I will return. Development priorities were also disadvantageous to women's employment in the 1950s. Resources in the first Five Year Plan were concentrated in heavy industry. The greatest growth in employment therefore occurred in the sphere where women by reason of lack of skills, education, and tradition were least equipped to compete for jobs. It seems, however, that the crucial limitation may have been the slow pace of growth of industry and employment,

---

[44] †'What should you do when you can't manage a job on top of the housework?', RMRB (22 Jan. 1958.)

[45] †'Should we give up our jobs and go back home to do the housework?', *RMRB* (9 Feb. 1958).

caused by the relative scarcity of capital. Because of the existence of a fairly high level of male unemployment, a more rapid increase in the proportion of female employment would have been potentially disruptive to political support, social cohesion, and thus to economic development. Given this situation, the increase in female employment which did take place, and the laudatory publicity given not only to those engaged in what was already regarded as 'women's work' in the textile industry, but even to those entering traditionally male preserves in heavy industry appear quite remarkable.

In development theory, it is desirable to minimize the ratio of dependants to workers in growing towns since the overheads of new urbanization such as housing, the supply of public utilities, welfare, education, food supply and road construction are thus reduced. This may be achieved either by the migration of young (and in practice usually male) workers who leave their families in the countryside, or by maximizing the employment of the urban population of working age, which of course implies a high rate of female employment.[46]

In the 1950s, many young migrants into the towns were either single, or came alone, leaving families in the countryside, though after the advent of the higher co-operatives in 1956, the families of some urban wage-earners who had owned land but were labour-short and could no longer therefore expect any income from the land, began to move to the towns. A survey published in 1957 classed 60 per cent of the population of the fifteen major cities as non-productive and showed that the rate of growth of this section was higher than that of the 'productives'. Considerable effort was then devoted to reversing this flow.[47] It may be that the higher rate of female employment found by Richman indicates an attempt to reduce the dependency ratio by maximizing female employment, but this was clearly not the main development strategy of the 1950s.

Very great publicity has been given to the special employment structures of the new agricultural-industrial developments of the 1960s, of which the Daqing (Taching)

---

[46] For a lucid presentation of this theory see Ester Boserup, *Woman's Role in Economic Development*, pp. 206-9.
[47] Howe, *Employment and Economic Growth in China*, pp. 122 and 131-2.

oilfield is the best known. It had a high level of female employment, though men and women were usually engaged in different occupations. Such development strategy was feasible because these were pioneering and rapidly expanding settlements without the problems of residual unemployment and because migration could be limited to chosen recruits.[48]

Women in paid employment were of course far easier to reach with propaganda and organization than were women who never left their homes, and, though numerically a small group, they were given a disproportionate amount of attention by the Party, the Women's Federation and the trade unions at the time of liberation. They were quickly attracted by improved working conditions and promises of 'equality' which had little meaning to the housewife, for under the old regime they had been the victims of low pay, long hours, insecurity, and job discrimination. More importance was attached to the mobilization of women factory workers than of any other group, in part because they were members of what the Party taught was now to be the leading class in China, and also because they had an immediate role to play in the restoration of the economy.

Trade unions which were set up in both factories and offices had women's sections (*funübu*) to press the special interests of women. Enterprises with more than fifty female employees were required to have a women's committee of the trade union, and those with fewer elected a women's representative to the general trade union committee. Women's representative congresses were to be elected periodically to discuss specific issues in enterprises with a considerable number of women employees. Branches of the Women's Federation were also

[48] This development lies outside the period on which I have focused, but is of interest for the purpose of comparison. The wives of the oil-workers of the Daqing and Yumen oilfields are celebrated for having brought virgin lands under cultivation to solve the problem of food in the remote settlements, and for having set up light industrial and chemical enterprises which use the waste products of the oil refinery to produce such things as chemical fertilizer, soap, candles, and light bulbs (Taching, *Red Banner on China's Industrial Front*, pp. 12-14 and 31-3, and Rewi Alley, 'Oilfield Wives from the Gobi', *China Reconstructs* (Dec. 1973), pp. 32-5). Although the women's enterprise and resolve have been enormously praised, they are playing a role which must be seen not only as complementary but also as secondary to that of their husbands. There is a parallel to be drawn with the juxtaposition of neighbourhood factories and large-scale industry. Very recently, teams of women oil-drillers have also been formed.

formed within enterprises to link working women with other women all over China.[49]

The Women's Federation and the trade unions shared the tasks of urging women to go out to work and to do their jobs efficiently, and of pressing the implementation of welfare legislation which affected women and assisting them with their family problems. Immediately after liberation, when the most pressing need was the restoration of the economy, the first of these tasks was the vital one, and writings on women were mainly concerned with it. Since it was in the north-east, an area of heavy industry, that this need was first faced, much of what was written was intended either to encourage the establishment of small, lightly capitalized workshops producing textiles, clothes, shoes, and other desperately needed military supplies, or to glorify pioneer women who were training for jobs which women had not done before.

A book of reportage published in 1949 contains some very good examples of the sort of propaganda which was being directed at women at the time. One of the most interesting is an article on the padded clothes industry in Harbin which was given very high production targets in June 1948.[50] In the following four months, nine factories were set up employing 2,000 women who made between them 225,505 winter suits. The article describes the chaos which at first arose because the women completely lacked labour discipline. Some came early and some late, some brought small children who played in the workshops making a mess and distracting their mothers who sat around chatting . The factories were jointly supervised by the district government, the military supplies bureau, the processing industries bureau, and the Women's Federation. Each of these organizations at first had its own quality requirements which gave rise to much trouble. The processing industries bureau was especially strict, and kept demanding that garments which it considered too big should be unpicked and remade. This upset the women, and one of the older ones tried to walk out saying: 'Damn it, I'm fifty years old. Why should I learn these kids' methods? If this won't do then I'm

---

[49] For details of these structures see †*Regulations on the organization of trade unions*, pp. 64–6.

[50] †*New women workers of the new society*, part II.

going home.' When a cadre from the Women's Federation tried to reason with them, the irate women demanded: 'How about democracy? Why are we still being ordered around?'

Pilfering was also a problem in the factories. The workers concealed and carried out cotton wadding in their chignons, in spectacle cases, and in the points of shoes made for bound feet. These troubles were overcome gradually as much effort was devoted to giving the women a sense of involvement in and commitment to the new society. Talks were given at the factory on the importance of their role, a system of production bonuses was arranged, the local newspaper carried items about them daily. Finally their story was told in a documentary film. After all this publicity, shopkeepers and officials began to recognize them from the fluff which stuck to their clothes and to give them priority treatment. The children's league helped them with their housework and their status within their families was greatly improved by fame and the money which they earned.

Another article first published in 1948 described how women in Jixi county, Jilin (Kirin) province, became miners.[51] They were the dependants of coalminers who began to work in the pits picking stones out of the coal carried by a conveyor belt. When the management investigated the possibility of starting to work some seams which had been blocked off by the retreating enemy, they decided that they did not have enough trained labour for the job. Hearing of this, the Women's Association organized 100 women to clear the shafts, repair sabotaged machinery and restore electric track. The women got very dirty crawling into the machine chutes to clean them and packing the piled-up coal on to the trains, but when they finished the job many of them stayed on to work at the coal-face as loaders and even blasters. They paid older women to care for their children at home until the trade union set up a nursery.

Not all women were so determined. Out of fifteen girl graduates sent to a factory by an institute of electrical engineering in the north-east in March 1949, only six remained after two months.[52] Of those who had left one

---

[51] Ibid., part III.
[52] †*Experience of city women taking part in production*, p. 4.

complained that the wages were too low and stopped work entirely, one went to a teachers' training college, one said she could not manage the machines and went home and another 'lost her watch'. The writer of the article believed that the basic trouble was that wages were low and that the girls had either intended to work only until marriage, or were willing to continue after marriage only for the sake of getting two wage packets.

The large numbers of women workers who had to be organized after the liberation of Tientsin and Shanghai probably presented fewer problems of morale. They were accustomed to hard work and bad conditions and could be won over by the limited amelioration which was possible in the short term.

Jobs in industry were popular with women because workers were an élite. Even before liberation many girls had valued the independence conferred by a job in a mill, despite the fact that it was bought with long hours of work in bad conditions. The labour code of the People's Republic of China decreed equal pay for equal work, and a working day of between eight and ten hours. Maternity benefits gave 56 days' leave with full pay, an additional 14 days for a difficult birth or for twins, and a cash payment of 4 yuan. Pre-natal examination and hospital confinement were paid for by the enterprise. A woman who suffered a miscarriage got 30 days' paid leave. They had access to canteens, crèches and nurseries, and special diets when they were pregnant or unwell.[53] Since women who worked usually belonged to families with more than one wage-earner, they tended to live in comparatively good accommodation and to eat well. Recruitment to factories was intensely competitive and new workers were quite often even selected by examination, especially if there was a need for large numbers of them as when a new plant was being opened.[54] Nor were the advantages enjoyed by women workers

[53] *Labour Laws and Regulations of the People's Republic of China*, pp. 42–4.
[54] For example, in a story which though fictional is probably realistic in much of its detail, Kaixia, a village girl, considered taking a competitive exam to enter a textile mill near Xian (Sian) in 1953. She discovered that the Central Committee had issued a directive to factories to give preference to city girls who had failed to get into middle school. The exam, held in a county seat, she had intended to take was to be the last of its kind since it was thought to make country girls restless. Learning all this, she felt that it would be more progressive to stay and work in the countryside so she returned to her village. (Liu Ching, *The Builders*, especially pp. 443–5.)

purely material ones. Even during the periods when the role of the housewife was being glorified it could not rival for prestige that of the worker in a society where such a high value was placed on production.

However, working women also had to face problems. The first, their lack of self-confidence and the contempt in which they were held might not affect women in industries such as the textile industry where they had long been accepted, but these were serious problems for women in heavy industry, for women cadres, and for all other women doing jobs which had formerly been the preserves of men. Difficulties remained even for women who had overcome their own doubts and family opposition, since they often had to face mockery from their fellow workers' amongst whom they were a minority. The first women apprentices in heavy industry often found that the men who were to teach them their jobs regarded their task as hopeless.

Women cadres suffered, though perhaps less acutely, from a similar lack of confidence on the part of their colleagues and superiors, and had also, if they worked in management or administration, to cope with the doubts of those who worked under them. This problem was treated as an ideological one and was met with a determined propaganda effort. The successes of working women were given enormous publicity and small numbers of carefully selected women were trained for jobs which would have the maximum possible effect on the popular consciousness. These women then received awards before huge meetings, and were idolized in newspaper articles and documentary films.

Famous amongst such women were the steelworkers of Anshan,[55] but the most celebrated of all were the women train crews who worked as drivers, stokers, firemen, and guards on some of the principal trains of China.[56] To make the point even more strongly, some expresses were run exclusively by women. Although it is the case that women do some jobs in China which they do not normally do in the West, women train drivers are certainly still the exception there; such

---

[55] See Xu Fang, †*Women on the iron and steel production front.*
[56] See 'Woman Engine-driver, Tian Guiying', in †*Accounts of visits to model workers.* pp. 228-32.

publicity stunts were not intended to draw huge numbers of women into the railway or comparable industries. Rather they were intended to show women, and the men they might work with, that women might do anything that they wished to, and to associate the whole idea of women working with modernity, progress, and the concept of the 'New China' with which the Party had already succeeded in mobilizing much support for its policies. Countless women were encouraged by these examples to take up mundane but equally necessary jobs in many other fields.

Though the first three or four years after liberation saw the greatest effort to break down the old attitudes which were the cause of this problem, they tended to reassert themselves in various forms for many years afterwards, and continued to be the subject of frequent attack in the press. However, the technique of refuting these prejudices with reality really did slowly undermine them, as people were forced not only to accept working women, but to admire them.

Moreover, though it was still only exceptional women who worked in heavy industry, many more did so, and there was a general diversification of the type of industrial jobs performed

TABLE 4
Female workers and employees in China, by selected speciality, various years

Speciality	Women as % of total work force
Industry	
Light industry (1960)	30
Textile industry (1960)	75
Iron and steel industry (1958)	15
Machine building industry (1958)	15
Railway system, passenger service, (1962)	50
Education	
College teacher (1956)	20
Secondary school teacher (1956)	35
Primary school teacher (1960)	35
Doctor of western medicine (1961)	20
Professional health worker (1961)	35
Art (1960)	35
Urban communes, industrial worker (1961)	65

Source: Cheng Chu-yuan, 'Scientific and Engineering Manpower in Communist China', in Joint Economic Committee of the United States Congress, *An Economic Profile of Mainland China*, p. 539.

by women. At the same time the enormous increase in educational and welfare facilities provided many employment opportunities for women. Table 4 shows their representation in different branches of employment for various years.

This diversification is a healthy trend in an industrial economy which has been directed away from its early dependence on textiles and light industries, and in which both employment and remuneration in heavy industry have been raised more than in other sectors.[57] Another way in which it would be desirable to break down total female non-agricultural employment would be by age. We know that women factory workers of the 1930s in China were very young: a study of 368 women in 102 factories produced the following age break-down:[58]

18–21 years of age	42·4%
14–17 years of age	25·3%
22–25 years of age	16·6%
14–25 years of age	84·3%

The median age of the women was 19, 83 per cent of whom were single and only 16·5 per cent married.[59] This seems to indicate a strong tendency at that period for women to give up their employment on marriage or pregnancy[60] which would obviously militate against their acquiring a high level of skill, or entering types of industry which required such skills. Unfortunately I have no recent figures for the age of women workers, but I believe they would be somewhat more evenly spread across a wider span.

Since 1949 there has been a sustained effort to help women overcome the difficulties of pregnancy and child-care (see above). A trained industrial worker would take maternity leave, but would not be expected to resign from her job.

[57] Christopher Howe, *Wage Patterns and Wage Policy in China*, pp. 43–5.
[58] Cora Deng, 'Economic Status of Women in Industry in China', 1941, an unpublished thesis for Nankai University quoted by Nym Wales in *The Chinese Labor Movement*, p. 17. Cora Deng's survey reports are on a microfilm in the YWCA library in New York.
[59] Ibid. I was not able to obtain a copy of this microfilm, so I could learn nothing of the 0.5 per cent of women who appear to have been neither married nor unmarried, but even if only approximately correct, the figures are useful.
[60] In many factories they were in fact required to do so.

Women are thus more inclined to undertake lengthy training, and enterprises are able to encourage them to do so in the anticipation that they will make a lifetime's use of them.

Though it is uncommon for a skilled worker or an educated professional to be driven out of employment by the burdens of housework or child-care, in the towns as in the countryside they do still pose considerable difficulties which fall mainly on the shoulders of women and hold them back politically and professionally. Though, following Lenin, the Chinese Party recognized that 'as long as women are engaged in housework their position is still a restricted one', economic difficulties prevented the establishment even of adequate canteen and nursery facilities let alone the achievement of a 'full social economy' which he had advocated as the solution for women.[61]

Women continued to be held primarily responsible for the housework and the children in the urban household, although this was less easily justified than in the Chinese countryside where the differing physical capacities of the sexes give the traditional division of labour some rationale. Though there was some pressure on the husbands of working women to take a share of the chores, it was light in a society where social pressure could be a strong and even coercive regulator of behaviour. Moreover, the man was more often urged to 'help his wife' rather than to take his share of the work, and the discussion did not really challenge the idea that housework was regarded basically as the women's responsibility.[62]

For the childless couple housework was not too great a burden.[63] Canteens were notably more successful in the towns than in the countryside where the rhythm of life was so different. In the towns people were more accustomed to 'clock-watching' than in the countryside, and their hours of work

[61] Lenin, *Women and Society*, pp. 26–7.

[62] See for example an article, †'Women and the family' which explained that in *socialist* society women were still slightly disadvantaged because although many feudal bonds had been swept away, some household duties remained and prevented them reaching absolute equality with men in the cultural and economic spheres (*ZGFN*, 1 Jan. 1959). It was not until 1973 that the forumla of 'sharing household chores' (rather than the husband 'helping' his wife) appeared in a *People's Daily* editorial ('Working Women are a Great Revolutionary Force', *Peking Review*, 16 Mar. 1973: see Appendix 3), but this does seem to have set a new tone for the 1970s.

[63] The following section is drawn largely from observations during two years' residence in China (1963–5).

were regular as was their work place, so they could more easily eat at set times. For many it would have been very difficult to return home at midday. Young city workers who were recent immigrants to the towns and lived in dormitories created a hard core of customers for canteens, but they might also be preferred by young families living in cramped quarters with inadequate cooking facilities. Most working people ate in canteens at midday and unless some member of the family stayed at home all day they often found it easier to eat there in the evening too.

Since city homes were small, usually consisting of one, two or three rooms, and were very simply furnished, they were not difficult to keep in order. Domestic life became easier as piped water was extended to many households which had formerly relied on a lane tap, pump, or well. A young couple might be kept busy on Sunday by their laundry, cleaning, sewing, and perhaps shopping and cooking, but the work would not bring them great problems.

The arrival of the first child considerably altered the situation. Aside from the obvious problem of day-care which is discussed later, the amount of laundry and sewing which had to be done would obviously increase enormously. Subsequent children, and there were usually more than one, aggravated the situation. However, the evidence is that working women are seeking relief to this problem by limiting their families.

A letter in a Shanghai paper from a woman factory worker gives us a glimpse of her long hard day.[64] She had two children one of whom she left in a nursery on her way to work. The other she took with her to the factory crèche because she was still breast-feeding him. When she got home after her eight-hour day she still had to wash the clothes and do the housework. At first her husband had helped her, but when his fellow workers laughed at him and said that he was 'unmanly' and 'henpecked' he became embarrassed and stopped. She began to find exhaustion a real problem and wrote to the paper to ask for advice. The editorial comment condemned the attitude of the husband's workmates as a remnant of old ideas and contrary to the spirit of the Marriage Law. Rather

[64] 'Does a man lose face if he does housework?', *Labour Paper* (Shanghai), 7 July 1956.

inconsistently it claimed that some tasks such as knitting and sewing really were more suitable for women, but that it was nonsense to claim that men could not do any housework at all; if they did not know how to do it, they could always learn.

Complaints like this were printed quite frequently, and another sign of the changing climate was that in glowing descriptions of the lives of model married couples, the point is nearly always made that the husband did some of the housework.[65] By the end of the 1950s it was probably normal for the husband to perform some of the household tasks if his wife worked, but unusual for them to share them equally.

As to child-care itself it was provided in many different ways. Most large factories, some small ones, and many street committees opened crèches, nurseries, and kindergartens.[66] Crèches were most often at the place of work so that the babies might be fed by their mothers. For older children a kindergarten as near as possible to home would usually be preferred so that long journeys with sleepy children could be avoided. For this reason they were more often organized by the street committee. But throughout the 1950s there were complaints that child-care facilities were not nearly adequate to the need, and it appears that many, perhaps even most, working mothers relied on the help of a relative.[67] Though this might be a sister, sister-in-law, or cousin who lived nearby, it was most likely to be a mother or mother-in-law who shared the home of the working couple. Ageing parents might even be brought into the city from the countryside to join the household on the birth of a child. Thus the fact that a mother worked could sometimes strengthen the solidarity between the

---

[65] Similarly husbands who were reluctant to help were satirized:

Pregnant wife. How about going to buy some food?

Husband. Darling, you don't really want me to go, do you? The shops are so crowded on Sunday.

Wife. But it's so awful for me to go out now I'm so heavy.

Husband. That's silly. It's just the time people will be nice to you.

Wife. What do you mean?

Husband. They're bound to let you to the front of queues and give you seats on buses. In this new society everyone knows how to treat expectant mothers.

The New Fortnightly Examiner, (Xinguancha banyuekan), Peking, 16 July 1958.

[66] For detail on crèches and nurseries see Ruth Sidel, *Women and Child-care.*

[67] See for example †'They need help', *ZGFN* (1 July 1957), an article which contains a strong plea for more nurseries and accuses some factories of promising them but doing nothing.

parents and the grandparents, and militate against the trend towards the simple conjugal family group, which was otherwise strong in the towns where there were many recent immigrants from the countryside and where there was a critical shortage of accommodation.

Even when children were left in crèches or nurseries during the day, or when they were already of school age, their parents might find life easier if a grandparent lived with them. However good the facilities for day-care, problems remain when both parents work. Taking them to, and collecting them from, the crèche added to the length of the working day, school holidays were a problem, and difficulties arose during the illnesses which are so frequent in early childhood.

For those families with enough money, a servant was a possible solution and indeed one frequently resorted to. There were plenty of illiterate, unskilled middle-aged women who needed money or a home and who could not find jobs in industry. The morality of employing personal servants so that both husband and wife might work was not in question, indeed the cadre stipend had early given it official recognition. In pre-liberation and early post-liberation China, cadres did not receive wages, but only rations and a small allowance for covering personal expenses. Women cadres of a certain rank were granted money to allow them to keep a servant so that they might work.[68] Wages and hours of servants were discussed to some extent in articles in the press which seemed at least equally sympathetic towards the employer as they were towards the employed. Such articles urged maids to remember the revolutionary content of their work, which, although not directly productive, 'enabled others to take their place on the productive front'. They were reproached with a tendency to skimp housework and neglect children when they thought they could get away with it; faults which were grave because they were likely to make the work of their employers deteriorate.

Cadres were urged to treat their maids as equals but were asked not to turn a blind eye to their faults, or to try to win their loyalty by paying more than the average wage since this would upset the stability of the labour market. An article of

[68] Peter Townsend. *China Phoenix*, p. 207.

1956 advised employers that maids could be expected to work
more than the standard industrial day of eight hours, since
their work was not intensive.[69] It went on to comment that the
custom followed by some employers of giving their maid a free
day every fortnight was a good one. (Traditionally in China,
maids did not get a regular day off.) The life of servants was
probably not as hard as this perhaps implies; it was usual for
them to eat with the family, and to identify to a large extent
with its interests, and some really occupied a position not
unlike that of a grandmother although with less authority.
Their employers were considered responsible for their medical
expenses since they were not covered by industrial labour
insurance.

However, since the wage for a full-time maid was a third to
a half of what a skilled worker might expect to receive, only a
minority of working women could afford to employ one.
Cadres, teachers, and industrial workers could employ help or
use nurseries and crèches. But poorly-paid women such as
those in handicrafts and services sometimes found the price of
communal child-care too high, especially if they had several
small children, and gave up their work to care for them.

Even the many mothers who managed to keep their jobs
were at a disadvantage with respect to their male colleagues
because in China, perhaps even more than in the West, the
ambitious must be prepared and able to give up much of their
free time to their work.[70] For ordinary workers the working
week of 48 hours was frequently lengthened by an evening of
political study or a meeting, and these were a regular feature
of life for all cadres and teachers.[71] The heaviest burden was
borne by party members who had to attend party meetings
and to be especially active politically at their place of work.
They were also expected to show an interest in spare-time
education, and to give an example if there was extra work to
be done or if a colleague needed help. At times of intensive
political activity they might have to give up every evening of

[69] †'Concerning the work and wages of maids', *ZGFN* (1 Sept. 1956).
[70] For a general analysis of how housework and child-care affect women and their
relationship to the economy and society see Isabel Larguia and John Dumoulin,
'Towards a science of women's liberation'.
[71] †'Build up a regular work and life routine. How to guarantee the women personnel
of enterprises the time to take care of their housework'. *RMRB* (29 Jan. 56).

eir week. Obviously women who had to clean and wash and are for children after work would find it hard to get to evening meetings.

No mass-scale attempt to sever permanent child-care from the family unit was ever made, but significantly the boarding schools and residential kindergartens which did exist were mainly attended by children from families where both parents were cadres. No doubt claims made during the Cultural Revolution that in such cases power had obtained privileges were true,[72] but it was equally true that such privileges made it easier for women in senior positions to get promotion or to preserve their power.

This problem was sometimes raised in the press. In 1956 the *Peking Workers' Daily* published a letter from a man whose wife had said sadly on his admission to the Party: 'You men can make such progress, but we are just women.'[73] He claimed that this had made a deep impression on him and had made him feel that although their relationship was superficially good, they were in fact growing apart. Yet it does not seem to have affected his behaviour, for, according to the letter, his wife was later refused admission to the Youth League on the grounds that she was too busy at home and had a poor work record in the factory. She thought about this and realized that she really had too much housework to do. She asked the League secretary to advise her and he referred it to the Party branch. It was brought up at a branch meeting and the husband was criticized and asked to reform.

Inadequate education is another factor which has disadvantaged women. We know that far more women than men were illiterate in 1949, and that inequality existed at every level of the educational system. Table 5 below shows that inequality had been reduced but still persisted at the end of the first decade of the People's Republic. Table 6 shows the small percentage of women amongst those who had completed their

[72] See 'The first school system for children of high-ranking cadres: the ten great crimes of the August 1st School', by Mao Tse-tung's Thought Revolutionary Rebels' Joint HQ August 1st School, Capital City, and 'The reactionary bloodline theory and boarding schools for cadre children', by the 'Wind and Thunder' Combat Team of the August 1st Middle School, Canton, big-character posters translated in *Chinese Sociology and Anthropology*, 1, No. 4 (summer 1969), pp. 3-37.

[73] †'Between husband and wife,' *GRRB* (10 July 1956).

education, a consequence of past discrimination with obvious employment implications for the future.

TABLE 5

Number of female students in education institutions, various levels, as percentage of enrolment, intervals 1949–1958

YEAR	Higher educational institutions		Secondary specialized schools	
	number	%	number	%
1949	23,000	19·8	158,000	n.a.
1952	45,000	23·4	158,000	24·9
1957	103,000	23·3	206,000	26·5
1958	154,000	23·3	397,000	27·0

YEAR	Secondary general schools		Primary schools	
	number	%	number	%
1949	n.a.	n.a.	n.a.	n.a.
1952	585,000	23·5	16,812,000	32·9
1957	1,935,000	30·8	22,176,000	34.9
1958	2,667,000	31·3	33,264,000	38·5

n.a.: not available.
Source: State Statistical Bureau, *Ten Great Years*, p. 201.

TABLE 6

Percentage of male and female students in higher and secondary education before and after 1949

	Higher educational institutions				
	Male	%	Female	%	Total
Pre-1949	102,000	82	23,000	18	125,000
Post-1949	385,000	77	115,000	23	500,000
Total	487,000	78	138,000	22	625,000

	Secondary educational institutions				
	Male	%	Female	%	Total
Pre-1949	574,000	82	126,000	18	700,000
Post-1949	1,872,000	72	728,000	28	2,600,000
Total	2,446,000	74	854,000	26	3,300,000a

a Includes the 625,000 who went on to higher educational institutes.
Source: Leo Orleans, *Professional Manpower and Education in Communist China*, p. 145.

Since education was neither compulsory nor free and fees might involve parents in financial hardship,[74] it could be expected to be a particularly stubborn area of sex discrimination. As long as marriage continues to be patrilocal, or as parents look to their sons rather than daughters for support, and find satisfaction and prestige in the career achievements of boys rather than girls, this will persist. Such tendencies are no doubt stronger in the countryside. Probably female primary school attendance would be almost universal in the cities, and the percentages above are distorted by the rural element. Almost all secondary schools and tertiary institutions were in the cities in the 1950s, and their syllabus was planned to prepare pupils for urban employment. The statistics do therefore indicate that women suffered discrimination in education even in the towns, and that they were not being adequately equipped to compete equally with men on the urban job market. Only in medicine and pharmacy where the female share of student enrolment in 1958 was 40·2 per cent was the proportion of women students respectable. Such a situation in the late 1950s will obviously have effects on the proportion, level, and remuneration of women in the work force for many years to come.[75]

Looking back on the 1950s, it is clear that urban women were hampered in their attempts to work by <u>the whole heritage of male-orientated ideology</u>. It was this heritage which made it unthinkable to increase women's employment too obviously at the expense of putting men out of work, which made discrimination in education so hard to fight, and which meant that housework was still often perceived as the women's 'natural' responsibility. Discrimination in work and education feed each other. If it is hard for a woman to have a career her education may be seen by her parents or even by the state as unprofitable, and if a woman lacks education it will be hard for her to work.

Compromises made necessary by the gap between what was

---

[74] For details of the effects of fees and competitive entrance on the class origins of the pre-Cultural Revolution enrolment see Marianne Bastid, 'Economic Necessity and Political Ideals in Educational Reform in the Cultural Revolution', *The China Quarterly* (April-June 1970), pp. 16–46.

[75] Leo Orleans, p. 146.

realizable in a difficult economic situation and the ideals posed by theory characterize policy towards women in the towns in the 1950s. Theory proposed that economic independence alone could make women's liberation a possibility, but there was a limit to the rate at which the demand for labour, especially for unskilled and inexperienced labour, could be expanded. Moreover, beyond a certain point, it turned out to be expensive, in the Chinese situation, to replace the woman's unpaid labour in the house with collective facilities.

However, the majority of city women who remained housewives, whether by choice or the lack of any other option, could hardly be ignored as members of the new society. They had no escape from their role which was an essential one, and the Party could not therefore allow them to feel despised. Even the attempt to make such women play a larger role in society by organizing them to work together for the community in such bodies as residents' committees held no promise of complete liberation according to the theory since they did not involve them in productive activity. The glorification of the housewife's role in making a comfortable home for her family and feeding it well and economically illustrated clearly the dilemma of the Party. It accorded ill with the principle that the emancipation of women remains an impossibility as long as the woman is shut out from social productive labour and restricted to private domestic labour.[76]

But even employed women did not achieve full equality with men although thanks to economic independence and social respect they came nearer to it. So long as there was neither a completely comprehensive system of canteens, child-care facilities, and communal services, nor a truly radical attack on the idea of women's special responsibility to the home and the family, they were bound to carry the double burdens of which Alexandra Kollontai had warned in the context of the Soviet Revolution. Though doubtless there were other factors at work, I suspect that this is the one that best explains the failure of

---

[76] F. Engels, *The Origin of Family, Private Property and the State*, p. 221. (This quotation is well known in China and has been much used in the Women's Movement, e.g. Soong Ching-ling, speech to the Asian Women's Conference, Peking, 11 Dec. 1948, reprinted in *The Struggle for New China*.)

women in China to achieve high position in large numbers in
China in the 1950s.

CONCLUSION

The proper scope for a study of woman in China would once have been her roles as a daughter-in-law, wife, and mother in the family, the group within which the lives of women were then almost entirely confined. It is a measure of the changes which have taken place that a study of women now necessitates consideration of the whole economy and society of China. The complexity of the roles of modern Chinese women not only within the family, but also in the economy as a worker or a peasant and in the political field as a member of a community grouping like the street committee or a mass organization like the Women's Federation, makes a simple characterization of women's position impossible.

The basis of the Marxist position on women's emancipation was set out by Engels in these words: 'The emancipation of woman will only be possible when woman can take part in production on a large, social scale, and domestic work no longer claims anything but an insignificant part of her time.'[1] In the important formative years of the communist women's organizations the whole orientation of woman-work was based on this tenet. We have seen that there were considerable departures from this principle in woman-work in the mid-1950s but that they were temporary, and the old emphasis is now restored.

The rate of female participation in employment therefore seems one criterion by which to judge the achievements of policy towards women in China. The data which we have for the period ending about 1958 indicate a limited success in this sphere. In the countryside, women were making a greater contribution to agricultural production than they had made before 1948. The provision of some communal facilities to reduce domestic burdens has made it easier for them to do so, and the obstacles of tradition and prejudice have been fought with propaganda and education. Nevertheless although we lack recent statistical information, it is quite clear that even

[1] F. Engels, *The Origin of the Family, Private Property and the State*, p. 221.

now, sixteen years after the establishment of the communes, women's contribution to productive work, or more precisely their ability to earn extra work-points, is considerably less than that of men. The work that they are allocated is frequently of a type perceived as subsidiary to that of men, and their participation is particularly seasonal.

For non-agricultural occupations there is a similar dearth of statistical information after 1959–60. Although an impressive rise in the absolute numbers of women workers and employees was achieved in the first decade after liberation, they still represented rather less than 20 per cent of all workers and employees. This compares really well only with those countries belonging to the Muslim, Hindu, or Chinese cultural tradition where the idea of the seclusion of women is still strong, and with African countries where few women work in the modern sector. In Latin American countries the percentage of women amongst employees in modern occupations is usually several points higher, and in advanced Western countries it is commonly about 30 per cent.[2] The Soviet percentage had already surpassed this level in 1926 when it stood at 31 per cent. By 1959 it was as high as 47.3 per cent.[3] In China since 1960 efforts to raise the numbers of women in employment seem to have been rather better sustained than they were in the 1950s. In the absence of statistical information we cannot be certain, but it seems that the Chinese have succeeded in increasing the proportion of women in the employed population, although institutional limitations still restrict the rate of increase. Any assessment of the achievements in this field must take account of these limitations. This is especially necessary if cross-cultural comparisons are to be put in a proper context.

In the Chinese countryside, the burden of domestic work and child-care is still heavy. The old lines of division of labour between the sexes are less sharp than they were, but are still far from obliterated. Here again it may be useful to consider the Soviet case. In the Soviet Union in 1959, 57 per cent of the

[2] For comparative data on women's employment in various countries see E. Boserup. *Women's Role in Economic Development*, p. 181.

[3] N. Dodge, *Women in the Soviet Economy*, p. 44, Table 27 under Workers and Employees (non-agricultural).

work-force on the collective farms was female, but women contributed only 46.4 per cent of the total man-hours expended on the farms.[4] However, when all agricultural activities are taken together, including work on private plots, women contributed 55.5 per cent of total labour inputs measured in man-hours.[5] On the collective farm of Viriatino 200 miles south-east of Moscow in Tambov province, women form an even higher proportion of the work-force. When it was surveyed in 1957, 312 women and 172 men were actively engaged in agricultural work.[6] The average number of labour-days credited to able-bodied workers in 1955 was 269.[7] (The 'labour-day' like the work-point is a measure not just of time worked, but also of the type and quantity of labour performed.) Only women employed in the care of livestock, which is highly paid, accumulated more than the average number of labour days. They got as many as 340–60. However, women who worked in the fields accumulated only 120–60 labour days, and women doing heavier work got up to 230; very considerably below the average.[8] Women who worked in the fields did very little on the collective farm in winter, and this was true not only for mothers, but for younger women as well. The exceptions were widowed mothers who were the sole supporters of their families. Women whose husbands were in well-paid jobs tended to work less than others.

We have of course much less detailed information about women in China. Presumably their share of work on private plots is greater than their share of collective work as it is in the Soviet Union and for the same reasons; work on private plots is more easily combined with child-care and cooking, and the household budget will suffer less if it is women who abandon their collective earnings since they are generally lower paid than their husbands.

Strong forces operate in agriculture to make women's contribution to farm work marginal. Women's proportional

---

[4] Ibid., p. 166.

[5] Ibid., p. 167.

[6] Sula Benet (ed.), *The Village of Viriatino*, p. 182.

[7] Ibid., p. 192.

[8] The rules of the kolkhoz required 200 labour days from men as against only 150 from women or 120 from women with children (ibid., p. 192).

participation may be expected to rise significantly only when the demand for labour is more evenly distributed throughout the year, when domestic work can be lightened, collectivized, or shared with the family, and when more women do jobs which are well remunerated in terms of work-points. Closely linked with this last point is the training of women in the skills required by modern agriculture. The modernization of agriculture is often associated with declining participation by women. So far such a decline has been avoided in China, and the reverse has even been achieved. However, if the trend is to continue women must take a share of the more skilled jobs in agriculture. To do this they require a fairer share of school places, and more chance to train. Since, as we have seen, one of the obstacles to this is the patrilocal marriage system, fundamental changes are necessary to achieve it.

Comparisons between different countries in the sphere of non-agricultural occupations are also difficult because such different conditions obtain. As we have seen, the percentage of women in the employed population in China compares favourably with that in other countries where women were traditionally secluded, but badly with industrialized countries and especially with the Soviet Union. However, the comparison with the Soviet Union raises difficulties since, in spite of a shared ideological commitment to the employment of women, cultural, historical and demographic conditions differ sharply. Women in Russia were more easily accepted in employment, especially in the professions, even before the Revolution. The employment of women in the eastern republics where conditions were in some ways more comparable to those in China is known to be much less than in European Russia. Furthermore the sex ratio in the Soviet Union (number of men per 100 women) has undergone a catastrophic decline in the twentieth century. Even in 1926 it was as low as 94, by 1939 it had fallen to 92 and in 1947 it was only 74.[9] These figures, which reflect the tragic history of the country, imply conditions which would favour the employment of women. Another important feature of recent Soviet history has been the demographic transition from a relatively high fertility in 1926 to exceptionally low fertility

[9] N. Dodge.

during and even after the Second World War. In spite of the pro-natal policies of the government the birthrate continues to decline. One source claims that urban women average one child and rural women only 1.25 children at the present birth rate.[10] Obviously such small families make it easier for women to work. They also cut the time a woman takes off from her job for maternity leave and for child-rearing. When the difference in length between men's and women's working lives is thus reduced, a major argument against training equal numbers of men and women in complex skills, namely that investment in women's education does not give equal returns, is greatly weakened. The birth rate in China is falling, but fertility is still higher than in the Soviet Union, and this of course has special implications for women's employment.

Although the proportion of women in the urban work-force is still quite low in China compared with advanced industrialized countries, women in China may have the advantage in the variety of jobs which they do. The largest concentration of women is employed in jobs often identified as 'female preserves' such as textile manufacture, food-processing, and banking. However, by 1958 they had also established themselves in smaller numbers in the iron, steel, and machine-building industries, and recently they have been entering the construction industry in increasing numbers. Though women engineers like women in the other professions are still a minority, their numbers are rising. A girl who wishes to study engineering certainly occasions no surprise. Between 1949 and 1961, 14 per cent of the 9,000 students who graduated from Qinghua (Tsinghua), China's most famous school of science and engineering, were women. In 1959 they represented 23 per cent of the graduates.[11] However, in all spheres of education, even at primary level, women were still at a disadvantage a decade after liberation. Their share of education put them in a less favourable position for employment than men. Even if their share is now equalized, it will be a long time before the disadvantage suffered by women who were of school age in the 1950s ceases to affect the figures

[10] W. Mandel, 'Soviet Women and their Self-Image', *Science and Society* (Autumn 1971), p. 299.

[11] Cheng Chu-yuan, *Scientific and Engineering Manpower in Communist China, 1949-1963*, p. 140.

for women's employment, promotions, and holding of skilled jobs or posts of responsibility.

We have seen the significance attributed by the Chinese communists to productive work as a means of liberating women. However, without specifically rejecting the principle that the divorce of women from commodity production is the basis of women's special oppression, the Chinese have in fact experimented with other ways of giving women power and importance in society. Mao Zedong's inscription for the magazine *Chinese Women* (*ZGFN*), written in 1949, reads: 'Unite and take part in production and political activity to improve the economic and political status of women'.[12] As we have seen, political work—taken in a very wide sense so as to cover war work done by women, struggles led by the women's organizations against the oppression of women, and the sort of community work performed by the street committees—has certainly made an enormous contribution to women's liberation. It would be hard to overestimate the importance of women's organizations in the struggle to establish women's equality in the family. The old authoritarian structure of the family has died hard, indeed remnants of it still survive. Without the Women's Federation these might have been stronger. The Women's Federation, and indeed the whole Party propaganda machine, seem also to have achieved considerable success with women's image of themselves as a group. If some women still lack confidence it is in themselves as individuals rather than because they are women. Formidable attacks have been made on old beliefs about women's inferiority. Mao Zedong's words, 'What men comrades can accomplish women can too',[13] have received dramatic confirmation in the achievements of such national heroines as the women oil-drillers, bridge-builders, and high-tension power-line workers.[14]

The implications of community work and even indeed of enterprises at the fringe of the productive sector like the neighbourhood factories seem to me complex and uncertain. As a short-term expedient they have undoubtedly been

[12] *ZGFN* No. 1. (1949).
[13] Quoted in †'Train women cadres enthusiastically', *RMRB* (16 Jan. 1974).
[14] See *New Women of New China*.

excellent. They have taken women from their houses, drawn them into public life, given them experience and authority in their communities, and, in the case of neighbourhood factories, have brought them a wage. However, street committee work, being voluntary, does not confer economic independence, and even employment in a neighbourhood factory brings in less money, less job security, and fewer fringe benefits than a regular job. The danger of such developments is that they may become institutionalized. If this happened a large proportion of urban women would be excluded from the most productive and rewarding sector of economic activity. In effect such women would be offered a 'separate but equal' path which would deny them real independence for ever.

In spite of official assertions that in China men and women are equal, statements and documents also show a clear awareness that equality is still far from complete. The press regularly publishes attacks on cadres who denigrate women as backward or useless and who neglect to train or promote them. One of these, an article in the *People's Daily* in 1971, charged that cadres in the countryside sometimes failed to train women because, once married, they would be burdened with household work, and others opposed training women because they would be lost to the brigade when they married away.[15] Even more authoritative was the *People's Daily* editorial for Women's Day 1973.[16] It criticized the failure to train women cadres in proper numbers, unequal pay for equal work in rural areas, unwillingness to accept women as workers in some factories, and the surviving feudal influences in marriage. It urged that nurseries should be well run, families planned, and household work shared between men and women in order to enable women to take a more effective part in political activities, production, work, and study. Thus in spite of all the progress made by women in China it is officially recognized that their struggle is far from complete. As long as this is so, their progress will surely continue, for inequality and discrimination can hardly become rigidly institutionalized so long as a critical consciousness of them exists.

[15] 'Pay attention to the development of female Party members', *RMRB* (13 Sept. 1971); see also N. Diamond, 'Collectivisation, Kinship and the Status of Women in China'.
[16] *RMRB* (8 Mar. 1973), see appendix 3.

APPENDIX 1

Decisions of the Central Committee of the Chinese Communist Party on the present orientation of woman-work in all the anti-Japanese base areas (1943)

In the past five years, relying mainly on the Eighth Route Army, the New Fourth Army, and the broad masses of the people, of whom the 50 per cent who are women have played an important part, we have set up anti-Japanese bases in the enemy rear, kept up the Resistance War, fought bitterly with the puppet troops, overcome innumerable difficulties, and achieved unprecedented successes. Our work amongst women has been effective, yet in this work we have lacked both the spirit of seeking truth from reality and a true mass outlook. In our work we have neglected to go right down, plunge ourselves into really tough work, and make ourselves one with the masses.

We have not really grasped the great importance of economic construction for continuing the Resistance War and building up the base areas. We have not regarded economic work as the most relevant for women, or grasped that the mobilization of women for production is vital to safeguard their special interests. We have not investigated and researched into women's circumstances properly, or formed a profound appreciation of their feelings. We have not considered their home commitments, their physiological limitations, or the hardships of their daily lives. Instead of thinking what women can and should do at a given time in a given place, we have coined the slogans of the women's movement, drawn up projects, set up organizations, got women to go to frequent meetings and wasted their labour power and material resources, mobilizing them unnecessarily all in accordance with our subjective views. Consequently the work is too general and the organization too formalized and both lack a real mass basis. It is these tendencies to subjectivism and formalism which isolate us from ordinary women and are the basic cause of the stagnation and stunted growth of woman-work.

As victory draws daily nearer and things get daily tougher in all the anti-Japanese bases, we are faced with three necessary tasks; fighting, production, and education. Of these tasks, it is production at which women can and should particularly excel, and their part in it is as glorious a struggle as that of the soldiers at the front. Moreover, progress towards women's liberation through an amelioration in their educational level, their political position, and their living standards will arise from their economic independence and prosperity. If they produce plenty and are very thrifty, women and their families will be able to live better. Not only will this play a big part in building up the economy of the base areas, it will give women the material conditions which will enable them gradually to escape from feudal oppression. This is the essence of village women's special interests in all mass work and is also a new orientation for work amongst women in all the anti-Japanese base areas.

In order to put this orientation into effect, the form and procedures of woman-work must undergo a big change. We must make thorough investigations in order to understand the life, needs, and feelings of ordinary village women. Centres should be chosen with an eye to their subjective potential and their objective conditions, in which to start work and from which the neighbouring areas will gradually be influenced until every area is stirred up.

I. Every local women's association or women's salvation association ought to treat investigating and organizing women's individual and collective production as their primary task. They should go deep into the countryside to teach and give help in solving the difficulties of women on the production front. Whether women do well in production work or not is the measure by which to judge woman-work.

II. Whether village women weave, breed silkworms, work on the land, or look after the home should be planned in accordance with the specific situation in each place. But their production must be planned in accordance with that of the rest of the family. They should not just go off to work regardless of anything. The mistakes of certain places where formalistic proclamations were made, full of figures for land-clearance and tree-planting by women, but which in fact had no practical content, must not be repeated. Women must be mobilized to go amongst the masses and play a real part in production.

III. Organize in accordance with the needs of ordinary women in the base areas and correct the old method of forming organizations in name only. Use production co-operatives and all forms of production (e.g. weaving etc.) as ways of organizing women. These should become the basic organizations of the women's associations or women's salvation associations. Do not create groups and societies which exist only in name.

IV. Strive to reduce the unnecessary pressures on village women, to cut down on meetings, and husband their labour power and material resources so as to make them stronger for production.

V. In matters which affect women's health and are thus detrimental to production, such as foot-binding, or inattention to hygiene, women should be encouraged to carry out reform.

VI. Women should be educated culturally and politically through production, for example they should improve their production techniques, learn characters connected with production and compose songs for work.

VII. Women cadres must get rid of the incorrect idea that political and productive work are unimportant. They must understand that production is one of the most important political tasks in the base areas, and that moreover if those who do woman-work are to get a close relationship with the villagers, they must start by going right into the villages to organize women for production, solving their difficulties and promoting their economic interests. If they want to do this they must themselves study the details of the rural economy and understand women's production from the inside, for only then can they really organize and lead it. A lot of able women comrades should go to work in co-operatives, and a lot of women party members should go to work in public economic enterprises to make the public sector of the economy develop. It is absolutely wrong to float along doing nothing and, instead of feeling ashamed about it, to be arrogant.

The theme for commemorating International Working Women's Day this year will be the mobilization of women to take an active part in production. Detailed plans should be drawn up everywhere according to the specific situation.

26 February 1943.

Decisions of the Central Committee of the Chinese Communist Party on woman-work at present in the countryside of the liberated areas (1948)

After keeping up the fight against the Japanese for eight years the Chinese people finally defeated Japanese imperialism. Now they have been fighting the People's Liberation War for two and a half years and have won unprecendentedly great victories. The reactionary Kuomintang regime can basically be defeated in about another year. These victories were gained relying on the Party's correct leadership, the fighting skill of the People's Liberation Army, and the bitter struggles of the ordinary people. Women, who form half the population, have played a big role and have become an indispensable force for defeating the enemy and building a new China. Woman-work has been especially successful since February 1943, when the Central Committee issued 'Decisions of the Central Committee of the Chinese Communist Party on the present orientation of woman-work in all the anti-Japanese base areas'. This gave a clear direction to woman-work in the liberated areas, and where it was put into practice there were noticeable changes in the work. Ordinary village women of the liberated areas were further mobilized and organized to work in handicrafts, supplementary enterprises, and agriculture, and to contribute to the war effort with all their strength. In land reform all the liberated areas mobilized even more women to take an active part in the sharing out of land and the struggle to eliminate feudalism. In the districts where land reform is already complete there has been a fundamental change in class relations in the villages, land has been distributed to both men and women, young and old, and quite a few women have become district or village representatives, and have even been elected village heads, deputy heads, or cadres above the village level. Women have become much more aware and enthusiastic, and consequently there has been a fundamental change in their political and economic position and in their position in the family and in society, opening the way to complete liberation.

But there are certain shortcomings in woman-work in the liberated areas. In a few places the Party organization and the women's associations have not given enough recognition to the Central

Committee Decisions of February 1943 or have not understood them properly. The central task in woman-work is to organize women to take an active part in production. This is also a guarantee of women's special interests and the key to freeing them from the constraints on them which still survive. Some areas have even completely disregarded these decisions and so have not carried them out conscientiously or thoroughly. Moreover, in some districts conscientious care has not been given to eliminating the survivals of feudalism which hold women back or to satisfying women's special interests and demands in the course of mobilizing women for production, land reform, and work to aid the front. It has been supposed that when women are mobilized for production and land reform, everything will naturally be solved in consequence. Woman-work has also been mechanically isolated from other work. Because of this, many of the special sufferings of women cannot be ended when they should be, and their full mobilization is thus obstructed. In a few areas the old erroneous tendencies to carry out woman-work in an isolated detached way still exist, and these have built up internal antagonisms between men and women peasants and between young and old women and have even alienated the masses. Since 1943 the latter mistake has for the most part been overcome and in the few places where it has survived it is now being corrected. Up to the present the former is still rather a common phenomenon everywhere. These shortcomings are largely due to the fact that in some places some cadres of the Party and the women's organizations do not have an over-all idea of work amongst the masses, have not realized the general importance of woman-work, do not properly understand it as a part of the whole relation to revolutionary work, and cannot reconcile mobilizing women adequately for production with protecting women's special interests.

Apart from this, in some places the Party organization and the women's organizations have not given nearly sufficient attention to the glorious task of leading women to aid the war effort and consolidate the army. Either they have not been conscientious about helping and caring for the dependants of army personnel, or they have not offered suitable criticism and education to those backward army dependants who hold the soldiers back and generally undermine the consolidation of the army. They have not made ordinary women understand that without victory in the People's Liberation War there can be no true liberation for the mass of women, and so they cannot fully arouse the enthusiasm of women for the war effort. Since work was not checked when it should have been, and since experience was not summed up and mistaken tendencies were not corrected, these shortcomings could not be overcome.

The orientation of woman-work in the liberated areas should still be based on mobilizing and organizing women for an active part in production. The basic policies laid down by the Central Committee decisions of February 1943 are still completely appropriate. The whole party, all cadres engaged in woman-work, and all women activitists must understand that under New Democratic Government, all the laws of the old society which constrained or mistreated women and forced them into a humiliating position of obedience have ceased to exist. The new laws guaranteeing absolute equality of the sexes in the economy, in politics, and in society have been formulated or basically formulated in the first period of New Democratic power. The question is whether these laws can truly be realized. The attitude of valuing men and despising women handed down from the old society, all kinds of constraining feudal customs, especially the economic dependence of women on men and the handicaps of not excelling at all sorts of labour and even despising it, have obstructed the rapid realization by women of the rights already granted to them in law. So if women's rights are to be properly realized, the work must be done. In the first place women must not only be given equal economic rights and position with men, and in the countryside get and keep an equal share of land and property, above all they must be made to understand fully the importance of labour and must look on it as glorious. They must participate actively in all the productive jobs which are within their physical capabilities and become the creators of wealth in both the family and society. Only by going to work with a will, so that they gradually become economically independent, can women gain the respect of their parents-in-law, their husbands and society at large, and increase the harmony and unity of the family; only thus can the economic, social and political position of women be easily consolidated and only thus can all the laws concerning sex equality acquire a strong base on which to be implemented. The experience of the last few years has proved this completely. That is to say, where women have taken an active part in productive labour and regarded it as glorious, given education on sex equality, opposed the feudal constraints and divided up the land, the position of women is clearly completely different from before. They are happy and respected and quite a few activists have been elected as representatives or have taken part in other social or political activities. And it must be recognized that women's participation in labour is not simply the key to their liberation: whether for the present war effort or New Democratic economic construction or the future victory of socialism, women's labour is absolutely indispensable.

Therefore in the villages of the liberated areas we must go on doing our very best to mobilize and organize women for agriculture, handicrafts and supplementary production. As to the orientation and needs of the restoration and development of all sorts of production, and to what sort of work the women in each place should concentrate on (agriculture, handicrafts or supplementary enterprises), concrete proposals for this suited to the locality and the time should be made in accordance with the unified local government-party production plan, the labour power ratio between men and women, and what women customarily produce.

As land reform is completed, all problems connected with women should be solved in accordance with the correct policies of the local government and the directives for dealing with problems left over from land reform, so as to confirm and increase women's enthusiasm for production. There must be government orders to guarantee women's rights to land. When the family is taken as a unit for issuing land deeds, a note must be made on the deeds that the men and the women have equal rights to land. Every member of the family has democratic rights in the disposal of possessions. When necessary, land deeds for women can be issued separately. At the same time there should be a considerable period of publicity and education for all peasants so that both men and women fully understand the importance of protecting women's rights to land.

To promote the healthy development of women's production, we must carry out the policy 'get organized' correctly, and do our best to get women to take part in all sorts of co-operatives (e.g. production co-operatives such as mutual-aid groups and weaving groups etc.). In agriculture women find that inter-household co-operation and mutual-aid groups in which both men and women can participate are convenient. In handicrafts and supplementary enterprises they find supply and marketing co-operatives convenient. As to methods, our principle must be that all is done voluntarily in the interests of both sides, to promote the democratic spirit and foster the creativity of the masses, and we must restrain ourselves from interfering too much and refrain from commandism and formalism, but at the same time, we should not just let things drift.

Take production as the focal point, and in the course of production improve educational work amongst women, raise their political consciousness and cultural level and mobilize them to participate in New Democratic Government. Improve health standards among women and children (e.g. by organizing training classes for infant and maternal health-workers, Chinese and western medicine co-operatives etc.) and safeguard the special interests of women. Step by step we must purposefully eliminate the feudal thought, constraints, and customs which prevent women's participation in political, cultural, and economic activities (of which the most important is production). It should not be thought that once women take part in production all the remnants of feudalism in society which still constrain them will just naturally disappear and there will be no need to do any more work. This way of just letting things drift ignores the special interests of women and is erroneous. In the course of production, at all mass meetings and in the mass organizations, all peasants should be given constant ideological education on the equality of the sexes; feudal thought, constraints, and customs must be criticized, and it should be pointed out that all the feudal customs constraining women must be eliminated. The small number of backward elements who want to preserve old feudal customs and who constantly oppress women must be suitably struggled against where necessary. But it must be understood that this sort of struggle is an ideological struggle amongst the peasants and should be radically different from the class struggle against feudal landlords. Moreover, the purpose of ths type of struggle is to educate all the peasants more effectively and to help to mobilize women to engage in production and other constructive enterprises and to build a truly democratic and harmonious family. It should also strengthen and further consolidate the unity between the peasants. At the same time it must also be recognized that this is work to change the peasants' ideas and is a long, demanding job which cannot be hurried. We should oppose both just letting things drift and impetuosity. The government must issue orders against foot-binding, infanticide, purchase marriage, taking in child brides etc., and must also educate the masses so as to bring about the realization of these laws. In the past, in some places in the liberated areas the marriage laws contained sections opposed to the principles of the equality of men and women and freedom of marriage. These should be changed quickly.

The direction of woman-work in the villages of the newly liberated areas should be based on the directives of the Central Committee on work in the newly liberated areas. The Party's policies (including those on woman-work) should be publicized. The Party's influence should be enlarged, the false rumours and black slanderous arbitrary propaganda of the enemy denounced, and social order maintained. In areas where rent and interest reduction or land reform are being carried out, ordinary women should be mobilized to take an active part, and should be led and organized to participate in productive construction and to contribute to the war effort. In these new areas after rent and interest reduction or land reform has been completed, productive labour remains the pivot of the women's movement. As for feudal traditions and customs which constrain women, these will be serious in the new areas and so they must be eliminated purposefully and steadily, in accordance with the level of consciousness of ordinary people, by educating people on the equality of the sexes and making them more aware.

As to the problem of the form of women's organizations, the elimination of independent women's organizations or their existence in name only which occurred in some places in the past was inappropriate. Because of the actual situation of women in China at present, they need independent organizations to lead and inspire woman-work to unite and educate ordinary women and to serve them constantly.

Women's congresses are the best form of organization to bring women together on a larger scale and more democratically. These organizations should exist everywhere at every level. The basic organization of this sort of congress is the village women's congress. Its delegates should be democratically chosen by ordinary women and should include women members of the people's congress, delegates from the women's organizations (such as women representatives of weaving groups, co-operatives and literacy groups) and delegates elected directly by the women (the number of women electors being settled by residential conditions). The role of this sort of congress is to represent the opinion of ordinary women, to discuss the policy and important tasks in local woman-work, to publicize the policies, orders, and resolutions of the Democratic Government and higher authorities, and to mobilize women to carry them out. There should also be a committee chosen by the congress to carry out resolutions, deal with day-to-day work, and decide when to convene a congress. What the committee should be called depends on the wishes of the masses. Where women are already very familiar with the women's association, it can be called the committee of the women's association. In order to have a fully organized mass basis the women's association committee ought always to make use of all sorts of organizational forms, such as literacy classes, co-operatives, mutual-aid groups etc., to organize all the ordinary women with their different requirements. At the same time it should maintain constant contact with, and serve the mass of women who do not belong to any organization.

At county level and above, women's congresses should also be called in accordance with the above-mentioned principles and should choose women's association committees to lead woman-work.

In the past in a small number of places the women's associations did not base themselves on the real circumstances of ordinary women. They were formalistic in organization, laid stress on increasing membership, and held too many group meetings but went without holding congresses for a long time. In work they went in for commandism and they performed as they said 'the tasks passed down by higher authority' formalistically but did not serve the masses. In practice this caused the divorce of the association from the masses, and it became monopolized by a small number of people. In future this bad phenomenon must be earnestly corrected.

In the newly liberated countryside, where the general situation begins to become stable, women's associations can be built up, but first there must be steady, planned preparatory work. Women's organizations should be built up gradually, taking into account the needs and level of consciousness of the masses, and ordinary women should be united and educated. These women's organizations must be based on labouring women.

In accordance with what is necessary to the development of the present revolutionary situation, a large group of party and non-party women cadres must be boldly educated and fully utilized and pushed forward to take up posts of every sort and reinforce the cadres in women's organizations at every level. The same work should be allocated and the same training and educational opportunities given to men and women cadres of equal ability without discrimination. Moreover, taking into account the special position of women cadres, greater attention should be given to raising their political, theoretical, and cultural levels and their ability at work. In order to assist with their special difficulties, crèches and nurseries should be set up and mutual-aid groups of women cadres should be organized to care for children. This will not only lighten the burden of the women cadres, it will also be a start in the nursery care of children by society. The education of the new, labouring women cadres in the villages, especially those who have already held posts before, should be improved. They should be given patient training and steady encouragement with special attention to increasing the number of Party members. In the new liberated areas, pay special attention to training local women cadres. All levels of Party schools and training classes set up by the government should take in women cadres as students according to a plan. Party organizations and propaganda departments at all levels should include the teaching and training of women cadres in their work. And the women cadres themselves under the leadership and guidance of the Party ought to work with purpose and enthusiasm, plunging really deeply into their work and becoming more unified and more efficient. They should study theory, politics, and general knowledge, and knowledge and skills connected with production industriously, and should initiate criticism and self-criticism, overcome their handicaps as women, resolutely seek to progress and strengthen their ideal of serving the people. This is the basic condition for turning oneself into a cadre valuable to the Party.

After the National Land Conference of 1947, Party committees at every level generally regarded leading woman-work as more important than before, and there have been various changes, but they have not yet realized regular and planned leadership of woman-work. The passive phenomenon of efficient leaders having efficient subordinates but lax leaders having lax subordinates is still apparent in woman-work, and a small number of Party committees still despise woman-work and just let it slide. From now on the whole Party must recognize properly that the mobilization of ordinary women for revolutionary struggle is indispensable to revolutionary victory in the whole country. It must further reinforce the leadership of woman-work and carry out the policy of getting the whole party to do woman-work. Party committees at all levels should make woman-work a part of general Party-work, and when check-ups or summaries of work are being planned, woman-work should be included. Party papers and publicity offices at all levels should increase propaganda reportage on woman-work. Party committees at county level and above ought to build up and strengthen the organization of women's committees and give them regular guidance and help. At district level and below, woman-work should be led through the branch and a particular person should be made responsible for it. The duties of women's committees are, under the leadership of the Party committee at the same level, to investigate women's problems and policies concerning women, to check woman-work, to give their opinions to the Party committee, and to direct and stimulate woman-work.

The Party ought further to correct the feudal ideology which values men and despises women that still survives both inside and outside the Party, and to correct the negative idea of cutting woman-work off from all other work, and the mistaken tendency to do woman-work in an isolated, detached way. At all levels Party organizations should intensify their study of Marxism-Leninism and the thought of Mao Zedong and put it into practice more in the way they do woman-work. They should cultivate a complete mass outlook and get a correct grasp of the policy on the women's movement and should overcome lawlessness and anarchy in woman-work. Those who do woman-work should seek truth from reality more often, go right down amongst the masses, plunge into tough work, serve ordinary women with all their hearts and wills and lead the women's movement forward.

To satisfy the needs of national revolutionary development and to concentrate the fighting strength of women, the women's organizations of the liberated areas should actively bring together women all over the country who oppose US imperialism, feudalism, and bureaucrat capitalism, to struggle together to throw US imperialism out of China, strike down the reactionary ruling clique of the Kuomintang, and build a unified, democratic People's Republic. For this purpose it has been especially decided that the women's societies of the liberated areas should hold a national conference of women delegates in the spring of 1949, to set up a National Democratic Women's Federation to bring the women's movement all over the country under a unified direction and leadership, so that it can develop even more strongly in future.

20 December 1948

APENDIX 3

'Working women are a great revolutionary force'

RMRB editorial, 8 March 1973, translated in *Peking Review*, 16 March 1973

Today is March 8, International Working Women's Day. It is the glorious festival of working women the world over in unity for struggle. We convey our high respects to the revolutionary women of all countries and warm greetings to the working women of all nationalities in our country!

Women are a great force on all fronts of China's socialist revolution and construction. During the Great Proletarian Cultural Revolution, the masses of women in urban and rural areas, including those who seldom participated in political activities, have taken an active part in the fierce struggle between the two lines, denouncing the revisionist line. Never before have women been mobilized on such a scale and to such an extent as in this movement. Their consciousness of class struggle and the struggle between the two lines has been rising steadily. Large numbers of activists have come to the fore, and many outstanding women of worker and peasant origin have become members of leading bodies from national to local levels.

In the mass movements *'In industry learn from Taching'* and *'In agriculture, learn from Tachai'*, women have played a role worthy of 'the other half'. The overwhelming majority of urban women have left the confines of their homes to take part in communal work and productive labour, and work in 'May 7' productive organizations. The number of women workers and staff members has increased considerably. In many rural areas, women are the main labour force. Many organizations on the industrial and agricultural fronts, such as 'March 8 work teams', 'March 8 railway groups', 'iron-willed girl detachments' and 'red women companies' have become a shock force in production. Women in commercial, financial, cultural, educational, health and other fields, including large numbers of 'barefoot doctors', have achieved new successes in serving the people. The militant militiawomen have contributed to the defence of our socialist motherland. The storms of the Great Proletarian Cultural Revolution have tempered the working women of all nationalities, bringing new progress to the women's movement in China and tremendous changes in women's outlook.

Women's emancipation is a component part of the cause of liberation of the proletariat. The success of the socialist revolution and construction would have been impossible without the active participation of women, who account for half the population. Likewise, women's emancipation would be out of the question without the victory of the proletarian revolution. The fundamental tasks for the women's movement are to grasp class struggle and the struggle between the two lines, use Marxism-Leninism-Mao Tsetung Thought to educate the masses of women, eliminate the remaining influence of the revisionist line of Liu Shao-chi and other political swindlers on women's work, and mobilize women to take an active part in the struggle between the two classes, the two roads, and the two lines. It is wrong to look at and handle women's work without taking into consideration class struggle and the struggle between the two lines, for that will make it impossible to lead the women's movement on to a correct path. At present, criticism of revisionism and rectification of the style of work is the task of prime importance to the whole Party and country. Doing a good job of it is the key to doing the work well in every department or place. In women's work too, it should be given priority. The masses of women should be mobilized to read and study seriously so that they can grasp and thoroughly criticize the essence of the revisionist line pushed by Liu Shao-chi and other political swindlers, raise their ability to distinguish between genuine and sham Marxism, and enhance their consciousness of implementing Chairman Mao's proletarian revolutionary line.

While carrying out criticism of revisionism and the rectification of the style of work, it is necessary to give the women a better understanding of the political situation and use the domestic and international political situation and the new successes achieved by women in various fields to inspire their political and labour enthusiasm. The Chinese revolutionary women should concern themselves not only with the revolution and construction at home but also with the revolutionary struggles of the people and women of all countries, keep the interests of both the motherland and the world at heart, display proletarian internationalism and strive to contribute to the complete emancipation of all mankind.

The victory of China's democratic and socialist revolutions has opened up a broad road for women's emancipation. Women and men hold equal positions in the political, economic and cultural fields and in family life. But China was under feudal rule for 2,000 years and the exploiting classes left behind deep-rooted ideas discriminating against women and looking upon them as slaves and appendages. Today, classes and class struggle still exist in our society and it is still impossible to eliminate completely the remnants of the old ideas of looking down upon women. Neglecting to train more women cadres, giving men and women unequal pay for equal work in rural areas, showing unwillingness to accept women as workers in some factories, and the remaining feudal influences in marriage — all these are a reflection of such old ideas. It is necessary to wage a protracted struggle against them so as to overcome the idea of looking upon women as inferior. With regard to remuneration for labour, *men and women must be given equal pay for equal work*. No factory should discriminate against women when recruiting new workers. We must do away with old customs and habits in marriage and establish new socialist standards.

Large numbers of women cadres have come to the fore. This is an important indication of the emancipation of China's women and a demonstration of the superiority of the socialist system. A number of women cadres have tempered themselves and matured in protracted revolutionary struggle; they are a valuable asset to the revolution. But the number is far from meeting the needs of the developing revolutionary situation. More women cadres should be trained so as to give still better leadership to the masses of women in their advance. Leading bodies at all levels should have a certain percentage of women members, and let them temper themselves in the great storms of struggle, use them boldly, train them warmheartedly, and develop their talent so that they will mature faster.

In order to enable women better to take part in political activities, production, work, and study, it is necessary to help them approach such questions as love, marriage, family, and the education of children from the proletarian point of view and resist the influence of bourgeois and feudal ideas on these questions. Attention should be paid to women's specific characteristics and to showing concern for and solving their special difficulties. Every possible effort should be made to run nurseries, kindergartens, and nursing rooms well and do a good job in maternity and child care. Late marriage and planned parenthood should be promoted, and men and women encouraged to share the household work. It is important, as Lenin taught us *'to get women to take part in socially productive labour, to liberate them from "domestic slavery", to free them from their stupefying and humiliating subjugation to the eternal drudgery of the kitchen and the nursery.'*

Party committees at all levels should pay great attention to women's work and strengthen their leadership over it politically and ideologically. Some of their members should be assigned to take charge of the work. Women's organizations at all levels should be consolidated and their work improved so that they can act as capable assistants to Party Committees in carrying out women's work and as militant organizations in mobilizing the masses of women. It is necessary to assign a certain number of cadres to take charge of work concerning women, educate them to foster the idea of doing it well for the revolution, and overcome the erroneous idea of disdaining such work. In planning the central work, it is necessary to take into account women's specific characteristics, make proper arrangements and implement the policy of mobilizing both men and women.

Chairman Mao has said: '*Times have changed, and today men and women are equal. Whatever men comrades can accomplish, women comrades can too.*' Chairman Mao has always given great encouragement to women. The women of our country must live up to our great leader's earnest expectations. They should aim high, study hard, and strive to make new and still greater contributions to socialist revolution and socialist construction!

8 March 1973

BIBLIOGRAPHY

BOOKS AND PAMPHLETS IN CHINESE

Accounts of visits to model workers, Laodong mofan fangwenji (New China Bookstore, Peking 1951).

Agricultural production heroines of the north-east, Dongbei nongye shengchan de nüyingxiong. North-Eastern Democratic Women's Federation, Dongbei minzhu funü lianhehui (New China Publishing House, North East 1950).

Answers to questions about the Youth League, Qingnian tuan wenti jieda. South China Work Committee of the New Democratic Youth League of China, Zhongguo xinminzhu zhuyi quingniantuan Huanan gongzuo weiyuanhui (July 1950).

Answers to some questions about marriage, Jige hunyin wenti de jieda. Work Committee of the Guangdong Provincial People's Court (ed.), Guangdong sheng renmin fayuan bangongshi (South China People's Publishing House, Canton 1953).

Basic programme of the Chinese Agrarian Law, Zhongguo tudifa dagang, promulgated by the Central Committee of the CCP, Zhongguo gongchandang zhongyang weiyuanhui (Harbin 1948).

Battling against nature on many fronts, Xiang da ziran quanmian kaizhan (People's Daily Publishing House, Peking 1958).

Booklet of explanatory pictures about the Marriage Law, Hunyinfa tujie tongsu ben (East China People's Publishing House, Shanghai 1951).

Cai Chang, *Greeting the new orientation of woman-work, Yingjie funü gongzuo de xin fangxiang* (n.p., Mar. 1943). LA documents 1.

The campaign for women of the liberated areas of China to take part in the war, Zhongguo jiefangqu funü canzhan yundong. Preparatory Committee of the National Democratic Women's Federation (ed.), Quanguo minzhu funü lianhehui choubei weiyuanhui bian (n.p., Mar. 1949). LA documents 3.

Cao Zige, *Stories of old and new marriage, Xinjiu hunyin de gushi* (Cultural Supplies Publishing House, n.p., Aug. 1952).

Chen Dongyuan, *A history of the life of Chinese woman, Zhongguo funü shenghuoshi* (Commercial Press, Shanghai 1937).

Chen Shaoyu, *Marriage Law of the PRC: report on the course and reasoning of its drafting, Guanyu Zhonghua renmin gongheguo hunyinfa qicao jingguo he qicao liyou de baogao*, in *Marriage Law of the PRC, Zhonghua renmin gongheguo hunyinfa* (Peking 1952).

Chinese women stand up, Zhongguo funü da fanshen (New Democracy Publishing House, Hongkong 1949).

Circular No. 14 of the Central Burea of the CCP of the Soviet Areas: Prepare the commemoration of International Working Women's Day and correct the errors in woman-work, Zhonggong suqu zhongyangju tongzhi dishisihao: Zhunbei 'sanba' jinianjie bing jiuzheng funü gongzuozhong de cuowu (16 Feb. 1931). CC collection reel 4. 008. 2411.3021.

Circular No. 74 of the Central Government: The women's movement and preparatory work for Labour Day, Zhongyang tongzhi diqishisi hao, Wuyue gongzuo yu funü yundong (5 Apr. 1930). CC collection reel 4.008.2411.1071.

Collection of documents from the national representative congress of the dependants of industrialists and merchants and female industrialists and merchants, Quanguo gongshangye zhe jiashu he nügongshangyezhe daibiao huiyi wenjian hui bian (Finance and Economics Publishing House, Peking 1956).

Comparative illustrations of old and new marriage, Xinjiu hunyin duibi tu (South China People's Publishing House, Canton 1952).

Compendium of reference materials on marriage problems, Hunyin wenti cankao ziliao huibian. Legal Committee of the Central People's Government (ed.), Zhongyang renmin zhengfu fazhi weiyuan hui bian (People's Publishing House, Peking 1950).

Decisions of the CC of the CCP on the present orientation of woman-work in all the anti-Japanese base areas, Zhongguo gongchandang zhongyang weiyuanhui guanyu ge kangrigenjudi muqian funü gongzuo fangzhen de jueding (Feb. 1943). LA documents 1. Appendix 1, referred to as CC decisions 1943.

Decisions of the CC of the CCP on woman-work at present in the countryside of the liberated areas, Zhongguo gongchandang zhongyang weiyuanhui guanyu muqian jiefangqu nongcun funü gongzuo de jueding (Dec. 1948). LA documents 1. Appendix 2, referred to as CC decisions 1948.

Decisions of the first joint meeting of the heads of the district committees to improve women's lives of Gonglüe county, Gonglüe xian gequ diyici funü shenghuo gaishan weiyuanhui zhuren lianxi huiyi jueyi an (8 July 1932?). CC collection reel 4.008. 2411.8067.c2.

Decisions of the joint conference of the Guangchang Central County Committee and the heads of the district women's departments, Guangchang zhongxin xianwei gequ funü buzhang lianxi huiyi jueyi (10 Jan., no year). CC collection reel 4. 008.2411.0065.2.

Deng Yingchao, *Land Reform and the new tasks of woman-work, Tudi gaige yu funü gongzuo de xin renwu* (Dec. 1947). LA documents 1.

Deng Yingchao, *Report on the present direction and tasks of the Chinese women's movement, Zhongguo funü yundong dangquian de fangzhen renwu baogao* (1949). Congress documents 1.

Ding Ling, *Diary of Miss Sophie, Shafei nüshi riji,* in *In the darkness, Zai heian zhong* (Shanghai 1928).

Ding Ling, *A Yanan collection, Yanan ji* (People's Literature Publishing House, Peking 1954).

Documents of the Third National Congress of Chinese Women, Zhongguo funü disanci quanquo daibiao dahui zhongyao wenxian (Peking 1957). Congress documents 3.

Documents of the women's movement of the liberated areas of China, Zhongguo jiefangqu funü yundong wenxian (New China Bookstore, Shanghai 1949). LA documents 1.

Dong Bian, *Changes in rural marriages in the old liberated areas, Lao jiefangqu nongcun hunyin de bianhua,* in *Collected reference materials on marriage problems, Hunyin wenti cankao cailiao huibian* (People's Publishing House, Peking 1950).

Draft decisions of the standing committee of the National People's Congress on model regulations for the agricultural producer co-operatives, Quanguo renmin daibiao dahui changwu weiyuan hui guanyu nongye shengchan hezuoshe shifan zhangcheng caoan de jueyi (9 Nov. 1955).

Educational materials on women activists in the towns, Chengshi funü jijifenzi jiaocai. Peking Democratic Women's Federation (ed.), Beijingshi minzhu funü lianhehui bian (North China People's Publishing House, Feb. 1954).

Emulate the most advanced people in implementing the Marriage Law, Xiang zhixing hunyinfa mofan kanqi (People's Publishing House, Jan. 1953).

Er Dong, *Women and children do important work, Funü ertong dingle dashi* (Aug. 1947). LA documents 4.

Experience in mobilizing women during the land reform movement in Beiyue district, Beiyuequ tudi gaige yundong zhong fadong funü de jingyan (July 1948). LA documents 2.

Experience of city women taking part in production, Chengshi funü canjia shengchan de jingyan. All-China Democratic Women's Federation, Quanguo minzhu funü lianhehui (Peking, Sept. 1950).

The experience of Dongyan agricultural producers' co-operative in getting women to work in the fields, Dongyan nongye shengchan hezuoshe fadong funü canjia tianjian laodong de jingyan, in *Work experience in the countryside of Zhejiang (Chekiang) in 1955, Yijiuwuwu nian Zhejiang nongcun gongzuo jingyan huibian* (Hangzhou (Hangchow) 1955).

Experience of welfare work among women and children, Funü ertong fuli gongzuo jingyan. All-China Democratic Women's

Federation, Zhonghua quanguo minzhu funü lianhehui (Peking 1952).

Experience of work amongst the dependants of workers and employees, Zhigong jiashu gongzuo jingyan (Workers' Publishing House, Peking 1957).

Explanation of problems of matrimonial property, Hunyin fangwu zhaiwu deng wenti jieda (Central South New China Bookstore, Hankou 1950).

Fang Ming, *How the women of Beiguan village, Lincheng, are struggling free from the bonds of feudal tradition, Lincheng Beiguancun funü zenyang zhengtuo fengjian chuantong shufu* (July 1948). LA documents 2.

The First National congress of Chinese women, Zhongguo funü diyici quanguo daibiao dahui, referred to as Congress documents 1 (New Democracy Publishing House, Hongkong, June 1949).

'Florence Nightingales' of the liberated areas of China, Zhongguo jiefangqu de nandinggeermen. All -China Democratic Women's Federation (ed.), Quanguo minzhufunü lianhehui bian (New China Bookstore, n.p., Oct. 1949).

The forward leap of Shanghai women, Yuejin zhong de Shanghai funü. Education Bureau of the Shanghai Women's Federation (ed.), Shanghai shi funü lianhehui xuanchuan jiaoyubu bian (Shanghai 1958).

Friendship, love and marriage, Youyi, aiqing he hunyin (Chinese Youth Publishing House, Peking 1956).

Fully develop the activist role of women from the business world in socialist transformation, Chongfen fahui gongshang jie funü zai shehui zhuyi gaizao shiye zhong de jiji zuoyong (Finance and Economics Publishing House, 1956).

Guo Hancheng, *Discussing 'The women's representative', Tan funü daibiao* (Popular Arts Publishing House, Peking 1956).

Han Suyin(g), *Women, the family, and the new life, Funü jiating, xinshenghuo* (Hongkong 1971).

Handbook for women workers, Nügong gongzuo shouce. Women Workers' Bureau of the All-China Federation of Trade Unions, Zhonghua quanguo zonggonghui nügongbu bian (Workers' Publishing House, Peking 1951).

The happiness brought by the Marriage Law, Hunyinfa dailaide xingfu. Legal Committee of the Central People's Government (ed), Zhongyang renmin zhengfu fazhi weiyuanhui bian (People's Publishing House, Peking 1953).

Happy marriage, Meiman hunyin (East Liaoning People's Publishing House, Dec. 1952).

High tide of socialism in the Chinese countryside, Zhongguo nongcun shehuizhuyi gaochao. General Staff Office of the CC of the CCP, Zhonggong zhongyang bangong ting (People's Publishing House, Peking 1956).

How to do marriage registration work well, Zenyang zuohao hunyin dengji gongzuo. Civil Administration Department of the Ministry of the Interior, Neiwubu minzhengsi bian (Peking Village Readers' Publishing House, Peking 1963).

Hu Delan, *Recollections of some revolutionary women in the old red bases of north-east Jiangxi, Yi Gan dongbei lao hongsequ jige geming funü*, in *Stories of the revolutionary struggle of Jiangxi women, Jiangxi funü geming douzheng gushi*. Jiangxi Provincial Women's Federation (ed.), Jiangxi funü lianhehui bian (Chinese Women's Magazine Press, Peking 1963).

Huang Zuying and Huang He, *The literacy class and the future of women, Shiziban yu funü qiantu*, in Bai Tao, *Seeing the educational work of the liberated areas through the example of one village, Cong yige cun kan jiefangqu de wenhua jianshe* (Hongkong 1949).

Important documents of the campaign to implement the Marriage Law, Guanche hunyinfa yundong de zhongyao wenjian (People's Publishing House, Peking 1953).

Important documents of the Chinese women's movement, Zhongguo funü yundong de zhongyao wenjian. Educational Bureau of the All-China Democratic Women's Federation, Zhonghua quanguo minzhu funü lianhehui xuanchuan jiaoyu bu bian (People's Publishing House, Peking 1953).

Important documents of the national representative congress of the dependants of workers and employees, Quanguo zhigong jiashu daibiao huiyi zhuyao wenjian (Workers' Publishing House, Peking 1957).

Industrial construction heroines of the north-east, Dongbei gongye jianshe shang de nü yingxiong. North Eastern Democratic Women's Federation, Dongbei minzhu funü lianhehui (New China Publishing House, North East 1950).

Jin Qiaoqiao gets married, Jin Quaoqiao jiehun (South Jiangxi People's Publishing House, Oct. 1952).

The Labour Law of the Chinese Soviet Republic, Suwei'ai laodongfa, adopted by the 1st National Congress of the Soviets in Nov. 1931. CC collection reel 5. 008.2129.4077.

Letters on the problems of love, marriage, and the family, Guanyu lianai, hunyin, jiating wenti de tongxin. Shanghai Democratic Women's Federation, Shanghai minzhu funü lianhehui (Shanghai People's Publishing House, 1956).

Li Zhen, *Real Love, Zhenzheng de aiqing* (Youth Publishing House, Peking, Dec. 1956).

Liu Heng, *Zhehu, the village where every household weaves, Jiajia fangzhi de Zhehu cun.* LA documents 4.

Liu Lequn, *Why our marriage broke up, Women fufu guanxi wei shenmo polie* (Chinese Women's Magazine Press, Peking 1956).

Liu Mianzhi, *New China's women advance, Xin Zhongguo de funü zai qianjin* (Sanlian Bookstore, Peking 1953).

Liu Xiang, *Biographies of model women, Gu lie nüzhuan* (Commercial Press, Shanghai, 1936).

Lu Feng, *The people arise, Renmin fanshenji* (Hongkong 1947).

Lu Fu, *New talks about the woman problem, Funü wenti xinjiang* (New Democracy Publishing House, Hongkong, Apr. 1949).

Luo Qiong, *The cottage textile industry in the Shaan-Gan-Ning border region, Shaan-Gan-Ning bianqu minjian fangzhiye* (Chinese Women's Press, n.p., Mar. 1946).

Luo Quiong (ed.), *Documents of the women's movement, Funü yundong wenxian* (North-east Bookstore, Sept. 1949). LA documents 5.

Luo Qiong, *Production by rural women in the past year, Jinnianlai jiefangqu nongcun funü shengchan shiye* (n.d.). LA documents No. 4.

Luo Yijun, *New words on the Marriage Law, Hunyinfa xinhua* (Labour Publishing House, Shanghai 1950).

Mao Zedong, *Collected works of Mao Zedong, Mdotakuto shu.* Research group on Mao Zedong's writings, Motakuto bunken shiryokenkyu-kai (Tokyo 1970-2).

Mao Zedong, *Investigation into Caixi district, Caixi xiang diaocha* (reprinted in *SW* 1947 and in *Maotakuto Shu* (Tokyo 1970-2)).

Mao Zedong, *Investigation into Changgang district, Changgang xiang diaocha* (reprinted in *SW* 1947 and in *Maotakuto Shu* (Tokyo 1970-2)).

Mao Zedong, *Selected Works of Mao Zedong, Mao Zedong xuanji.* Jin-Cha-Ji Central Office of the CCP, Zhongguo gongchandang Jin-Cha-Ji zhongyangju bianyin (n.p., 1947, referred to as *SW* 1947).

Marriage handbook, Hunyin Wenti shouce, issued by the *Progressive Daily, Jinbu Ribao* (Tientsin 1951?).

The Marriage Law and related documents, Hunyinfa ji qi youguan wenjian. Legal Committee of the Central People's Government (ed.), Zhongyang renmin zhengfu fazhi weiyuanhui bian (New China Bookstore, Peking 1950).

The Marriage Law of the Chinese Soviet Republic, Zhonghua Suweiai gongheguo hunyinfa, in Compendium of Soviet laws, Suweiaifadian (Ruijin 1934).

Marriage problems in New China, Xin Zhongguo de hunyin wenti

(Co-operative Bookshop, Hongkong 1950).

The Martyr Xiang Jingyu, Lieshi Xiang Jingyu (Chinese Women's Magazine Press, Peking 1958).

Mother and child welfare in new China, Xin Zhongguo dailai gei muqin he haizi de fuli. Child Welfare Department of the All-China Democratic Women's Federation (ed.), Quanguo minzhu funü lianhehui ertong fuli bu bian (Peking 1952).

The Movement in which the women of the liberated areas of China are standing up, Zhongguo jiefangqu funü fanshen yundong (n.p., 1949), in LA documents 6.

New forms of women's organization emerge in land reform, Tugaizhong chuxianle xinxingde funü zuzhi xingshi (1 Oct. 1948). LA documents 2.

A new stage in our country's women's liberation movement, Woguo funü jiefang yundong de xin jieduan (People's Publishing House, Peking 1960).

The new type of housewife, Xinxing de jiating funü (Chinese Women's Magazine Press, Peking 1956).

New women of new China. Introducing the delegations and the outstanding personalities of the 1st national congress of Chinese women, Xin Zhongguo de xin funü. Zhongguo funü diyici quanguo daibiao dahui daibiaotuan ji dianxing renwu jieshao. Education Bureau of the All-China Democratic Women's Federation (ed.), Zhonghua quanguo minzhu funü lianhehui xuanchuan jiaoyubu bian (New China Bookstore, Mar. 1949).

New women of new China, Xin Zhongguo de xin funü (Masses' Bookstore, Peking 1951).

New women's reading book, Xin funü duben (New Democracy Publishing House, Hongkong, July 1950).

New women workers of the new society, Xin shehui de xin nügong. Preparatory Committee of the All-China Democratic Women's Federation (ed.), Quanguo minzhu funü lianhehui choubei weiyuanhui bian (Peking 1949).

Niu Zhi, *The great revolution in marriage, Hunyin da geming* (New Democracy Publishing House, Canton 1951).

Notification No. 7 of the Ningdu central county committee of the CCP: mobilize labouring women for the struggle against feudal oppression, Zhonggong Ningdu zhongxinxianwei tongzhi diqihao: fadong laodong funü fandui fengjian yapo de douzheng (16 July, no year). CC collection, reel 4. 008.2411.1229.

On love, marriage, and the family in a socialist society, Lun shehui zhuyi shehui de aiqing hunyin he jiating (New China Women's Publishing House, Peking 1955).

On the spring ploughing front, Chungeng zhanxian. Soviet Education Bureau of Jiangxi province, Jiangxi sheng Su jiaoyubu.

CC collection, reel 8. 008.478.5056.

Order No. 10 of the Gan county soviet government, Xunling dishihao Ganxian suweiai zhengfu (20 Oct. 1932). CC collection, reel 4. 008.2411.2213.

Our marital relationship, Women fufu zhijian (Peking Publishing House, Peking 1957).

Outstanding examples of women taking part in production and construction, Funü canjia shengchan jianshe de xian jin bangyang. Educational Bureau of the All-China Democratic Women's Federation, Zhonghua quanguo minzhu funü lianhehui xuanchuan jiaoyubu bian (Youth Publishing House, Peking 1953).

Pan Lang, *Love, marriage, and the family in the new society, Xin shehui de lianai hunyin yu jiating* (Hongkong 1949).

Pang Dunzhi, *Basic knowledge of the new Marriage Law, Xin hunyinfa jiben renshi* (Overseas Chinese Book Company, Kowloon 1950).

Points for propagandizing the Marriage Law, Hunyinfa xuanchuan tiyao (South China People's Publishing House, Canton 1953).

Points to which Youth League members should give attention in carrying out the Marriage Law, Zai guanche hunyinfa zhong qingnian tuanyuan yinggai zhuyi xie shenme (Youth Publishing House, Jan. 1953).

Popular explanatory materials for the Marriage Law, Hunyinfa tongsu jiangjie cailiao (People's Publishing House, Jan. 1953).

Popular talks on the 'Five Goods Movement', 'Wuhao' tongsu jianghua. Education Bureau of the Shanghai Democratic Women's Federation (ed.), Shanghaishi minzhu funü lianhehui xuanjiao bu bian (Shanghai People's Publishing House, Oct. 1956).

The problems of love and marriage of young people, Qingnian de lianai hunyin wenti (Youth Publishing House, Peking 1950).

Programme and methods for promoting the struggle of the labouring women of east Jiangxi, Fadong Gandong laodong funü douzheng de gangling he fangshi. Ningdu Central County Committee of the CCP, Zhonggong Ningdu zhongxin xianwei (14 July, no year). CC collection, reel 4. 008.2411.1220.

Programme for the organization and work of labouring women's representative congresses, Laodong funü daibiao huiyi zuzhi ji gongzuo dagang. Central Bureau of the Soviet Areas, Suqu zhongyang ju (undated). CC collection, reel 4, 008.2411.9924.

Qian Tang, *Revolutionary women, Geming de nüxing* (Great Learning Publishing House, n.p., 1949).

Qian Xiuqing and Jiang Jinhai, Qian Xiuqing yu Jiang Jinzhai (cable of the NCNA from north Shaanxi, 28 Jan. 1948). LA documents 3.

Questions and answers on the Marriage Law, Hunyinfa wenda. Judicial Office of the Higher People's Court of Anhui (ed.), Anhui sheng gaoji renmin fayuan sifa xingzheng chubian (Hofei 1964).

Regulations of the Women's Federation of the People's Republic of China, Zhonghua renmin gongheguo funü lianhehui zhangcheng, in Congress documents 3.

Regulations on women's property and rights of inheritance, Nüzi caichan jicheng quan tiaoli, in *Collection of political measures and regulations of the Shaan-Gan-Ning border region, Shaan-Gan-Ning bianqu zhengce tiaoli huiji* (n.p., 1944).

Regulations on the organization of trade unions, Gonghui gongzuo zuzhi tiaoli (North-eastern Workers' Publishing House, 1951).

Resolutions on the summoning of the provincial representative congress of women workers and peasants, Zhaoji quansheng nügongnong daibiao huiyi de jueding. Jiangxi Provincial Committee of the CCP, Zhonggong Jiangxi shengwei (11 Oct. 1933). CC collection, reel 4. 008.2411.2728.

The rural women's production movement in the liberated areas, Zhongguo jiefangqu nongcun funü shengchan yundong. Women's Association of the Liberated Areas of China (ed.), Zhongguo jiefangqu funü lianhehui (New China Bookstores, 10 Feb. 1949). LA documents 4.

Selected Documents of the women's movement, Funü yundong wenxuan. Woman-work Committee of the Tientsin Municipality Party Committee (ed.), Zhonggong Tianjin shiweihui funü gongzuo weiyuanhui bian (n.p., 8 Mar. 1949). LA documents 6.

Selected essays on divorce problems, Lihun wenti lunwen xuanji (Law Publishing House, Peking 1958).

Self-determination in marriage, Hunyin zizhu (North-west People's Publishing House, 1953).

Selected autobiographies of women writers, Nü zuojia zizhuan xuanji (n.p., c. 1945).

Socialist construction in rural Shaanxi, Shaanxi nongcun shehuizhuyi jianshe. Shaanxi Provincial Committee of the CCP, Zhonggong Shaanxi shengwei bangongting bian (Sian 1956).

Songs about the Marriage Law, Hunyinfa ge (Central South People's Publishing House, Hankou 1953).

Stories of the movement in which the village women of the liberated areas of China are standing up, Zhongguo jiefangqu nongcun funü fanshen yundong sumiao. Preparatory Committee of the National Democratic Women's Federation, Zhongguo minzhu funü lianhehui choubei weiyuanhui bian (1949). LA documents 2.

Stories of the revolutionary struggle of Jiangxi women, Jiangxi funü geming douzheng gushi. Jiangxi Provincial Women's Federation (ed.), Jiangxi sheng funü lianhehui bian (Chinese Women's Magazine Press, Peking 1963).

Study Handbook for the Marriage Law of the PRC, Zhonghua renmin gongheguo hunyinfa xuexi shouce (Shanghai 1950).

Study materials for the campaign to implement the Marriage Law thoroughly, Guanche hunyinfa yundong xuexi cailiao. Issued by the Peking Committee for the Campaign to Implement the Marriage Law, Beijingshi guanche hunyinfa yundong weiyuanhui bianyin (Dec. 1952).

Sun Ming, *Talks on husband-wife relations, Tan tan fufu guanxi* (Shanghai People's Publishing House, Shanghai 1957).

Three-character reader for workers and peasants, Gongnongbing sanzi jing. CC collection, reel 8. 008.5542.1057.

Trade union work with women workers, Gonghui nügong gongzuo. Woman Workers' Bureau of the Shanghai Trade Union Federation, *Shanghai* zonggonghui nügong bu bian (New China Bookstore, Shanghai 1951).

Wang Naicong, *Compendium of questions and answers on the Marriage Law, Hunyinfa wenti jieda huibian* (Cultural Supplies Press, n.p. 1951).

What do women live for? Furen huozhe wei shenme? (Chinese Women's Magazine Press, 1963).

When you marry, marry in the new style, Jiehun yao jie xinshi hun (South Jiangsu People's Publishing House, Nov. 1952).

Wherever my country needs me, Zai zuguo xuyao wo de difang (Workers' Publishing House, Peking 1956).

Women in rural co-operativization, Nongye hezuohua daolu shang de funü (New Knowledge Publishing House, Shanghai 1956).

The Women of Peking are making progress, Beijing funü zai qianjin. Peking Democratic Women's Federation, Beijingshi minzhu funü lianhehui bian (Peking Masses Publishing House, 1955).

Women on the Industrial Front, Gongye zhanxian shang de funü (Chinese Women's Magazine Press, 1956).

Women's reading primer, Funü duben. Issued by the Education Bureau of the Shanghai Democratic Women's Federation, Shanghai minzhu funü lianhehui xuanchuan jiaoyubu bianyin (Shanghai, Aug. 1953).

Women who have won revolutionary awards in their work, 'Sanba' hongqi shou (Chinese Women's Magazine Press, Nov. 1960).

Women workers of China, Zhongguo nügong (Workers' Publishing House, 1956).

Work experience in the countryside of Zhejiang (Chekiang) in 1955, Yijiuwuwu nian Zhejiang nongcun gongzuo jingyan huibian. General Office of the Zhejiang (Chekiang) Provincial Committee of the CCP, Zhongguo gongchandang Zhejiangsheng weiyuanhui bangong ting bian (Zhejiang (Chekiang) People's Publishing House, Hangzhou (Hangchow) 1955.)

A work plan for the Ningdu county women's movement, Ningdu xian funü yundong gongzuo jihua (21 May 1932 (?); year calculated from internal evidence). CC Collection reel 4. 008.2411. 3047.

Xie Bingying (Hsieh Ping-ying), *Autobiography of a woman-soldier, Nübing zizhuan* (Shanghai 1936).

Xu Dixin and others, *The emergence of new China, Xin Zhongguo de dansheng* (San Francisco 1949).

Xu Fang, *Women on the iron and steel production front, Gangtie zhanxian shang de funümen* (Youth Publishing House, Peking 1956).

Zhang Fan, *Love, marriage, and married life, Lianai, hunyin, yu fufu shenghuo* (Shanghai 1952).

Zhang Shanzeng, *Cross-talk on marriage problems, You guan hunyin wenti de xiangsheng* (Peking, Dec. 1951).

Zhang Xuewen, *Hygiene in New China, Xin Zhongguo de weisheng shiye* (Sanlian Bookstore, Peking 1953).

Zhang Yun, *Build up the country economically, manage the household thriftily, and struggle for socialism, Qinjian jianguo, qinjian chijia wei shehuizhuyi er fendou* (1957). Congress Documents 3.

Zhou Jiaqing, *Talks on the Marriage Law, Hunyinfa jianghua* (Youth Publishing House, Peking 1964).

ARTICLES IN CHINESE-LANGUAGE PERIODICALS

An Ziwen, 'The problem of the retirement of women cadres must be understood correctly', 'Yinggai zhengque renshi funü ganbu de tuizhi wenti', *ZGFN* No. 2 (1958).

An Ziwen, 'Carry out the Marriage Law and destroy the remnants of feudal thinking', 'Guanche hunyinfa suqing fengjian sixiang canyu', *RMRB* (30 May 1950), reprinted in *The Marriage Law and related documents, Hunyinfa jiqi youguan wenjian*.

'Attend to special problems which women have at work', 'Zhaogu funü zai laodong zhong teshu wenti', *Southern Daily, Nanfang Ribao* (20 July 1957).

'Be a revolutionary changing old habits and customs', 'Zuo yifeng yisu de gemingpai', editorial in *Gungming Daily, Guangming Ribao* (12 Apr. 1966).

'Be skilled and work well'. Xuehao benling, zuohao gongzuo', *XHYB* (Apr. 1950).

'Build up a regular work and life routine. How to guarantee the women personnel of enterprises the time to take care of their housework', 'Jianli zhengchang de gongzuo he shenghuo zhixu. Zenyang baozhong jiguan nügongzuo renyuan you liaoli jiawu de shijian'. Education bureau of the Women's Federation, Quanguo fulian xuanjiao bu, *RMRB* (29 Jan. 1956).

'Can women workers and employees who have children continue to make progress?', 'Nüzhigong you haizi nengbuneng jixu jinbu?', *GRRB* (26 June 1956).

'Carry out woman-work with enthusiasm', 'Renzhen zuohao funü gongzuo', *XHYB* (Apr. 1950).

'Clothes problems of women today', 'Jintian de funü fuzhuang wenti', *ZGFN* No. 3 (1955).

'Concerning the work and wages of maids', 'Guanyu baomu de gongzi, gongzuo', *ZGFN* No. 17 (1956).

'Decisions of the State Council of the Central People's Government on employment problems', 'Zhongyang renmin zhengfu zhengwuyuan guanyu laodong jiuye wenti de jueding', *RMRB* (4 Aug. 1952).

Deng Yingchao (Teng Ying-ch'ao), 'Report on the present orientation and tasks of the Chinese women's movement', 'Zhongguo funü yundong muqian de fangzhen renwu baogao', *ZGFN* No. 5 (1953). Congress documents 2.

Deng Yingchao, 'Comrade Deng Yingchao reports on the Marriage Law', 'Deng Yingchao tongzhi guanyu hunyinfa de baogao', *RMRB* (26 May 1950).

'Denounce the crimes of the black gang element Dong Bian', 'Jiefa heibang fenzi Dong Bian de zuixing', by 'The revolutionary working personnel of this press', 'Benshe quanti geming gongzuo renyuan', *ZGFN* No. 7 (1966).

Ding Ling, 'Thoughts on March 8th', 'Sanbajie yougan', *Liberation Daily, Jiefang Ribao* (9 Mar. 1942).

'Directive of the All-China Democratic Women's Federation to all levels of the organization to co-operate in the implementation of the decisions on employment of the State Council of the Central People's Government', 'Zhonghua quanguo minzhu funü lianhehui wei xiezhu zhixing zhongyang renmin zhengfu zhengwuyuan guanyu laodong jiuye wenti de jueding gei geji fulian de tongzhi', *RMRB* (10 Aug. 1952).

'Do housework and child-care count as work?', 'Guan jiawu, dai haizi, suanbusuan laodong?', *GRRB* (16 Dec. 1956).

'Documents of the Second National Congress of Chinese Women', 'Zhongguo funü dierci quanguo daibiao dahui zhongyao wenxian', *ZGFN* No. 5 (1953).

'Does a man lose face if he does housework?', 'Nanzi zuo jiawu shi diulian ma?', *Labour Paper, Laodong Bao* (Shanghai, 7 July 1956).

'Frugality and clothes beautification', 'Pusu yu fuzhuang meihua', *Heilongjiang Daily, Heilongjiang Ribao* (10 Feb. 1957).

'How to deal correctly with equal pay for men and women', 'Zenyang zhengque liaojie nannü tongzhou', *RMRB* (9 Sept. 1956).

'Implement the new democratic marriage system', 'Shixing xin minzhu zhuyi de hunyin zhidu', *RMRB* (16 Apr. 1950).

'Is it domestic slavery to be considerate to your wife?', 'Titie qizi jiu shi jiating nuli ma?', *GRRB* (8 Dec. 1956).

'Marriage Regulations of the Chinese Soviet Republic', 'Zhonghua Suweiai gongheguo hunyin tiaoli', *Red China, Hongse Zhonghua* (18 Dec. 1931).

'Mobilize women's energies and develop their active role', 'Diaodong funü liliang, fahui funü jiji zuoyong', *Liberation Daily, Jiefang Ribao* (13 Dec. 1956).

'Oppose contempt of women, housework is glorious too', 'Fandui qishi funü, jiawu laodong ye shi guangrongde', *Shenyang Daily, Shenyang Ribao* (5 June 1957).

'The problem of female employment can only be met gradually', 'Funü jiuye wenti zhi neng zhubu jiejue', *Liberation Daily, Jiefang Ribao* (13 Dec. 1956).

'The Provincial Women's Federation calls an enlarged executive committee meeting to agree on future tasks for women in our province', 'Sheng fulian zhaokai zhiwei kuoda huiyi queding jinhou bensheng funü gongzuo renwu', *New Hunan paper, Xin Hunan bao* (Changsha, 7 Apr. 1957).

'Recollections of the struggles of past life', 'Huiyi guoqu de shenghuo de douzheng', *GRRB* (3 July 1957).

'The Red School youth team beats the women's team', 'Hongxiao qingniandui dazhan nüzi dui', *QNSH* (21 May 1933). CC collection reel 19.

'Red Woman', 'Hongse Funü', *Combat Issue, Zhanbao*, No. 1. Produced by the Red Rebels' League of the National Women's Federation, Quanguo fulian hongse zuofan zongtuan (19 May 1967).

'Resolutely enforce the Marriage Law, guarantee women's rights', 'Jianjue guanche hunyinfa, baozheng funü quanli', *RMRB* (29 Sept. 1954).

'Should we give up our jobs and go back home to do the housework?', 'Gaibugai tuizhi huijia congshi jiawu laodong?', *RMRB* (9 Feb. 1958).

'Some special problems of women at work which need attention', 'Bixu zhuyi jiejue funü canjia laodong yixie teshu wenti', *Fujian (Fukien) Daily, Fujian Ribao* (30 Mar. 1953).

'Some views on village wives', 'Guanyu "tulaopo" yidian yijian', *Democratic Youth, Minzhu Qingnian* (Dalian, 29 Mar. 1950).

'They need help', 'Tamen xuyao bangzhu', *ZGFN* No. 13 (1 July 1957).

'Train women cadres enthusiastically', 'Jiji peiyang funü ganbu', *RMRB* (16 Jan. 1974).

'What attitude should one take to a backward wife?', 'Dui luohou de qizi caiqu shenme taidu?' *GRRB* (2 Dec. 1956).

'What should you do when you can't manage a job on top of the housework?, 'Gongzuo he jiawu wufa jian gai zenme ban?', *RMRB* (22 Jan. 1958).

'The women of Lankao denounce the criminal acts of the black gang element Dong Bian', 'Lankao funü tongchi heibang fenzi Dong Bian de zuixing'. Lankao County Women's Federation, Lankao xian fulian, *ZGFN* No. 8 (1966).

Wu Yuanqi, 'The great plot of false discussion and real poisoning', 'Jia taolun zhen fangdu de da yinmou', *ZGFN* No. 8 (1966).

Xiang Jingyu (Hsiang Ching-yü), 'Three matters to which the women's rights movement in Shanghai should give attention from now on', 'Shanghai nüquan yundong hui jinhou ying zhuyi de san jian shi'. *Women's Weekly, Funü Zhoubao* (31 Oct. 1923), reprinted in *The Martyr Xiang Jingyu, Lieshi Xiang Jingyu* (Chinese Women's Magazine Press, Peking 1958).

Xiang Jingyu, 'Three types among China's women intellectuals', 'Zhongguo zhishi funü de sanpai', *Women's Weekly, Funü Zhoubao* (28 Oct. 1928), reprinted in *The Martyr Xiang Jingyu, Lieshi Xiang Jingyu* (Chinese Women's Magazine Press, Peking 1958).

Yang Lianying, 'Representative congresses of women workers and peasants and their work', 'Nügongnong fudaibiao huiyi jiqi gongzuo', *QNZH* (28 May 1933). CC collection reel 19.

Zhang Zhe, 'When getting married don't have betrothal gifts', 'Jiehun bu yao caili'. Yongwang hamlet brigade, Zuoshan Commune, Changyi county, Shandong Province, Shandongsheng Changyixian Zuoshan gongshe Yongwang dun dadui, *Chinese Youth, Zhonguo Qingnian*, No. 2 (1966).

Zhang Zhirang, 'A much-needed marriage law', 'Qiehexuyao de hunyinfa', *XHYB* (May 1950).

'Zhongshan County draws up a woman-work plan for the next two years', 'Zhongshan xian dingchu liangniannei funü gongzuo de jihua', *Southern Daily, Nanfang Ribao* (19 Mar. 1956).

BOOKS IN WESTERN LANGUAGES

All-China Democratic Women's Federation, *Chinese Women in 1950* (Peking 1950).

J. N. D. Anderson, *Family Law in Asia and Africa* (Allen and Unwin, London 1968).

A. Appadorai, *The Status of Women in South Asia* (Orient Longmans, Bombay 1954).

Florence Ayscough, *Chinese Women Yesterday and Today* (Boston 1937).

Jack Belden, *China Shakes the World* (Harper, New York 1949).

Ester Boserup, *Women's Role in Economic Development* (Allen and Unwin, London 1970).

Hugh Brody, *Inishkillane: Change and Decline in the West of Ireland* (Allen Lane, Harmondsworth 1973).

J. L. Buck, *Land Utilization in China* (Nanking 1937).

J. L. Buck, *The Chinese Farm Economy* (Nanking 1930).

Chao, Buwei Yang, *Autobiography of a Chinese Woman* (New York 1947).

Central Committee of the Chinese Communist Party, *Resolutions on some questions concerning the People's Communes, 6th plenary session of the 8th Central Committee of the CCP* (Foreign Languages Press, Peking 1958).

William Caudill and Liu Tsung-yi (eds.), *Mental Health Research in Asia and the Pacific* (East-West press, Honolulu 1969).

Chao Shu-li, *Rhymes of Li Yu-tsai and other stories* (Foreign Languages Press, Peking 1955).

C. S. Chen and C. P. Ridley, *Rural People's Communes in Lien-chiang* (Hoover Institution Press, Stanford 1969).

Jack Chen, *A Year in Upper Felicity* (Macmillan 1973).

Jean Chesneaux, *The Chinese Labor Movement* (Stanford U. P. 1968).

Jean Chesneaux, *Secret Societies in China in the Nineteenth and Twentieth Centuries* (Heinemann, London 1971).

Jean Chesneaux, *Les Syndicats chinois 1919–1927* (Mouton, The Hague and Paris 1965).

Chou Li-po, *The Hurricane* (Foreign Languages Press, Peking 1955).

Chow Chang-cheng, *The Lotus Pool of Memory* (Michael Joseph, London 1961).

O. Edmund Clubb, *Twentieth Century China* (Columbia U.P., New York 1964).

Charlotte Bonny Cohen, 'Women in China' in Robin Morgan (ed.), *Sisterhood is Powerful, An Anthology of Writings from the Women's Liberation Movement* (Vintage Books, New York 1970).

Boyd Compton, *Mao's China, Party Reform Documents 1942–1944* (University of Washington Press 1966).

Isabel and David Crook, *Revolution in a Chinese Village* (Routledge and Kegan Paul, London 1959).

Isabel and David Crook, *The First Years of Yangyi Commune* (Routledge and Kegan Paul, London 1966).

Dymphna Cusack, *Chinese Women Speak* (Angus and Robertson, Sydney 1958).

Deng Yingchao (Teng Ying-ch'ao), 'On the Marriage Law of the People's Republic of China', in the English edition of the Marriage Law (Foreign Languages Press, Peking 1950).

Norton T. Dodge, *Women in the Soviet Economy, Their Role in Economic, Scientific, and Technical Development* (The Johns Hopkins Press, Baltimore 1966).

Mary Douglas, *Purity and Danger, An Analysis of Concepts of Pollution and Taboo* (Routledge and Kegan Paul, London 1966).

Alexander Eckstein, Walter Galenson, and Liu Ta-chung, *Economic Trends in Communist China* (Aldine Publishing Company, Chicago 1968).

U. R. Ehrengels, 'The Anthropological Background of Matrilineal Societies', in A. Appadorai (ed.), *The Status of Women in South Asia* (Orient Languages, Bombay 1954).

John Philip Emerson, *Non-Agricultural Employment in Mainland China 1949–1958* (International Population Statistics Reports, US Bureau of the Census, Washington D.C. 1965).

J. P. Emerson, *Sex, Age and Level of Skill of the non-agricultural labour force of Mainland China* (US Bureau of the Census, Foreign Demographic Analysis Division, Washington D.C. 1965).

Frederick Engels, *The Origin of the Family, Private Property and the State* (International Publishers edition, New York 1972).

Fei Hsiao-t'ung, *Peasant Life in China* (Routledge and Kegan Paul, London 1939).

Maurice Freedman (ed.), *Family and Kinship in Chinese Society* (Stanford U.P. 1970).

Tadashi Fukutake, *Asian Rural Society; China, India, Japan* (University of Washington Press, Seattle and London 1967).

Sidney Gamble, *Peking, A Social Survey* (George H. Doran, New York 1921).

Lionel Giles, *Ch'iu Chin: A Chinese Heroine* (East and West Ltd., London 1927).

Kathleen Gough, *The Origin of the Family* (New Hoytown Press, Toronto 1973).

Emily Hahn, *The Soong Sisters* (New York 1945).

Fannina W. Halle, *Women in Soviet Russia* (Routledge, London 1933).

Fannina W. Halle, *Women in the Soviet East* (Secker and Warburg, London 1938).

Handbook on People's China (Foreign Languages Press, Peking, April 1957).

William Hinton, *Fanshen* (Monthly Review Press, New York 1966).

William Hinton, *Hundred Day War: The Cultural Revolution at Tsinghua University* (Monthly Review Press, New York 1972).

Ho Ping-ti, *Studies on the Population of China, 1368–1953* (Harvard University Press, Cambridge, Mass. 1959).

Charles Hoffman, *Work Incentives, Practices and Policies in the People's Republic of China 1953–1965* (State University of New

York Press, New York 1967).

Rudolf Hommel, *China at Work* (M.I.T., Cambridge Mass. 1964) (first published 1937).

Christopher Howe, *Employment and Economic Growth in China*, (Cambridge U.P., Cambridge 1971).

Christopher Howe, *Wage Patterns and Policy in China 1919-1962*, (Cambridge U.P., Cambridge 1973).

Hsiao Tso-liang, *The Land Revolution in China, 1930-1934* (Washington U.P., Seattle 1966).

Important Labour Laws and Regulations of the People's Republic of China (Foreign Languages Press Peking 1961).

Institute of Differing Civilisations, *Women's Role in the Development of Tropical and Sub-tropical Countries* (Brussels 1959).

Joint Economic Committee, Congress of the United States, *An Economic Profile of Mainland China* (US Government Printing House, Washington 1967).

Alexandra Kollontai, *Communism and the Family* (Pluto Press Edition, London 1972 (first published in 1920)).

Bela Kun (ed.), *Laws of the Chinese Soviet Republic* (Lawrence, London 1934).

Labour Laws and Regulations of the People's Republic of China, (Foreign Languages Press, Peking 1956).

Olga Lang, *Chinese Family and Society* (Archon Books reprint, 1968 (first published in 1946)).

V. I. Lenin, *Women and Society* (International Publishers, New York 1938).

Marion Levy, *The Family Revolution in Modern China* (Octagon Books reprint, New York 1963 (first published in 1949)).

John Wilson Lewis (ed.), *The City in Communist China* (Stanford U.P., Stanford. California, 1971).

Li Ju-chen, *Flowers in the Mirror,* translated and edited by Lin Tai-yi (Berkeley 1965).

Liu Ching, *The Builders* (Foreign Languages Press, Peking 1964).

Leonora Lloyd, *Women Workers in Britain* (Socialist Woman Publications, London 1973).

Trygve Lotveit, *Chinese Communism 1931-1934, Experience in Civil Government* (Scandinavian Institute of Asian Studies Monograph Series, No. 16, Lund 1973).

Lu Xun (Lu Hsun), 'What happens after Nora leaves home?' (26 Dec. 1923), a talk given at the Women's Normal College, Peking, 26 Dec. 1923, in Gladys Yang (trans. and ed.), *Silent China* (Oxford University Press, 1973).

Louise E. Luke, 'Marxian Women: Soviet Variants', in Simmons (ed.), *Through the Looking Glass of Soviet Literature* (New York 1953).

Henry McAleavy, 'Some Aspects of Marriage and Divorce in Communist China', in J. N. D. Anderson (ed.), *Family Law in Asia and Africa* (Allen and Unwin, London 1968).

Mao Zedong, *Selected Works of Mao Tse-tung* (Foreign Languages Press, Peking 1965).

Marriage Law of the People's Republic of China (Foreign Languages Press, Peking 1950).

Sir John Maynard, *The Russian Peasant and Other Studies* (Collier Books, New York 1962 (first published 1942)).

M. J. Meijer, *Marriage Law and Policy in the Chinese People's Republic* (Hongkong University Press, Hongkong 1972).

Raymon Myers, *The Chinese Peasant Economy* (Harvard U.P. 1970).

Jan Myrdal, *Report from a Chinese Village* (Heinemann, London 1965).

Jan Myrdal and Gun Kessle, *China: the Revolution Continued* (Random House, New York 1972).

New Women in New China (Foreign Languages Press, Peking 1972).

Leo Orleans, *Professional Manpower and Education in Communist China* (National Science Foundation, Washington 1960).

Robert Payne, *Journey to Red China* (Heinemann, London 1947).

Dwight Perkins, *Agricultural Development in China 1368–1968* (Edinburgh University Press 1969).

Ida Pruitt, *A Daughter of Han, The Autobiography of a Chinese Working Woman* (Stanford University Press, 1967 (first published in 1945)).

Victor Purcell, *The Boxer Uprising, A Background Study* (Cambridge University Press 1963).

J. R. Quinn (ed.), *Medicine and Public Health in the People's Republic of China* (US Dept. of Health , Education and Welfare, Washington D.C. 1973).

Mary B. Rankin, *Early Chinese Revolutionaries* (Harvard University Press 1971).

Resolutions on some questions concerning the People's Communes, 6th plenary session of the 8th CC of the CCP, 10 December 1958, in Chao Kuo-chun, *Agrarian Policy of the Chinese Communist Party* (Asia Publishing House, New Delhi 1960).

Barry M. Richman, *Industrial Society in Communist China* (Vintage Books, New York 1972).

Sheila Rowbotham, *Woman, Resistance and Revolution* (Allen Lane, London 1972).

Janet W. Salaff, 'The Role of the Family in Health Care', in Joseph R. Quinn (ed.), *Medicine and Public Health in the People's Republic of China* (US Dept. of Health, Education and Welfare, Washington D.C. 1973).

Rudolf Schlesinger, *The Family in the USSR* (Routledge and Kegan Paul, London 1949).

Peter Schran, *The Development of Chinese Agriculture 1950-1959* University of Illinois Press, Chicago 1969).

Franz Schurmann, *Ideology and Organization in Communist China* (University of California Press, Berkeley 1968 (revised edition)).

Mark Selden, *The Yenan Way* (Harvard U.P. 1972).

Vincent Y. C. Shih, *The Taiping Ideology, its Sources, Interpretation and Influences* (University of Washington Press, Seattle and London 1967).

Ruth Sidel, *Women and Childcare in China* (Penguin (US), 1972).

Agnes Smedley, *Battle Hymn of China* (Gollancz, London 1944).

Agnes Smedley, *China's Red Army Marches* (Lawrence and Wishart, London 1936).

Edgar Snow, *Red Star over China* (Gollancz, London 1937).

Helen Foster Snow *see* Nym Wales.

Soong Ching-ling, *The Struggle for New China* (Foreign Languages Press, Peking 1952).

A. C. Stafford, *Typical Women of China* (Kelly and Walsh, Shanghai 1899).

State Statistical Bureau, *Ten Great Years* (Foreign Languages Press, Peking 1960).

Gunther Stein, *The Challenge of Red China* (Pilot Press, London 1945).

Anna Louise Strong, *China's Millions, Revolution in China 1927* (New World Press, Peking 1965).

Sun Yü, *The Women's Representative* (Foreign Languages Press, Peking 1956). For a Chinese-language discussion of this play see under Guo Hancheng in the Chinese section of the bibliography.

Taching. Red Banner on China's Industrial Front (Foreign Languages Press, Peking 1972).

Peter Townsend, *China Phoenix, the Revolution in China* (Jonathan Cape, London 1955).

M H. van der Valk, *Conservatism in Modern Chinese Family Law* (E. J. Brill, Leiden 1956).

M. H. van der Valk, *An Outline of Modern Chinese Family Law* (Catholic University, Peking 1939).

Ezra Vogel, 'A Preliminary View of Family and Mental Health in Urban Communist China', in William Caudill and Liu Tsung-yi (eds.), *Mental Health Research in Asia and the Pacific* (East West Press, Honolulu, 1969).

Nym Wales (Helen Foster Snow), *Inside Red China* (Doubleday Doran, New York 1939).

Nym Wales, *The Chinese Communists. Sketches and Auto-biographies of the Old Guard* (Greenwood Publishing Company,

Connecticut 1972).

Nym Wales, *The Chinese Labor Movement* (The John Day Company, New York 1945).

Nym Wales, *Women in Modern China* (Mouton, The Hague 1967).

Arthur Waley, *Chinese Poems* (Allen and Unwin, London 1946).

Kenneth Walker, 'Ma Yin-chu: A Chinese Discussion on Planning for Balanced Growth', in C. D. Cowan (ed.), *The Economic Growth of China and Japan* (Allen and Unwin, London 1964).

Simine Wang, *Le Travail des femmes et des enfants en Chine* (Paris 1933).

Barbara E. Ward, *Women in New Asia: The Changing Social Roles of Men and Women in South and South-East Asia* (UNESCO, Paris 1963).

Wei Cheng Yu-hsiu (Mme Wei Tao-ming), *My Revolutionary Years* (Charles Scribner, New York 1943).

Roxanne Witke and Margery Wolf (eds.), *Women in Chinese Society* (Stanford University Press 1975).

Roxanne Witke, 'Women as Politicians in China of the 1920s', in Marilyn B. Young (ed.), *Women in China: Studies in Social Change and Feminism*.

Margery Wolf, *Women and the Family in Rural Taiwan* (Stanford U.P. 1972).

Shirley Wood, *A Street in China* (Michael Joseph, London 1958).

C. K. Yang, *The Chinese Family in the Communist Revolution* (M.I.T. Press, Cambridge Mass. 1959).

Gladys Yang (transl. and ed.), *Silent China* (Oxford University Press, 1973).

Marilyn B. Young (ed.), *Women in China, Studies in Social Change and Feminism* (Centre for Chinese Studies, University of Michigan 1973).

ARTICLES IN WESTERN-LANGUAGE PERIODICALS

Rewi Alley, 'Oilfield Wives from the Gobi', *China Reconstructs* (Dec. 1973).

Marianne Bastid, 'Economic Necessity and Political Ideas in Educational Reform during the Cultural Revolution', *The China Quarterly*, No. 42 (Apr.–June 1970).

Charlotte Beahan, 'The Woman's Press in China prior to the Revolution of 1911' (unpublished paper).

Deng Yingchao, 'Chinese Women Help to Build a New China', *People's China*, No. 6 (1950).

Deng Yingchao, 'The Women's Movement in new China', *People's China*, No. 5 (1952).

Norma Diamond, 'Collectivisation, Kinship and the Status of Women in Rural China'. *Bulletin of Concerned Asian Scholars.* (Jan–March 1975).

Norma Diamond, 'Women under Kuomintang Rule: Variations on the Feminine Mystique', *Modern China Quarterly* (Jan. 1975).

C. T. Hsia, 'Residual Femininity: Women in Chinese Fiction', *The China Quarterly* (Jan.–Mar. 1963).

Hu Chi-hsi, 'Mao Tse-toung, la révolution et la question sexuelle', *Revue Française de Science Politique*, xxiii. 1 (Feb. 1973).

Isabel Larguia and John Dumoulin, 'Towards a Science of Women's Liberation', *Casa de las Americas* (Havana, Mar.-June 1971; reprinted in English as a Red Rag pamphlet, London 1973).

Lin Yutang, 'Feminist Thought in Ancient China', *Tien Hsia Monthly,* 1, No. 2 (Nanking, Sept. 1935).

William Mandel, 'Soviet Women and their Self-image', *Science and Society*, 35 (1971), pp. 286–310.

'Pay Attention to the Development of Female Party Members', *RMRB* (13 Sept. 1971), trans. in *Current Background* (Nov. 1971).

G. W. Skinner, 'Marketing and Social Structure in China. part 1', *Journal of Asian Studies* (Nov. 1966).

Soong Ching-ling, 'Women's Liberation in China', *Peking Review (11 Feb. 1972).*

John Weakland, 'Chinese Film Images of Invasion and Resistance', *China Quarterly* (July–Sept. 1971).

Arthur Wolf, 'Adopt a Daughter-in-law, Marry a Sister: A Chinese Solution to the Problem of the Incest Taboo', *American Anthropologist*, 70.5 (Oct. 1968).

'Working Women are a Great Revolutionary Force', *RMRB* editorial for 8 Mar. 1973, translated in *Peking Review* (16 Mar. 1973).

INDEX

adultery, 95–6
Africa, 1, 2, 192
Agricultural Development in China, 1368–1968, 137
agriculture, 117–22, 136–7, 138–44. *See also* work
Aird, John S., 72
All-China (Democratic) Women's Federation, 52, 54, 62, 63, **64**, 65, 157, 169
All-China Federation of (Democratic) Youth, 65
All-China Women's Federation, 65, 157; preparatory committee of, 54, 62
Alley, Rewi, 174
ancestor cult, 6, 112
Anhui, 126, 143
Anshan, 178
anti-Japanese War, 18, 32, 39, 40, 43, 45, 61, 154, 155, 158
An Ziwen, 170
army, women in, Taiping Rebellion, 7, 8; Boxer Uprising, 9; 1911 revolution, 13; Nanking 1912, 13; anti-Japanese War, 18, 44–5; Civil War, 18; Red Army, 31, 51–2, 86; films depicting, 86
Asia, 1, 167
Asian Rural Society: China, India, Japan, 5
Autobiography of a Chinese Girl, 11, 81
Autobiography of a Chinese Woman, 11, 81

Bastid, Marianne, 188
Battle Hymn of China, 95
Behan, Charlotte L., 11
Beiguan village, Lincheng, 97
Beiyue report, 55, 140
Belden, Jack, 48, 49
Benet, Sula, 146, 193
Benxi (Liaoning province), 159
bigamy, 83, 84
Biographies of Model Women, 12
Blue Lantern, 9
Boserup, Ester, 1, 35, 118, 167, 173, 192

Boxer Uprising, 9
Boxer Uprising, The, 9
bride-price, 72–3, 84, 97, 106, 107
brigade, 129, 197
Brody, Hugh, 9
Buck, J. L., 34, 70, 71, 72, 90, 117–18, 119, 120–1, 122, 124, 136
Builders, The, 177
Bureau of Public Safety, 165
Buwei Yang Chao, 11, 81

cadres, in liberated areas, 43, 44, 47, 52; and Women's Organizations, 53, 55, 57, 58, 64, 65, 68; implementing Marriage Laws, 85, 86, 87, 88–9, 91, 93, 94, 98, 101, 102–5, 107, 108–9; in countryside, 115, 127, 133, 139, 143; in towns, 155, 156, 159, 160, 170, 171, 175, 178, 184, 185, 186; retrenchment of (1958), 171, 197
Cai Chang, 14, 36, 37, 38
Caixi district, 32
canteen, 128, 151, 172, 177, 181, 182, 189
Cantonese women, 5, 86–7
Cao Ding, 147
Central Committee, *see* Chinese Communists Party
Chahar, 58
Challenge of Red China, The, 36
Changchun, 159
Changgang district (Jiangxi), 25, 29, 30
Chao Chen village (Shanxi province), 46
Chen, C. S., 113
Chen Dongyuan, 3
Chen, Jack, 93
Chen Shaoyu, 100
Cheng Chu-yuan, 166, 179
Chesneaux, Jean, 8, 81, 154
Chiang Kai-shek, 16
Chiang Kai-shek, Madame, 16
child betrothal, 73–5, 84
childbirth, 69, 79, 124, **131-2**, 133, 134
children, 84, 105, 107, 111, 112–4; custody of, 78, 85, 97; care of, 123–4,